T0309827

Fundraising the SMART Way™

The AFP Fund Development Series is intended to provide fund development professionals and volunteers, including board members (and others interested in the nonprofit sector), with top-quality publications that help advance philanthropy as voluntary action for the public good. Our goal is to provide practical, timely guidance and information on fundraising, charitable giving, and related subjects. The Association of Fundraising Professionals (AFP) and Wiley each bring to this innovative collaboration unique and important resources that result in a whole greater than the sum of its parts. For information on other books in the series, please visit:

http://www.afpnet.org

Fundraising the SMART Way™

Predictable, Consistent Income Growth for Your Charity

ELLEN BRISTOL

WILEY

*This book is dedicated to Riley, Cade, and Aaron,
the next, next generation.*

Contents

Preface

In this book, I propose that we revisit the way fundraising is managed, not the way fundraising is done. There's a big difference. The way fundraising, or any other business function, is *managed* is what leads to high levels of productivity and sustainability. Managing a business function, including fundraising, means identifying the results desired from the fundraising effort, establishing performance targets and indicators, developing methods of doing it that are effective and in keeping with the organization's corporate values, and holding the "do-ers" accountable.

The way fundraising is *done*, on the other hand, describes the tactical activities of the fundraising staff, be they employees, contractors, or volunteers. Many fine fundraising professionals have raised their tactical skills to the level of art. We all know outstanding practitioners who specialize in grant-seeking, major gift work, capital campaigns, corporate relations, special events, and the list goes on. If there are, in fact, so many high performers out there in the fundraising discipline, how come fundraising remains the problem child of the nonprofit sector?

I contend that the nonprofit sector as a whole would enjoy more sustainable levels of income if the management of all that talent and art were to become more sophisticated, adopting some of the practices that support performance excellence in the for-profit sector. In fact, many nonprofit organizations, such as those in the fields of healthcare and healthcare research, practice extremely sophisticated management when it comes to service delivery and related programs. Many of them are required to do so by their certifying authorities. But as far as I can tell from the data and observation, it's the rare development shop that is managed strategically, with a stated intention to improve productivity.

By contrast, fundraising is largely tactical. If you're lucky enough to staff your development shop with senior superstars who already have relationships with the community's most willing philanthropists, it might not seem as if rigorous management methods are terribly important. But if your nonprofit is more typical—with a budget of less than $10 million—it's more likely that you spend your share of sleepless nights worrying about how you're going to do better this year than you did last, afford to hire more experienced staff, upgrade your facilities, build capacity to serve more clients, or any of the other thousand-and-one issues that you'd like to handle, but aren't able to afford.

The only way to get out of this spiral, in my opinion, is to improve the management of the development shop. Sure, you might get an incremental bump by adopting some cool new tactics, or throwing another event. But such tricks aren't sustainable. If you rely only on tactics, it's pretty tough to figure out what's working or not working. In that case, all you can do is repeat the things you think might be working for you, or experiment with new tactical ideas. Your big event works? Throw another event. Nonprofit X uses online giving? Put up a PayPal page on your website. How well is it working? Well, it depends . . .

The problem of how to improve fundraising results doesn't start with tactics, however. Its origins lie way upstream in the organization's mission, and in the way its leaders interpret that mission. When it comes to defining the organization's mission, I really like the way John Carver, developer of the Policy Governance® model, breaks it down. He says that a well-defined mission shows the results the organization intends to achieve, describes the recipients of those results, and states *what it should cost* to achieve those results. To my way of thinking, working out what it should cost to achieve the organization's desired results is the springboard for fundraising success.

This doesn't mean that leadership has to do the work of fundraising. In spite of popular opinion, I think that having the board involved too intimately in fundraising activities can be counterproductive. Leadership should be involved in articulating desired outcomes, defining performance indicators and success targets, and thinking strategically about the agency's role in the community. Clarity about the "what"—"What do we wish to accomplish?"—leads to clarity about the "how"—"How do we know we're accomplishing it?" That's a very big job indeed, one that's better suited to the high-level "volunteers" who serve on the governing board than the role of philanthropic solicitor,

My experience with nonprofit organizations, especially the smaller ones (which make up the majority of nonprofits), is that they never address the "what it should cost" part of Carver's equation. It's more common for them to proceed on the unspoken assumption of, "Let's raise as much as we can and then figure out how to use it."

By contrast, if you and I were to set up a business and seek external investors, those investors would want to know how much money we planned to spend on hiring and compensating qualified executives and staff, and scrutinizing the way we planned to identify the market for our products, establishing reliable go-to-market strategies, and selling the heck out of our products and services. They would demand to know how we planned to plow sales income back into the business to build additional capacity. At the end, of course, they'd want to know how their investments would pay off to satisfy their personal interests.

Every part of this description applies to the not-for-profit sector, even the very last sentence. Nonprofits get virtually all their income from external investors, with the modest exception of earned income. Those "investors" or philanthropists should also want to know how the organization recruits top-notch talent, identifies the market for its programs, has effective strategies to become well known, and can raise enough income to sustain current operations and build capacity. They too want to know how their investments will pay off, but in terms of mission achievement rather than the creation of personal wealth.

I have always contended that acquiring income is the single most strategic function in any business, regardless of sector. Now that there are reliable ways to assess the effectiveness and efficiency—the productivity—of the fundraising function, let's use them. That's what this book is all about.

Acknowledgments

Above all, let me thank the Publishing Advisory Committee of the Association of Fundraising Professionals (AFP), especially its chair Steven Miller of Cornerstones Virginia, for selecting my book proposal and recommending it to the wonderful people at John Wiley & Sons. Your endorsement and validation mean more than I can ever say.

There are a few other people I'd like to acknowledge, and the first is Mrs. Douglas, my eighth-grade English teacher, who taught me how to create outlines. Even though I was a mediocre student, I really got into the outlining thing; it made so much sense! Mrs. Douglas, in whatever heaven you currently reside, you had no idea you were infecting me with a yen to master formal process management, so this thanks is long overdue.

Susan Galler, president of The Galler Group, a highly accomplished strategic planner, major-gift expert, and executive coach for nonprofit CEO's, had an enormous impact on this work. Susan heard about the sales version of the SMART Way model and immediately pursued me to repurpose it for the nonprofit sector, for which I owe her undying gratitude. Among many other things, she taught me to "speak nonprofit" fluently.

Terrie Temkin, PhD, governance expert and principal of Core Strategies for Nonprofits, paved the way by encouraging me to deepen my involvement in the nonprofit sector and introduced me to AFP, among other organizations. She also urged me to write as much and as often as possible. Terrie, you were right; it does get easier.

On a more personal note, my friend and sometime business partner Dr. Rebecca Staton-Reinstein made sure I stuck to it. My husband Mike Perillard kept me sane and tolerated me when I wasn't. My brother Mike Bristol, a Shakespeare scholar who's written a few books himself, provided terrific insights about writing book-length works. Mike Antonelli, the third Mike, gave great entrepreneurial advice and encouragement. Pat Dobbs and Dell Harmsen were the cheering section. My grandchildren Riley and Cade Ellis and grandnephew Aaron Bristol provided surprising support every time they forced me away from the computer to play with them instead. This workaholic salutes you; you've got your priorities straight.

Finally, a debt of gratitude goes to the many nonprofit executives and fundraising professionals I've worked with over the years. You put forth such great effort, often with too little reward, to serve the greater good. I hope that this book and the methodology it describes will ease your burden and support your efforts.

Introduction:
Why We Need a
Fundraising Revolution

Revolutions take place when there's a disconnect between those doing the governing and those who are governed. If that disconnect becomes intolerable, revolution may ensue. They are usually a bloody mess; both sides are convinced of the rightness of their cause and will fight, literally to the death, to prove it. While we may certainly agree that the American, French, and Russian revolutions, to name a few, have brought about desirable changes, we also have to acknowledge that they came at grave cost to lives and property. Just ask Marie Antoinette how she felt about it.

I wrote this book to reveal the need for a revolution in the discipline of fundraising and how to bring it about. Those governing the work—including the governing board and the organization's senior management—are not well connected to those doing the work of fundraising, whom I'll call "the governed." Evidence of this disconnect is obvious. Fundraising results are lousy, in general, and they're not getting a whole lot better. Pound per pound, nonprofits bring in considerably less money than their for-profit counterparts do, even when the organizations are of similar size, makeup, and even area of focus. Nonprofits often enjoy levels of market awareness and general admiration that many for-profit businesses would kill for. So why are they willing to tolerate such anemic flows of income when they could do so much better?

On the whole, I would argue, the entire nonprofit sector suffers from our collective difficulty with measuring, managing, and improving fundraising through the use of certain business disciplines and management controls considered mission-critical by successful commercial companies. Too bad those disciplines seem to have bypassed the nonprofit sector overall. Here are a few insights.

While Giving USA's research report of 2013 shows modest increases in most philanthropic categories (individual and major gifts, grants, and corporate support) ranging from 3.5 percent to 4.4 percent, total giving as a percentage of gross domestic product (GDP) was flat from 2010 to 2012, at 2 percent. In fact, the peak year for giving to charity was 2006, during the U.S. housing bubble, when it rose to a grand total of about 2.25 percent.

The 2012 Survey Report from the Fundraising Effectiveness Project, a collaboration between the Urban Institute and the Association of Fundraising Professionals (AFP) shows that "every $100 gained in 2011 was offset by $100 in gift attrition," and "every 100 donors gained in 2011 was offset by 107 in lost donors through attrition."

And I was stopped dead in my tracks by the June 19, 2013, GuideStar Blog on the "overhead myth" where several leading authorities in our field expose the weakness of using low overhead as a reliable indicator of an agency's performance. How many decades has it taken to figure out that the amount paid out in overhead has little to do with the agency's ability to achieve its mission or produce any results at all? If anything, low overhead is often a marker of poor performance, signaling that leadership has not invested properly in improvements.

When I first started my consulting practice in 1995, I was motivated to address the challenges that face people who raise money for a living (which includes corporate salespeople). It seemed to me that we were asking fundraising professionals and salespeople alike to do an extremely difficult job without a map or compass. We were asking them to navigate through an otherwise trackless wilderness to find those elusive prospects from whom they just might be able to extract money, and keep those people happy enough to continue funding us into the future. Our primary metrics were, and still are, based on how much we raised and not much else. If we raised or sold enough, we kept our jobs. And often the reward for such "good behavior" was for the boss to raise our targets for next year.

It's time to stop asking our development officers to work without a net. We need to give them the backing, guidelines, meaningful methods, and other forms of management support that will help them and their agencies thrive, regardless of the state of the economy, the competition, or the latest cool new gadget or online giving craze. I want us to be able to manage fundraising using reliable strategic ways to control the controllable and work with, or around, the uncontrollable.

The fundraising revolution is all about the way leaders lead and managers manage the income-acquiring function of their enterprises in order to produce optimal, sustainable results at manageable costs. This revolution will help us produce consistent, predictable income growth from fundraising, or at least reveal why we're not achieving such growth. We need this revolution because the tools that should clarify what's actually happening, point the way to needed changes, and improve development-shop account-ability are largely missing in action. Think about it: raising money is probably the most strategic thing you can do to achieve your mission and fulfill your vision, but it's managed, often, as a tactical afterthought.

When we talk about the fundraising "discipline," we tend to concentrate on campaign concepts, rely on trailing indicators—mainly income—and make knee-jerk decisions when results fall below desired levels. We don't spend a lot of time talking about what might have gone on "upstream" to affect results observed "downstream." We tend to throw more tactics, usually out of context, at the fundraising problem, such as holding more special events rather than digging into the data to see where we might have gone wrong, and then making informed decisions about how to rectify the situation. Or we play hot potato with fundraising, where the staff thinks it's the board's job, the board thinks it's the staff's job, and it ends up being nobody's job.

Regrettably, the data suggest that we actually do a lot of things that are counterproductive. Rather than relying on a standard benchmark for qualifying donor prospects, we wing it. Rather than setting targets for donor retention, we simply tell the staff it's a good idea but don't provide many tools to make sure retention actually happens. And don't get me started on the fantastic data we *could* be collecting—but probably aren't— from our web sites, e-newsletters, and social media, all of which could help us figure out what our donors actually want from us. Instead, we manage fundraising like we manage the weather. We complain about it.

No one can manage the weather. But we *can* manage fundraising, as long as we adopt some concepts that may seem revolutionary. We can equip the development staff with the benefits of performance management, tools that have driven immense levels of productivity and innovation in the for-profit sector, starting as long ago as the late 1940s, after World War II. These concepts have revolutionized businesses as diverse as major auto manufacturers and small accounting firms, retail operations, and medical device manufacturers. In the world of the charitable organization, the methods and disciplines of performance management applied to fundraising are still unfamiliar or unknown. Why shouldn't the charitable sector benefit from them too? All we need to do is to adopt them, making some modifications appropriate to our industry.

FUNDRAISING THE SMART WAY™

This book is about revolutionizing the fundraising function through the classic elements and disciplines of performance or, as it's often called, process management. Originally referred to as Total Quality Management (TQM), this methodology and its numerous offspring such as Six Sigma and Lean have brought about enormously improved productivity and innovation in all sorts of industries, including the ways we lead and manage improvement itself. Our methodology, Fundraising the SMART Way™, based on the classic disciplines of performance management, provides the management controls so sorely needed to acquire and sustain funding in a significantly more rational, objective, and productive manner. These techniques don't merely fix problems; they also open the door to innovation.

Fundraising the SMART Way is a formal methodology, containing the guidelines, benchmarks, reporting methods, performance metrics, analytics, and business intelligence needed to produce a particular outcome, namely continuous improvement of fundraising results. We define the acronym SMART this way:

- **S**trategic
- **M**easurable
- Donor-**A**ction focused (Yes, we know "donor-action focused" starts with a D, but we figured nobody could pronounce "SMDRT.")
- **R**ealistic
- **T**ime defined

A cautionary note: If you're reading this book to pick up tips and tricks about improving your events, making the "ask" to a new major donor, or running a capital campaign, then you've come to the wrong place. What you're going to learn about instead is how to wrap your organizational arms and minds around the persistently stormy nature of the fund-development climate, and how to prevent tsunamis, hurricanes, and tornados in favor of balmy breezes and warm climes, a fund development world where what you *want* to happen, happens.

How It Works

Since this book is not a mystery novel, we're going to give away the ending right here. The SMART Way^{TM} model establishes two critical components that tend to be ignored, overlooked, or undervalued. When you can document and quantify these two components, capture data against them, and then cross-reference the data, you will be far more capable of maintaining high levels of productivity, management control, visibility, and accountability for all engaged in the fundraising effort, including peer solicitors and even donors themselves. Here are the two magic components:

Component 1: The Ideal-Funder Profile, a benchmark for each category of funder (donor, grant maker, corporate giver) that lists factual, quantitative characteristics of your ideal funder; qualitative or values-based characteristics, and the danger signs that suggest that some donors, assuming you were to win them over, might cost more than they are worth, in terms of a return on the investment of your time and effort. A complex benchmark of this nature provides clear guidelines about which donors justify the most investment of time and effort, and which do not. In the SMART Way model, we call such profiles *Scorecards*.

Component 2: The Donor Moves, milestones that locate the gift/grant opportunity in the pipeline based on the donor's *giving* process, rather than your team's "getting" process. Virtually all gifts and grants evolve through a short, predictable, unvarying series of milestones that provide effective performance indicators, both leading and trailing.

Each of these components makes for effective metrics. The Scorecard produces a rank (A, B, C, or D) that describes the prospect's potential for long-term value. Donor Moves are numbered sequentially, from 0 to 8.

Once you cross-reference these two metrics, it's easy to see the health or productivity of the fundraising process. It's possible (actually it's pretty easy) to figure out which donor prospects and opportunities justify attention at all, which justify the attention of the executive director of board chair, which ones need to be nudged in the right direction, and which ones need to be left alone, at least for now.

Okay, this sounds fairly straightforward, right? And it is. However, defining the components and then putting them together to form your fundraising toolkit requires a little rethinking about fundraising, and some work.

Before we jump into the solution, let's review the data revealing the need for our fundraising revolution.

RESULTS FROM THE LEAKY BUCKET STUDY

Over the years, we've worked with hundreds of nonprofit development teams, trying to figure out what's really going on out there in fundraising land. Something must be happening; otherwise, why would there be so many articles, books, training programs, and software applications for fundraising? But there's also a huge amount of "water-cooler" conversations, general gossip, and endless postings and repostings about the frustrations of fundraising. Sometimes these conversations are positive, reporting on new initiatives, insightful research, and the like. But just as often, the reverse is true. We've seen more cries for help than we can even count: "Help! We lost money at our event!" "Help! Our grant money ran out!" "Help! We had to lay off our staff!" Not to mention the thousands of requests for ideas on how to run events, choose software, or make the proverbial *ask,* a term I deplore.

We have yet to meet any nonprofit executives, development officers, or board members who haven't said, at least once, that they're worried about fundraising and not sure what to try next to improve results. Unfortunately, panic often sets in, producing some fairly unsustainable concepts.

Raising money continues to be a stone in the collective shoe of the nonprofit sector. Since we're long-time lovers of research data, we wondered if there was any real evidence that fundraising was tough to manage, or if the impressions we were getting were merely symptomatic of the all-too-human desire to grouse and complain. So we snooped around, asked a lot of questions, and launched a survey, which we will discuss more later on. What we've discovered so far shows that it's common to run fundraising in an ad hoc, unplanned manner, without paying much attention to such strategic issues as donor-selection criteria, ways to identify the various stages of the cultivation process, and effective methods for handling things when fundraising falls below desired levels. In short, there is a disease lurking behind these symptoms.

Does this mean that fundraising professionals don't know their jobs? No. The outcomes we've just described are not the fault of the grant writer, major-gift officer, corporate relations team or direct-mail guru. They're not even the "fault" of the executive director or the governing board. They are organizational problems, and as such they require organizational solutions. They require the institution of appropriate management controls to maintain desirable performance. Such controls have become SOP (standard operating procedure) in many for-profit disciplines, including manufacturing, logistics and distribution. Even the field of corporate sales, another income-creating discipline that's notoriously difficult to manage, has jumped on the bandwagon, at least since the late 1990s. In the nonprofit world, there are plenty of management controls in such areas as client service delivery, at least those imposed by the reporting requirements of grant makers. Almost every significant grant comes with requirements, sometimes excruciating, to report on outcomes and other forms of evidence. But in the fundraising department, such controls tend to be unknown, distrusted, or ignored—which is a real shame.

Effective management controls could help nonprofit organizations of all shapes and sizes run their fundraising efforts at continuously improving levels of productivity, which means that gift income goes up, while costs and time go down. Since productivity measures both efficiency and effectiveness, it's hard to think of a better time than *right now* to bring such controls to the development shop. As the economy morphs from a miserable past into an unappetizing future, there's no time like the present to ensure that the nonprofit dollar can go absolutely as far as possible, including the investments needed to bring in those gifts, grants, and sponsorships. To achieve superior levels of productivity in a fundraising organization requires more than hard work. In fact, sometimes "hard work"—late hours, sweating out major grant applications, managing multiple events, worrying about how to optimize online giving—may actually stand in the way of true productivity.

IMPORTANT!

Working "hard" is not the same as working "smart." It takes effective methods, metrics, benchmarks, guidelines, and reporting methods to work smart.

STATISTICS FROM THE LEAKY BUCKET ASSESSMENT

We launched our Leaky Bucket Assessment for Effective Fundraising back in 2011. We designed it to help us figure out whether all that anecdotal evidence had any basis in fact. After a while, when you've heard the same hundred anecdotes from a hundred executives at a hundred agencies from all sectors, sizes, and locations, you start to wonder: are all these people just tired and cranky, or is there really a problem out there? So far, the Leaky Bucket Assessment suggests that there really—*really*—is a problem out there. Several problems, in fact. Fortunately, these are problems that can be resolved. But they also suggest that some nonprofits that were decimated or hurt by the recession of 2008 might well have survived, or at least limped through, if they had employed some of the basic business disciplines that our assessment evaluates. In keeping with the heavily scientific design of the assessment, we scored each participant at one of four levels:

- Leaking Like a Sieve!
- Call the Productivity Helpline!
- Time for Preventive Productivity Maintenance!
- Watertight!

To date, a mere 4 percent have come in at the Watertight Level.

Even though the Leaky Bucket study was conceived as an informal tool, the scores we are seeing for the individual statements in the assessment are surprising and sobering. Here they are:

- Qualifying prospects:
  - Thirteen percent have no criteria for qualifying prospects; they just try as hard as they can.

- Sixty-five percent say they have "preferences" for selecting prospects but no documented criteria.
- Fifteen percent say they qualify prospects based only on wealth profile and giving history or on granting guidelines.
- Only 7 percent say they use a benchmark describing wealth profile, giving history, and charitable motivations.
- Acquiring new funders:
  - Twenty-two percent have no standards or targets for new-donor acquisition.
  - Forty-three percent state that they have "preferences" for acquisition but no documented targets.
  - Twenty-two percent say that they have targets for amount of new income.
  - Only 13 percent say that they seek a targeted amount of new income from a targeted number of new funding sources.
- Retaining current funders:
  - Fifteen percent have no standards or targets for donor retention.
  - Fifty-eight percent say that they are "encouraged" to retain donors but don't measure retention rates.
  - Eighteen percent say that they pay attention to the amount of money retained from current donors.
  - Only 9 percent say that they maintain targets for amount of money retained and numbers of funding sources retained from year to year.
- Upgrading (up-selling and cross-selling) donors:
  - Twenty-six percent have no standard practices for upgrading their funders.
  - Fifty-three percent say that they are "encouraged" to do so, but nothing is documented.
  - Sixteen percent say that they have targets for upgrading funders.
  - Only 5 percent say that they have documented targets for upgrading their funders, *plus* they run specific campaigns to do so.

- Standards for funding diversification:
  - Seven percent report only one or very few funding sources.
  - Twenty-four percent report that almost all funding comes from a single category such as grants.
  - Fifty-one percent report that they obtain funding from a variety of sources, but funding is still not well balanced.
  - Only 18 percent report that they believe their funding to be well balanced and diversified.
- Staff resources for fundraising:
  - Twenty-five percent say that the executive director does all the fundraising (and everything else).
  - Thirty-three percent say that they have one staff member or contractor for fundraising, in addition to the executive director.
  - Sixteen percent say that they have two or more people, plus the executive director and help from the board.
  - Twenty-six percent say that they have a director of development with a staff, plus help from the executive director and the board.
- How fundraising is measured:
  - Only 60 percent report that they measure total income against a target.
  - Fifty-one percent report that they measure income by category (gifts, grants, corporate support) against a target.
  - Sixteen percent measure number of visits with donor prospects, against a target.
  - Twenty-four percent measure the number of grant applications and/or donor proposals produced, against a target.
  - Twelve percent chose "none of the above," which means they are not measuring anything—or they measure stuff we didn't think about.
- What's in the fundraising "toolkit":
  - Only 48 percent say that they have a documented strategic plan with specific objectives for fundraising.
  - Only 26 percent report that they use documented donor profiles.
  - Only 56 percent say that they use donor management software, or at least a spreadsheet

- Only 26 percent state that they have an up-to-date, documented case for support.
- Twenty-two percent said "none of the above."
- Responding to undesirable fundraising performance:
  - Fourteen percent chose the option "fire the development director."
  - Fifty-three percent chose "produce more events."
  - Fifty-one percent chose "pursue more grant applications."
  - Twenty-six percent chose "train staff, board, and peer solicitors."
  - Eighteen percent chose "improve, update the case for support."
  - Twenty percent chose "none of the above."

Though the Leaky Bucket study is relatively small, these numbers are suggestive indeed. For one thing, taken as a whole, they suggest that many nonprofits rely on hope and prayer, rather than a documented, measurable set of key performance indicators, so their development efforts rely on working harder, not smarter. Without such measurement, efforts to improve results are hit or miss, tactical solutions that might have worked for another agency in another sector at another time.

The lack of such business disciplines allows counterproductive tactics—the "tin-cup" mentality, which says "help us because we need the money"—to creep in and take the organization in one direction only: downward.

IMPORTANT!

The *less* you can measure fundraising performance, the *worse* it gets.

THE FOUR LAWS OF PERFORMANCE MANAGEMENT

Performance management is the science of defining the business disciplines, rules, guidelines, metrics, benchmarks, and reporting methods that drive specific, desired business outcomes, then using these tools to achieve desired results. One of the earliest performance management models was Total Quality Management (TQM), introduced by Dr. W. Edwards Deming back in the late 1940s, after World War II. Eventually, TQM evolved into an alphabet soup of management methodologies, including Six Sigma, Lean, Information Technology Infrastructure Library (ITIL), and the like. While these productivity models first addressed "hard" business functions such as manufacturing and distribution, in more recent years they have evolved to address the "softer" functions, including career advancement, team building, customer-service delivery, and so on. In the for-profit world, the very last business discipline to embrace these models has been that of corporate sales, which is still, at time of writing, on the rising curve of adoption. In other words, it's no longer a shockingly new concept, but it still has a ways to go before most sales teams use it.

The discipline of philanthropic fundraising is still behind the adoption curve when compared to corporate sales. In the development shop, there is plenty of room for improvement, as demonstrated by the Leaky Bucket results. In fact, when we roll up all the results from the Leaky Bucket study, we see that the overall scores place our participants in the following four categories of "leakiness" (see Exhibit I.1).

Performance management has become so popular, not to mention complex, that you could get a PhD in it if you wanted to. But you

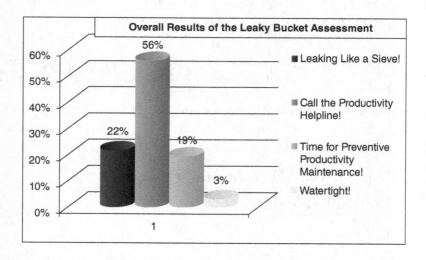

EXHIBIT I.1   **RESULTS OF THE LEAKY BUCKET STUDY, AS OF OCTOBER 31, 2013**
Source: Bristol Strategy Group

don't really need the advanced degree. Just learn these four laws and you can be a performance management superstar:

Law 1: You can't manage it if you can't measure it. The alternative to this law is "you can't improve it if you can't measure it." You can't improve your fundraising results if you can't measure them.

Law 2: What you measure is what you get. If you measure phone calls, you'll get lots of phone calls. Are you in the business of making phone calls or the business of raising charitable income?

Law 3: You can't figure out much by using a single measurement. You wouldn't build a house if the only measurement you had was for the bathroom window. You can't figure out much about your fundraising performance if you're only looking at how much money you dragged in.

Law 4: If the only thing you measure happens after the process is complete, then you haven't learned anything about the process. If you're only looking at how much you dragged in, you don't know how many no's it takes to get to yes. You don't know how long it takes the typical major gift to evolve through the cultivation process. You don't know where your opportunity pipeline encounters a predictable delay or how many opportunities convert from "nice to meet you" to "give me a proposal." And there are lots of other things you probably don't know.

Managing performance effectively is not only a management skill, it's an organizational mind-set, and it's a great one to cultivate. If your institution delivers medical care, early-childhood education, or community development, it's likely that you're already managing service-delivery performance. Outcomes measurements are a common requirement among funders and certifying bodies in these fields. You, your funders, and your clients rely on your ability to establish and maintain high standards of quality based on industry benchmarks.

Fundraising has been late to this particular party.

IMPORTANT!

Inexact measurement of the right things is more meaningful than exacting measurement of the wrong things.

In fundraising, it's common to report on activities (how many people attended the gala, how many grant applications were submitted, how many phone numbers were dialed) because they are relatively easy to count and track. But it's not so common to report on results. Activities—phone calls made, postcards delivered, e-mails opened, links clicked—are so easy to measure that your technology is already doing it for you. But if you're only counting up the number of activities, you might not really be making much headway.

However, if we can figure out which *results* to measure and how to measure them, then we will be more likely to measure the right things, things that actually give insight into the health of the fundraising process. Results—the outcomes of activity—are highly diagnostic and rewarding to measure, even if they tell you you're flunking Fundraising 101.

Once you've selected the right results to measure, you'll also need to measure some key activities. Emphasis is on the word *some*. Keep track only of diagnostic activities, those that provide meaningful insights into needed improvement. For example, if your organization has 10 major donors who each give at least $25,000 per year and you're determined to retain them at that level, then a useful activity to measure might be "schedule one annual planning session per year with every major donor."

Evidence, in the form of data collected from those famous metrics, reveals the level of effectiveness of your fundraising efforts. If you're on target, that's great; figure out what to do to stay there. If you're off track, figure out how to get back on.

And you're not the only one who wants the evidence. Funders of all sorts and sizes want, need, and often demand proof that their money is producing desired results, especially when the economy is weak. One way to improve fundraising results is to embrace the guidelines, metrics, benchmarks, reporting tools, and other methodological elements of effective performance management.

TARGET: CONSISTENT, PREDICTABLE INCOME GROWTH

Guess what keeps executive directors and board chairs awake at night. It's not simply the need for more money; it's *not knowing* if they're going to bring in the level income they need. If income is neither predictable nor consistent, bad things happen. We'll never forget the founding board chair who admitted, at the organization's 20th annual board retreat, that the agency had *never* been able to predict whether they would make budget or not. It's no surprise that the agency lost both its development director and its CEO in the same year.

Sometimes being sure that income is consistent and predictable is even more important than knowing that it's growing, especially during a weak economy. However, as shown in the Leaky Bucket results, it's not uncommon for nonprofit organizations to capture few (if any) meaningful metrics that demonstrate the level of consistency or predictability. Lack of insight increases levels of anxiety and may even make fundraising results look worse than they actually are.

Without accurate and timely reports based on key performance indicators, we hear demands for better results; we observe long anecdotal reports describing each opportunity one at a time; we endorse events without knowing if they'll bring in more than they cost; we launch marketing campaigns and then fail to follow up on the leads they produced. While it's certainly desirable to see results improve, it's best to have evidence that shows if results are actually improving, declining, or staying flat, at which times and under what conditions. Reliable evidence takes the worry out of fundraising and converts negative conversations into positive ones.

Let's compare philanthropic fundraising to corporate sales. For the most part, the corporate sales team is expected to produce a predictable amount of income every week, month, or accounting period. While the sales team's income targets may vary a bit from month to month to accommodate seasonality or special campaigns, salespeople learn early in their careers that they are expected to deliver their assigned results week after week, month after month, year after year. It's their ability to deliver *consistently* that gives them job security. Salespeople whose numbers fluctuate wildly may find themselves seeking career challenges elsewhere. Although corporate executives hate it when major events like expos and conferences fail to produce good leads, they're a lot more concerned about meeting forecast consistently. Corporate sales organizations are able to function this way because their metrics, guidelines, benchmarks, reporting methods, and even compensation practices have been designed specifically to produce such results.

It's impossible to overstate the importance of consistency and predictability in managing fundraising performance. If your measurements and reporting methods don't demonstrate how well or poorly your development team produces consistent, predictable income, then you risk wasting scarce, precious resources of time, energy, and money. Whether income is improving, flat, declining, or fluctuating wildly, you're a lot better off if you know what's going on.

EFFECTIVE FUNDRAISING AS COMPETITIVE ADVANTAGE

If all this seems like fuss and bother over something you "can't" manage anyway (like the weather), you are wrong. Effective fundraising produces significant competitive advantages.

211 Broward is a midsize agency in Florida, providing 24/7 phone support for crisis prevention and information and referrals to health and human services providers. Its CEO, Sheila Smith, was one of the first Leaky Bucket participants to score her agency at the Watertight level. We visited with Sheila because we were so impressed with her scores and discovered that:

- She has sufficient time and energy to plan for the future, consider innovations, and build capacity effectively.

- Her board of directors focuses its time and attention on major strategic issues—including peer solicitation—and demonstrates confidence in her ability to manage the agency effectively.

- Her programming and administrative staff receive competitive pay and benefits, with room for advancement.

- She maintains a small but sophisticated development team that gets appropriate support, time for training, and useful supportive technology.

In short, this organization has invested appropriately to manage fundraising for predictability and consistency. It's a great organization; people love their jobs, and the community benefits from their work. The fact that they're able to raise money on a consistent and predictable basis has freed the entire agency—and its governing board—to focus on service delivery and innovation.

What strikes me most about Sheila's experience is the *strategic* impact of effective fundraising. In my experience, nonprofit types often talk about fundraising as if it were a necessary evil, a distasteful act that has to be endured, like certain bodily functions. As I developed the Leaky Bucket Assessment, I expected that Watertight agencies would simply experience a *lack* of complaints about fundraising. Instead, it seems they have the leisure to concentrate on mission achievement and innovation, instead of worrying about paying the rent.

We manage all business processes, including fund development, not simply to reduce time, cost, and risk, but also to clear out the underbrush, facilitate insight, and find ways to innovate while responding to the shifting demands of the marketplace.

CASE STUDY

STORY FROM THE WORLD OF CORPORATE SALES

Another example, this time from the world of corporate sales, is illustrative. Just think "major donor," "major gift," and this anecdote will make total sense to you.

We were called in to work with a global manufacturing company. Because this company is privately held, we're keeping its name to ourselves. They manufacture stuff that's not very glamorous: industrial seals and gaskets for the petroleum and aviation industries. Their technology experts are chemical engineers, not computer nerds, who had traditionally been measured by the number of products and product types they could make and keep in inventory.

The company had reached the point where growth was becoming difficult. So rather than creating a bunch of new gaskets and seals, they launched a major-accounts sales program based on the idea "together we can make your business more successful and competitive." The company believed that both partners—the manufacturer and the customer—would benefit from this approach.

We helped them define the criteria that a sales account would have to meet in order to be considered a major account. They created a Scorecard or ideal customer profile, including the criterion "prospect willingly shares their latest SWOT analysis and strategic plan with us." In practice, this means that the account manager has to ask for a copy of the strategic plan at an early stage in the relationship and assess whether to continue to invest effort in the account. To our surprise and the delight of our client, this criterion was a major differentiator;

if the executive handed over the documents, our client knew they had very good odds of winning long-term loyalty and profitability. (We were all surprised by how many prospects were willing to share this confidential information.)

Along the way, we also asked our client to analyze the alignment between sales and manufacturing, to make sure that the sales force could sell what the engineering team could make and vice versa. After six months, the corporate project manager responsible for the major-account program gave us some welcome feedback:

- There was a $750,000 reduction of costs associated with commercial conferences and expos. They figured out which events helped and which didn't.

- There was a 6 percentage-point rise in overall corporate profits, just by concentrating on deeper relationships with strategic accounts.

- Significant reduction and streamlining of the number of individual items maintained in inventory led to substantial savings in costs and time.

- Engineers became part of the sales force, contributing as technical advisers and consultants and helping to raise profitability per account.

What was most meaningful to us, however, was an off-the-cuff remark made by the chief sales officer. He said, "The whole company is lining up behind this new strategic-account program. We never thought the engineers would want to be part of the sales team, and now they're vying with each other to go on calls."

What we hope you'll take away from this introduction is this: fundraising that is productive (efficient and effective), needs to be well documented, provided with the correct set of metrics, and reviewed regularly using the specific techniques of continuous improvement.

When fundraising works, you don't simply remove worries about making budget. You gain unanticipated advantages in how to achieve your mission, deliver value to your clients, and drive the promise of your vision.

Effective fundraising means more than simply raising money at reasonable costs. It frees you to drive your organization to levels of innovation and service that you might not otherwise be able to achieve.

ADOPTING THE SMART WAY MODEL

The SMART Way model adds two critical components to the discipline of fund development. The first is a clear benchmark for qualifying prospective funders that is unique to your agency, derived from collaborative effort, and based on the prospect's potential for long-term value. This benchmark or Scorecard allows you to manage and prioritize the time invested in selecting and cultivating prospects by guiding officers to concentrate on those with the highest potential. It keeps your development officers accountable for pursuing well-qualified opportunities, and allows them to avoid wasting scarce, precious, and unrecoverable time and money on those that are poorly qualified. We cover everything related to building your Scorecard in Part 1.

The second component is the subject of Part 2, with its focus on the opportunity pipeline. We manage the pipeline by defining stages of the process based on the donor's giving behavior, called *Donor Moves* in honor of the classic concept of Moves Management. In the SMART Way, we assign performance targets to these Donor Moves, and then capture and report on the frequency with which they are achieved. The list of possible Donor Moves is short, and all elements occur in an unvarying sequence, thus providing powerful leading indicators, metrics that are easy to understand and offer great insight into the health of the cultivation process. The development officer can easily determine whether the prospect has achieved a particular Donor Move, because the answer is always yes or no. Donor Moves describe key milestones covering the entire arc of cultivation, from prospecting through gift acquisition to stewardship. In Part 2, we cover everything related to adopting Donor Moves and establishing Donor Move targets.

However, there is a third component that is vital and without which the new model cannot deliver improved productivity. That component is the implementation phase, covered in Part 3. To our everlasting regret, we have discovered that the fact that we know *how* to do something doesn't mean we're actually going to do it, so we put a lot of energy into learning what it takes to adopt the new model and convert it to business as usual. In Part 3, we'll cover what it takes to validate the choices you made in developing your Scorecards and creating your donor move targets, and introduce the formal skills of continuous improvement, techniques that make a real difference in the way you raise your gross charitable income and reduce your bottom-line costs.

The SMART Way model delivers on the promise of the fundraising revolution.

Which Funders Are "Right" for You?

The first of the two major SMART Way™ components is the ideal-funder profile, a reliable way to evaluate lifetime donor value, so that's the subject of Part I. (Part II focuses on the cultivation process.) You will learn how to develop criteria that demonstrate the difference between funders offering high potential lifetime value and justifying a high level of effort, and those that don't. After all, those who meet your criteria already want to give to you. So why would you throw your scarce and precious time and money at funders who *don't* want to give to you? It's all about knowing which is which.

By providing more objective controls over prospect selection, you take the first step toward revolutionizing fundraising performance.

We all want funders to give generously to our causes. We agonize over those who don't give. We try to think up cool new ways of convincing them to give. We work our wiles, leverage our connections, and try to get the compromising photos that will guilt-trip them to give to us. Unfortunately, many of us don't seem to have mastered what I call the Cousin Judy approach.

When we were in middle school and high school, my cousin Judy (my real cousin) always had a line of boys trailing her down the hallways, calling her up at home, and hoping that she would agree to go out with them. I, however, sat home most weekends feeling sorry for myself, trying to understand why the boys didn't like me. To make things worse, you need to know that Judy was also a perfectly ordinary-looking person with a perfectly ordinary face and figure. She wasn't wealthy; she didn't come from a prominent family; she didn't have a cool car; she wasn't even a cheerleader. She was just nice, funny, and a great friend.[1] One fine day years later, I asked her why she was so popular at that time. I'll never forget her answer. She said, "Oh, I never worried about whether *they* liked *me*. I only wondered if *I* liked *them*."

Cousin Judy's approach to selecting a date translates very well to the world of fundraising. Maybe we shouldn't worry so much about whether the funder will "like" us or our agency, mission, programs. Maybe we should worry instead about whether that funder is *good enough for us*. Good enough according to an agreed-upon set of criteria that makes sense for our agencies, and good enough in terms of potential for lifetime giving, with a decent return on effort. When you flip the standard thought process upside down, things look mighty different, don't they.

Maybe that's why I haven't been surprised to discover that a huge proportion of nonprofit agencies—about 59 percent of respondents in the Leaky Bucket study—lack documented qualifying criteria to help the development team decide if their donor prospects are good enough. If such profiles were available, the development shop and the CEO and the board would be able to see if their development officers were using their time appropriately, investing in high-potential opportunities and *not* squandering their hours on prospects whose potential is only so-so or worse. When no such profiles exist, prospect selection may be very costly; it's hit or miss.

If you think your team is great at prospect research, that makes me happy. It means you've already developed some good disciplines. But conventional prospect research doesn't cover everything, so please don't skip Part I. The whole issue of how to select, cultivate, and acquire funders is the most likely part of the process to leak (hemorrhage?) productivity. The Leaky Bucket data show that if the agency has any kind of prospect profile, it's more likely to include "database-able" characteristics such as demographics and giving history only, while ignoring qualitative criteria such as charitable philosophy and motivations for giving. When those criteria are ignored, there's a high likelihood that development staff may spend significantly more time than is justified on prospects who may not give at all, may give at modest levels that don't meet the desired level of return on effort, or may even make you sorry you won their gifts altogether.

---

[1] We're grandmothers now and we *still* love each other.

The level of the donor's wealth has relatively little to do with the way they select the causes and charities they intend to support. That stuff comes from the donor's personal history, insights, and concerns. It's best if you actually know what those motivations may be.

Chapter 1 sets the context for fund development, with ways to calculate the true cost of achieving your mission, understanding the financial implications of your fundraising time, and articulating your unique value proposition (UVP) and value-added. Your value-added represents the strengths of your agency, cause, mission, and programs that are interesting to your ideal funders. They are what you're selling. If you have ever said anything like, "I hope you can give us money because we really need it," you need to read this chapter and take it to heart. Without a clear way to present your strengths to your target market, it's impossible to figure out which donors are going to be right for you and which aren't. Plus, you can't really begin to calculate return on effort if you don't have a way to articulate opportunity cost or organizational value.

In Chapter 2, you'll learn how to analyze your best funders' charitable motivations or "value-sought," then see how it aligns with your "value-added." This effort produces the exchange of value, the dynamic relationship between funder and agency. This exchange is the basis for your case for support, which in turn is the source for virtually all marketing messages from the personal conversation to the latest tweet.

This is the chapter where we can put the Cousin Judy approach to work and figure out what makes a funding prospect good enough for you. You'll also see why it's important to understand charitable motivations in each funding category, including smaller donors, grant seeking, and corporate giving. When you're clear on the ideal funder's value-sought, and you can see the dynamic play between value-sought and value-added, your team's productivity goes up.

Chapter 3 is where you'll build your SMART Way Prospect Scorecards, your qualifying benchmarks. Scorecards are weighted scoring matrices that calculate prospects' potential for lifetime giving, and rank them accordingly, a significant productivity gain because the A prospects justify much more investment of effort than the D's—and you and your team can see the difference. Now, this doesn't mean you'll stop trying to raise money from those with lower ranks; it just means you'll use less costly methods to do so. Since the pursuit of underqualified prospects has such a powerful negative impact on fundraising effectiveness, this chapter offers a great deal of food for thought.

Finally, in Chapter 4, you will learn how to validate and refine your Scorecard through regular use and review. You'll develop a set of suggested probing questions and use them for interviewing current funding sources. The insights you'll gain will enable you to tweak your Scorecards so that they—and you!—will be more persuasive and able to establish rapport more quickly. The Scorecards you build will be unique to your agency. They even include "cheat sheets," including suggested probing questions that help you find out how well the prospect matches your criteria, and even shorthand ways to figure out how well the prospect scores. That's important, because I want to make sure that you and Jane and Joe and Jack all score a given prospect the same way. The point is to make the subjective more objective.

CHAPTER 1

The Context for Fund Development

Nonprofit fundraising people and corporate salespeople share quite a few characteristics. They both tend to be outgoing, positive, oriented toward the future, and not afraid to ask for money. They are social beings. These characteristics, plus the ability to work late, are prerequisites for fundraising professionals; think of how many events they have to attend!

But there's also something that both share that's not so great, and that's the challenge of figuring out which prospects justify their attention. Both salespeople and fundraising people are heavily motivated by the desire, not to mention the need, to close the next deal. For the salesperson, there's usually a commission hanging on the end of the next sale. For the fundraiser, commissions are not the driving force, but the combination of altruism—your commitment to the mission—and practicality—keeping your job—replaces commissions reasonably well. But think of what happens if you win the gift, but the donor is impossible to deal with; you get the grant, but the reporting requirements are too onerous; or the corporation agrees to underwrite your event but demands unrealistic concessions from you.

A poor return on effort and a leakier bucket—that's what happens. These examples are all instances of fundraising effort that's more tactical than it is strategic. They hide the possibility that winning those particular deals might bring in some cash today but poke you in the eye later. That's not only unproductive, it's counterproductive. While your fundraising bucket gets leakier and leakier, you're eating more antacid tablets, your agency can't work as effectively as it should, and eventually your job is at risk.

Unfortunately, there's not all that much that you can do about it after the fact. But there is something that you can do *before*. You can figure out which funders are "right" or "best" for you, and which ones are most likely to make you sorry you bothered.

This requires some work on your part. You can't figure out which funders are right for you if you don't set the context for understanding—and improving—your fundraising productivity. To do so requires that you know four things:

1.   How much it should cost to achieve your mission.

2.   The value of your development time, or its "opportunity risk factor."

3.   What makes your best funders "best" in your eyes.

4.   Articulating your unique value proposition (UVP) or "value-added."

WHAT SHOULD IT COST TO ACHIEVE YOUR MISSION?

A few years ago, we worked with the executives of a nonprofit providing affordable housing in a poor neighborhood. The organization was chronically underfunded, but their strategic plan included ambitious fundraising objectives. Initially, that seemed fine and dandy, until we realized that they planned to raise about three times as much money in one year as had ever been produced collectively over the organization's lifetime. Considering that they had no development director, no donor database, and no donor management software, it seemed just a little unrealistic.

Now, funding an organization that builds houses is tricky. The budget for building the houses and fixing up the neighborhood is often separate from the budget that pays for staff and the administrative functions, and lots of it comes from government sources. Raising money to pay for office space, staff, and programs, however, is more likely to come from more conventional forms of philanthropy. The two budgets tend to be raised, spent, and accounted for separately.

Even before the project started, we talked with the chief executive officer (CEO) and chief financial officer (CFO), suggesting that they hire a development professional, but they became quite anxious. They said they couldn't find the money or justify the expense of such a hire. While money was available to build and renovate houses, they told us, there was no money to expand staff, compensate them properly, or pay for the information technology, professional development, and marketing outreach necessary to keep the lights turned on and continue achieving the mission. The board and senior leadership had tolerated the situation and believed that it was the only thing they could do.

Standard operating procedure for this group was "raise what we can, then we'll figure out how to spend it—and if we don't raise enough, we'll just tighten our belts and limp along."

The CFO and the CEO had never tried to figure out what it would really cost to fund the agency's operation because there was always enough, or nearly enough, to pay for building houses and revitalizing neighborhoods. They just couldn't manage the projects, do the marketing, or recruit and retain talented staff. As a result, organizational improvements weren't made, outreach wasn't conducted, staff were either not hired or were given little training, and there was never enough money to hire a development director.

Knowing what it costs to achieve your mission is the first thing you have to do if your fundraising is going to be productive and effective.

Increase the Income, Don't Cut the Budget

The temptation to underspend is endemic in the nonprofit sector. During the budget-planning cycle, it's appropriate to consider ways to save or reduce certain costs. But this is where the "overhead myth" rears its ugly head again. Nonprofit executives have been conditioned to keep their overhead costs so low that they squeak.

Not so long ago, when we were helping a client put their fundraising plan together, the CEO mentioned a revolving line of credit that kept costing them money. The total owed was about $70,000. But when staff and board started to figure out what they ought to raise for next year, they ignored the outstanding debt. Somebody (well, me) had to pound her shoe on the table and say, "Hey, raise enough to pay off that debt *and* pay for the other stuff you need!"

It's tough to raise money, whether you're raising it from sales or through philanthropy. Everybody gets that. And it's probably likely that nonprofit executives and fundraising professionals will continue to earn less than their corporate peers (and have cheaper furniture) forever. But it takes money to make money. Your nonprofit's CEO does the same kind of work as the CEO of a roughly equivalent for-profit enterprise, so executive compensation should be at least adequate. Your development team takes as much risk and works as hard as the for-profit sales team across town. Your needs for information technology, marketing, supplies, staff benefits, and professional development are just as important as they are to the corporate offices downstairs in your building.

The way I see it, though, it seems as if not spending money were some sort of badge of honor for nonprofit professionals. This is where the tin-cup mentality creeps in and makes a mess of things.

DEFINITION: THE TIN-CUP MENTALITY

The tin-cup mentality is the state of mind that says "We're a poor, lowly charity! Give us money because we need it!" Rather than signaling your value to the world, or inviting others to celebrate your triumphs, the tin-cup mentality emphasizes your neediness. Shouting about how poor you are does not inspire confidence among philanthropists. It also gives rise to a terrible fundraising habit, namely, "Let's raise whatever we can and then figure out how to spend it."

Trying to get by on low budgets (or no budgets at all in some cases) is a classic symptom of the tin-cup mentality. While it might sometimes be necessary to run on slim margins, forgo appealing projects, or wait for better times to launch new initiatives, it's a rotten idea to assume that just because you're running a nonprofit, you "can't afford" whatever it is.

Contrarian that I am, I always recommend that the board and CEO look carefully at the budget, asking, "Are we spending *enough* money? What would happen if we spent more?" Developing such a habit pretty well cancels out the tin-cup mentality, also known as the mentality of deprivation. Operating under this mentality, even if you're not consciously aware of it, can really hamstring your fundraising efforts. After all, you believe that your organization's mission delivers some benefit to the individual, the community, and the world, right? If your job is to make a positive difference in the world, what is that worth to the world? It should be worth reasonable levels of financial support. If you think it doesn't deserve such financial support, maybe, just maybe, you're not valuing your own agency the way it deserves to be valued and you should seek a career challenge elsewhere. I'm also going to assume that you work for your organization, serve on its board, or volunteer for it because you believe in it. You're proud of it. Many times, you have a personal connection to it because you or a friend or relative suffered from the negative conditions your organization works to eliminate, the disease it intends to cure, or the art form it celebrates. If you're so proud of the organization, its mission, its values, and its programs, then you need to believe that paying for it, including adequate staff compensation, is a very good thing indeed.

By all means, be prudent about your expenditures. But for heaven's sake, you and the rest of your team should not live on scraps when a professional, robust fundraising effort will get you the money you need to do the job right.

Reverse this mind-set by acknowledging to yourself that your case for support is strong, and that it's your job to make your agency worth raising money for in the first place. Yes, some major funders may want you to keep your overhead costs low and to put most of your money into programs. Those are the funders who still buy into the myth of the overhead ratio. That doesn't mean you should ration service delivery, cut programs, pay your staff less than a living wage, be unable (unwilling?) to provide them with benefits, scrape by using inadequate materials or equipment, or fail to conduct effective outreach because you can't afford the postage. Start your development planning based on what it *ought* to cost you to honor your mission and do it right. You may not be able to fulfill those fundraising goals in your first year or two, but with the right management controls—like the ones you'll learn about in this book—you'll know what to do to improve results every year.

IMPORTANT!

"Not-for-profit" doesn't mean you can't *make* a profit. It means you can't *distribute* your profits back to shareholders. You can, however, use it to improve your ability to serve clients, staff up appropriately, and stash money in a "rainy-day" fund. So please, plan to make a profit—and use it to achieve your mission.

ANALYZING THE TRUE COST
OF YOUR MISSION

To figure out what it should cost you to achieve your mission, start by looking at your current budget, paying careful attention to the expenses column. That should tell you your actual situation to date. But then, you will want to go back to your strategic plan. (If you don't have a strategic plan, shame on you; it will be more difficult for you to complete this assignment.)

Scrutinize your strategic plan as well as your actual budget. Ask yourself some questions like these:

- *Clients.* How many do we currently serve? Are there more people in our area who could benefit from our services? What would it cost for us to serve 50 percent more or 100 percent more individuals? *Note:* If you don't actually serve clients, ask this question a different way, by referring to the research, position papers, projects, grants you intend to make to others, or other things you do. What would it cost if you added more units of service delivery?

- *Program, technical, and administrative staff.* If we served more individuals or did more projects, would we be able to service them with our current staff? If not, how many more staff should we have, and how big should our payroll be then?

- *Facilities.* If we raised the number of clients, projects, and staff, would we have enough room, equipment, or supplies to do the job right? If we don't, how much will it cost us to get them?

- *Technology.* Ditto. Do we have the right technological resources, up-to-date software, and level of support that allow us to take full advantage of our applications and manage our affairs effectively? If not, what should we be spending?

For you non–financial experts out there, this is the way you create a pro forma budget. Pro forma budgets are "as if" exercises, designed to help you figure out how much money you would spend, and therefore would need to make over the next few years, in order to run the organization at its current level of capacity, a moderately larger level, and a significantly larger level. Typically, pro forma budgets look out two, three, or five years and show the anticipated budgets at low, moderate, and high levels. The pro forma exercise lets you speculate about what it would cost to operate your nonprofit at different levels of service capacity.

If you're thinking, "This is about capacity building," you are correct! Fundraising the SMART Way™ is all about capacity building, and about doing it using facts, not guesses, and evidence, not opinions. Thanks to the facts and evidence you'll capture and analyze, you'll gain greater insights and clarity. You'll also reduce the battle of wills that may occur among staff members or, worse, between board and staff, which often happens when differences of opinion are based on personal feelings and convictions rather than data or evidence. That battle of wills may actually be going on today, even if your staff or board members are too polite and diplomatic to let it show.

CASE STUDY	THE PRO FORMA BUDGET

We recently worked with the executive director (ED) of a nonprofit serving people with vision impairments. Every year, this ED struggled to raise about $1.6 million, much of it from state and county grants and contracts. When we asked her, "Are you serving all the people you could serve?," she said no. When we then asked, "What's holding you back?," she said, "Lack of money." When we asked, "If you can't serve more people, are you truly achieving your mission?," she said no again. "So how much more money should you raise in order to serve more people and offer more programs?" She said, "Wow—I never thought of it that way."

This agency is now working to put together a five-year pro forma budget.

YOUR OPPORTUNITY RISK FACTOR: THE REAL VALUE OF YOUR TIME

Figuring out how to build fundraising capacity requires an appreciation of the value of your time. Time is inelastic; you can't stretch the day beyond 24 hours or make an hour last longer than 60 minutes. Considering the constantly growing demands on your time, you have to recognize that it's not only precious, there's simply not that much of it. Unlike almost every other resource (talent, money, facilities, supplies), there is only so much time to go around, although we all know plenty of people who act as if they have unlimited time. Assuming, that is, that they don't spend any time on sleep, vacations, or sick days. Let's ignore that mistaken notion that you can do more stuff if you multitask. Multitasking doesn't work. Period.

The time you devote to fundraising comes with huge financial implications, often described as opportunity cost or its kissin' cousin "lost-opportunity cost." Opportunity cost includes stuff that's fairly simple to count up, such as meals, transportation, cost of collateral materials, travel, lodging, and other tidy line items you can expense with relative ease. It also should include the cost of your time. But I prefer to define the financial implications of fundraising time in terms of risk, rather than in terms of how much you're paid. I call it the *opportunity risk factor,* the amount of potential income you put at risk for every hour invested in fund development.

First, it's important to acknowledge that absolutely no one is able to spend 100 percent of their time on raising money. At least you have to sleep a few hours now and then, and there are other unavoidable drains on your time. So once you subtract the time devoted to those other things, from reporting to the board to taking your kid to the emergency room, you only have a certain amount left over to apply to the activities of fundraising, including such critical tasks as identifying appropriate prospects, writing grant applications, and meeting with major donors to convince them to raise their annual gifts to a higher level. Subtract all those nondevelopment hours from the total number of hours worked per year. Divide your annual fundraising target by the number of hours left over after you deduct hours

---

CASE STUDY	THE OPPORTUNITY RISK FACTOR

The opportunity risk factor is usually somewhere around $1,000 an hour, and often more. If you're the ED, it might be significantly higher than that. In one case, the fundraising team calculated their opportunity risk factors and discovered that theirs ran somewhere around $18,000 an hour, largely because their time management was so inefficient.

Unfortunately, the ED walked into the training room at the point where we had just calculated that enormous figure. When we explained the exercise to him, his face turned white and he actually staggered to a nearby table to hold himself up. We thought we might have to dial 911.

Calculate Opportunity Risk of One Hour of Fundraising Time
Estimate Number of Days You Devote to Each Activity. Place Your Cursor Over the Red
Triangles for Further Instructions and Explanations.

Days	Total per Year	Running Total
Total Number of Days in a Year		365
◥ Less Weekends	104	261
Less Holidays (State, Federal, Religious, etc.)	54	207
◥ Less Vacation	10	197
◥ Less Sick, Personal Days	5	192
◥ Less Days Devoted to Administration, Record keeping	94	98
◥ Less Days Devoted to Travel	6	92
Less Days Devoted to Training, Conferences, Offsites	12	80
◥ Less Days Devoted to Board Meeting Prep & Attend	12	68
◥ Less "Lost" Days	5	63
Total Number of Days Left		63
Total Number of Hours in a Year for Business Development (Number of Days Times 8 Hours)		504
Your Annual Fundraising Target in Dollars	$ 1,000,000	
Your Opportunity Cost (Income Target Divided by Number of Development Hours)		**$ 1,984.13**

If You Misuse One Hour of Opportunity Cost, Every Hour Left for Fundraising Is More Expensive and More Risky!

305-935-6676 | www.bristolstrategygroup.com | ellen@bristolstrategygroup.com

EXHIBIT 1.1   **THE OPPORTUNITY RISK CALCULATOR**
Source: Bristol Strategy Group

spent on all that other stuff. That's your opportunity risk factor. Use the calculator shown in Exhibit 1.1, or download the live spreadsheet from our web site.

If you've completed the exercise and learned your own opportunity risk factor, you may be thinking, "Hey, they're not paying me enough here!" Well, don't take it personally. The opportunity risk factor has very little to do with your payroll or benefits, and everything to do with the investment value of your time. When people make an investment, what do they look for? A return, of course! In terms of fundraising, you invest your time with the expectation that you will receive a considerable ROI—return on investment, or ROE—return on effort.

If you're carrying an opportunity risk factor of $1,000 or more an hour, you will think twice about which prospects justify the investment of your time. This is not to say that you don't show appreciation for those donors who give you small amounts of money. Of course you do. It's just not a good use of your time to spend hours and hours on a poorly qualified prospect when you could be investing those hours on donor prospects with a higher potential for lifetime donor value.

Establish the context for productive fund development by providing more objective criteria to differentiate between high-potential, moderate-potential, and no-potential donors. And that puts money right back onto your bottom line.

IMPORTANT!

Every hour you waste on unqualified funding prospects or unproductive development activities makes the opportunity risk factor of your remaining hours go *up*.

WHAT MAKES YOUR BEST FUNDERS "BEST"?

A common practice in corporate sales is to create something called a "loss report" if the deal you've been working on doesn't come through. The loss report is supposed to reveal why the prospect didn't buy from you. Most sales reps despise them, by the way, and I hated them with all my heart. They were tough to complete. For one thing, the buyer who blew you off was ill-inclined to spend more time telling you how you messed up. So they'd avoid you or lie to you out of politeness. The reports became exercises in creative writing for the sales team. I used to ask myself if we wouldn't be better off asking our happy customers, "Why did you buy from us? And will your experience lead you to buying from us again?" Now *that* practice would have been useful.

Figure out why your best donors give to you. Then clone them.

Classic prospect research doesn't really do a good job of telling you why your donors give to you. It tends to focus on the database-able information, the demographics, net worth, wealth profile, and giving history of the prospect. This information is useful, but it's not necessarily a good way to discover the kinds of qualitative insights you need in order to be persuasive. If the prospect doesn't give, your development officers may not complete loss reports, but they will speculate, sometimes endlessly, on why this person or that failed to make a gift.

So the real question is this: Why do your best donors give to you? What is it that inspires them to support your agency? And are there other funders who might share the same inspiration?

I'd like you to stop for a few minutes right now and think about the funders who currently support your agency. What it is that you like about them? Maybe it's just that they laugh at your jokes or give you expensive bottles of Scotch at Christmas. But, hopefully, what you like about your best funders includes such desirable qualities as:

- They give year after year after year.
- They raise the size of their gifts on a regular basis.
- They want some recognition but don't have unrealistic expectations.
- They love to brag about your organization and act as your booster club.
- They're happy to step forward, volunteer, and go the extra mile because they believe in what you're doing.
- They're the ones who tell you they want to leave their estates to you, so could you please figure out how to handle planned giving?
- If the development officer who acquired them leaves your shop, the donors don't follow the officer; they stick with your nonprofit.

Are these the things that describe the funders you like the most? Make up a list of all the desirable qualities you like in your current donor base. It's okay to do a little Frankenstein action here and cobble together qualities that exist in these donors over here, with others that only exist in those donors over there.

This exercise is often something of a surprise for the people we work with. They simply haven't thought about things this way. Maybe they've ignored those desirable qualities in the mistaken belief that wealth profile and giving history are somehow more important. But they're not. In fact, once you have gained clarity on the relationship you have with your best, happiest, most committed donors, your fundraising effectiveness is likely to increase, often dramatically.

The funders you like the most are usually the ones that like you the most in return. They don't always exhibit all the same characteristics. There are donors you adore, even though they might not give you the largest gifts. There are other donors you appreciate because of the amount they give you, even though you might not want to spend tons of social time with them. And there are still other donors you approve of because they're well connected, even if they don't give the most and you don't want to spend tons of social time with them. Write down a list of things that you love about your best funders. Be sure to include items that you may think of as frivolous or "too personal" for your standard business list. Sometimes the value of a donor is the enthusiastic sense of vision or potential that they bring you.

Characteristics of Your Favorite Funders

The idea here is to describe the relationship you want to have with your best funders *after* you acquire them. If you know what they ought to be, do, and give after the relationship has matured, it's easier to choose the right prospects in the first place. You'll now be cultivating with "the end in mind."

YOUR UNIQUE VALUE PROPOSITION: THE VALUE IN VALUE-ADDED

Before your start trying to raise money, you have to figure out what you're "selling" in the first place. It's surprising how often this basic step is given short shrift, but it's an investment of effort that will pay off handsomely.

After all, if you don't know what you're selling to your funders, you can't differentiate the good ones from the DOA's—the donors who are dead on arrival and make you sorry you cultivated their gifts in the first place. Sum up this value in a few words and it becomes your UVP. In the for-profit world, it's sometimes referred to as the unique selling proposition (USP). Maybe you've thought of it as your "elevator pitch."

Whether you think of it as selling or value, it's shorthand for your case for support, another important prospecting tool that gets short shrift, according to the Leaky Bucket study.

IMPORTANT!

The ideal donor is a donor who wants to support your nonprofit's mission and programs, at the level of giving you prefer, and who is satisfied with the kind of recognition you're good at delivering.

What is the UVP? It's a way to describe the value you bring to your two primary constituencies: clients and donors. The UVP will also play a role in attracting board members, staff members, and even volunteers, but we'll get to those applications later.

Defining your UVP requires thoughtful analysis. Avoid the temptation to put one together simply as an exercise in creative writing; that doesn't work. For now, please (PLEASE!) ignore everything you think you know about writing advertising copy. Follow the exercises in this chapter, preferably in a small group including members of your fund development team, program people, maybe even some board members or volunteers, rather than working alone. You'll get better insights.

And here's an important tip. Don't try to write the UVP without this analysis. If you think you can just dream up a brilliant piece of advertising copy, you're making a huge mistake.

SWOT Analysis with a Twist

The strengths, weaknesses, opportunities, and threats (SWOT) analysis is a great place to start articulating your UVP. We're going to add a twist at the end of this exercise, but for now, simply brainstorm to define the four components of the SWOT. Strengths and weaknesses are internal; they describe or characterize what's working well and not so well within the four walls of your organization. Opportunities and threats are external; they describe the market conditions within which you operate. Note that a strength can be a weakness and vice versa; opportunities can be threats and vice versa. But an opportunity cannot be a strength or a weakness because it describes something outside the boundaries of your organization.

For example, a strength might be your ability to provide a high ratio of teachers to students, while a weakness might be your challenges in retaining teachers because you can't pay them a competitive wage. Following this example, a desirable opportunity might be that the population of potential students is growing larger in your catchment area, while a threat would be the existence of schools offering higher teacher pay in the same area. We offer examples of the right way to do a SWOT so you can follow our lead.

While the SWOT analysis is most often used in strategic planning, we have adapted it just a little to make it useful for defining your UVP. First, conduct the SWOT in the conventional manner, as shown in the following example. We'll use The Arboretum as our fictional case study.

CASE STUDY	SWOT ANALYSIS FOR THE ARBORETUM

The Arboretum is a much-loved botanical garden in a midsized city. While attendance has been growing since a capital campaign helped to enlarge the facility and gift shop, donor retention and acquisition have fallen off. The Arboretum's senior leadership and development staff decided to analyze their UVP as a step in retaining current donors, reengaging past donors, and acquiring new donors. (See Table 1.1.)

TABLE 1.1   THE ARBORETUM: SWOT ANALYSIS

Internal Strengths	Internal Weaknesses
• 50-year track record	• Too much depends on ED
• Executive director well known	• Employee turnover is high
• Interactive environment appeals to all ages	• Information technology is out of date
• Strong research component; worldwide reputation for science	• We have a weak web site
	• We give too many fundraising events

- Scientists work well with volunteers, admin staff
- Practical resources for gardeners
- Peaceful oasis in busy city
- Reputation for sound management
- Known as a great place to work
- Recognized for educational programs for K–12 schoolchildren

- Working on a shoestring budget
- We don't market enough or consistently
- Case statement is out of date
- Internal communication is terrible
- Not enough training for nonscientific staff or volunteers

External Opportunities

External Threats

- Growing interest in gardening
- Local schools require extracurricular activities for students to graduate
- Lots of new houses going up in our neighborhood
- Local garden clubs are thriving
- County, state are favorable to funding zoos, arboreta, aquariums, etc.
- Economy is improving

- Economy is still shaky
- Local zoological society far more well-known than we are
- Stiff competition for state, local funding
- Still recovering from last year's superstorm
- Scientists predict another bad storm season for our region

Use questions like the following to complete your own SWOT analysis the right way. You can use our template or any other table format to answer the questions. Like several other exercises you have already done, the SWOT analysis is best performed in a group.

Strengths Questions

- What are our agency's competitive distinctions?
- What do our programs and services do better than/different from comparable programs and services from others?
- How well do we handle client service and outcomes? What, if anything, do we do in this area that's distinctive? What do we do well, even though others also do it?

- How well do we handle our fundraising process, from identifying funding prospects through cultivation and retention?
- Have we established reasonable financial goals for the agency, enough to cover costs and extra for growth?
- *Caveat:* Avoid using "fuzzy" abstractions such as "great people" or "committed staff." Instead, choose strengths that can be assessed by objective or quantifiable means.

Weaknesses Questions

- Are there gaps in our portfolio of programs/services that hamper our success?
- Are we slow, sloppy, or otherwise below par in client service delivery or program operations?
- Does our fundraising team understand how to promote our programs, services, and case for support?
- Are there operational glitches or obstacles within the agency that have a negative impact on our marketing or fundraising?

Opportunities Questions

- What's going on in our marketplace that presents us with new community needs or desires, especially ones that might be of interest to our current donors?
- Are there growth opportunities for us in other geographies or markets, especially ones we could penetrate with reasonable risk and expense?
- Are there opportunities to partner or collaborate with other agencies for fundraising purposes?
- Is there anything going on in the economy at large that could give us a boost?
- What information do we have (or need to have) about new or expanding market opportunities that would be right for our agency and its current suite of programs and services?

Threats Questions

- Have other nonprofits launched new programs and services or innovative marketing programs that are attractive to our current clients or donors?

- What's happening in the local market that would hamper our ability to sustain operations or build capacity?
- What's happening to interest rates and the credit environment; could it be detrimental to our ability to sustain operations or build capacity?
- Are there global or macroeconomic forces at work (war, energy prices, etc.) that could compromise our growth or drive up our operating costs?
- Are we vulnerable to weather disasters that could disrupt operations (blizzards in northern climates, hurricanes in southern climates)?

The Twist: Strengths the Competition Can't Touch

Now that you have completed your SWOT and filled out all four of those interesting quadrants, we want you to ignore everything except for your strengths. While it's important to understand your weaknesses, remember that your donors do not give to your weaknesses; they give to your strengths. Save the weaknesses, opportunities, and threats in a file somewhere and use them during your next strategic planning project.

Read your list of strengths to yourself and ask a critical question: which of these items motivates our donors to give to us? For example, many nonprofits are proud of their dedicated staff members. Do donors give because you have dedicated staff members, or do they give because you solve a social problem? Do they give because your hospital is considered a "great place to work" or because your hospital's expertise in dealing with heart disease (or whatever) is considered to be exceptional?

Be ruthless in this exercise. If you and the other people in your group can't agree that a particular item on the list actually motivates a donor to give, then strike that item off. Ask yourselves if there are other reasons why donors give that you haven't captured on your list. The items that remain after this ruthless pruning likely represent your UVP.

| CASE STUDY | THE ARBORETUM STRENGTHS ANALYSIS |

The Arboretum's leadership scrutinized the strengths quadrant of their SWOT analysis to identify their true competitive distinction.

Arboretum Strengths

- 50-year track record of preserving plant species.
- Interactive environment appeals to all ages.

- Strong research component, worldwide reputation.
- Practical services, resources for gardeners.
- Peaceful oasis in busy city.
- Strengthens our city's reputation as a world-class city.
- Reputation for sound management.
- Recognized for educational programs for K–12 schoolchildren.

Arboretum leaders agreed that these eight items represented the value-added they bring to their community, to plant science, and to conservation of the natural habitat.

What We Covered

- To revolutionize fundraising, start by describing what makes your best funders "best." To do so, concentrate on the relationship you have with these funders after you have acquired them.

- Learn to think like Cousin Judy and concentrate on knowing which funders are "good enough" for you, not the other way around.

- Your fundraising time is both scarce and precious. Invest it wisely.

- Seek a high ROE when you invest in cultivating funders. If the ROE is too low, you're chasing the wrong prospects.

- Understand why your best funders give to you. Their motivations for giving are much more important than their net worth, giving history, or capacity for giving.

- Understand what you're selling, and why it's motivating to the funders you like the most.

What You Can Do

- Complete a Leaky Bucket Assessment for your organization. Even better, have several members of the team—staff and board—complete the assessment and compare notes. If you don't know what's broken, you can't fix it. Go to www.BristolStrategyGroup.com/nonprofit-leakybucket to complete the live assessment.

- Figure out what it should cost to achieve your mission. If it should cost more than you currently raise, it's time to rethink the way you raise money. Remember—increase the income, don't cut the budget.

- Calculate your opportunity risk factor. It's easiest if you download a copy of the calculator from www.wiley.com/go/smartfundraising. Keep your risk factor in mind when you're prospecting.

- Describe your best funders by looking at the characteristics they share *after* you have acquired them.

- Conduct a SWOT analysis of your organization, emphasizing the strengths most sought after by donors.

CHAPTER 2

Funder Selection Strategies

We're now going to take up the challenge expressed so succinctly by Cousin Judy. How do we know if a funding prospect is good enough for us to pursue?

Through the use of the funder selection strategy.

The funder selection strategy is the step that comes before you conduct prospect research. It's the exercise where you identify the qualities, values, and other "soft" characteristics of your most beloved donors. You determine the motivations that drive those donors to engage and remain engaged, and describe the nature of the relationships you have with those donors once they are engaged. Funder selection strategies are based on the notion that, if you know what kind of relationship you seek with your best donors, and if you design your methods of cultivation and retention to maintain those relationships, more and more of the donors you acquire will match the ideal-funder profile.

If you develop your funder selection strategy carefully and then actually use it to drive development, eventually all your funding sources will come to resemble the ideal ones. In other words, all (well, most) funders will engage with your organization and remain engaged with it, regardless of the size of their gifts.

I wish I could say that corporate sales organizations have cracked the code of customer selection, but for the most part, they too are in the same boat as development professionals. Even when the boss provides reasonable standards and criteria for qualifying prospects, we still see more salespeople taking on any old prospect as long as there's an address and a pulse. So, fundraisers, it's up to you to break the mold here.

Funder selection criteria are based on characteristics of funders that represent ideal performance after you have acquired them. In other words, figure out how your best, favorite, "ideal" funders act like and talk like and give like today, so you can clone them. Donors who resemble your best funders are already motivated to select and stick with causes like yours, missions like yours, even your specific nonprofit. They will give to you based on the extent to which your organization addresses their charitable motivations and satisfies their desires for feedback, stewardship, and recognition. Once you have such a benchmark at your disposal, your prospect research will be more accurate and thus more useful. It will give you better return on investment (ROI) if you're buying or renting your lists, and better return on effort (ROE) regardless of the costs of your lists.

Chapter 1 focused on the context for fundraising effectiveness, an exercise that lays the groundwork for defining funder selection strategies. The formula goes like this:

- Figure out your opportunity risk factor, so you'll understand the importance of investing in the right donors and avoiding the wrong ones.

- Understand the real costs of achieving your mission, to make sure you raise enough money to support it.

- Define what makes a funding source "best" by looking at both qualitative and quantifiable characteristics

- Figure out and document the value-added strengths of your agency, the elements that attract prospective funders to you.

Now we'll move on to the next critical step, which is understanding the reasons why your best donors and other funders support your agency.

Good, accurate funder selection criteria aid the fundraising revolution by placing the focus of attention on donors, not simply in a tactical way, but rather by perceiving the effort from the donors' point of view. As Penelope Burke has said, this approach is "donor-centered." The deeper, more personal motivations that characterize your best funding sources today become the standards for new-funder selection. If you know what those motivations are, and if you can express them in the language your donors use, you are far more likely to engage new-donor prospects and move them through the relationship-building phase at a surprisingly rapid pace.

By contrast, fundraising that is *not* donor-centered keeps the attention on your agency. When they are in meetings with their prospects, development officers may be thinking more about meeting their assigned income targets; executives may be more concerned about the agency's need for money; board members may be trying to fulfill their funding obligations. Great funder-selection strategies, however, are all about engaging funders who are right for your agency—i.e., good enough for you—and downplaying the importance of those who are not. Which means you'll take their money if they give it to you, but you're not going to invest a lot of brainpower and cycle time in cultivating it.

WHY YOUR BEST FUNDERS SUPPORT YOU

Your best funders support your nonprofit because doing so does something for them. It scratches some sort of itch that can only be scratched properly through charitable giving, preferably to your agency. If you understand the itch and know how to scratch it, your fundraising results improve. Effective, efficient fundraising requires understanding what your donors want to accomplish with their charitable giving, not just how much money they want to give. Donors do not simply give you money because you asked politely. They invest in the impact your programs and services have in ways that relate to their own motivations. Itch, scratch.

Most donors give to achieve personal objectives. These may be entirely altruistic, such as those who give to alleviate a societal problem or discover a cure for a disease. Other personal objectives may seem self-interested, such as gaining community recognition or hobnobbing with the rich and famous. Often self-serving and altruistic motivations exist in the same donor. All of these motivations are entirely legitimate. Understanding and appreciating them will make your fundraising efforts more successful.

In the last chapter you articulated your nonprofit's value-added strengths. This chapter is all about the defining the "yin" to match the "yang" of the value-added. We call it the donor's value-sought. Value-sought spells out what drives your best funders' charitable motivations and philosophy. Value-sought criteria help donors and other funders to choose the charities they want to support. Uncover those values and you will improve the productivity of your fundraising efforts.

Giving capacity remains critically important, of course, but has less impact on your funder selection strategy. We'll discuss the role of giving capacity in Chapter 3 where you'll see how to develop the SMART Way™ Prospect Scorecard.

The things that motivate your major funding sources probably also motivate your minor funding sources as well. The only difference between a major donor and a "minor" donor, after all, is the size of their gifts. If I were raising money for your nonprofit, I'd like to make sure that all my donors, grantors, and corporate contributors shared similar motivations for giving; that would mean I'd always have a stable of minor donors whom I could gradually convert to "major" status over time.

Discovering Value-Sought

Value-sought criteria describe your donors' motivations for giving, including their passion for or commitment to your cause, as well as their personal self-interest above and beyond altruism. Every donor gives for complicated reasons reflecting their emotions and values. A common motivation for giving to a nonprofit battling cancer might well be the donor's personal experience with the disease. In fact, "personal connection to the mission" is one of the most common criteria we find in value-sought analyses.

DEFINITION: VALUE-SOUGHT

If the things that make our nonprofit distinctive or competitive can be called value-added, then we need a phrase to describe the desire to obtain such value, hence the term *value-sought*. It describes the attributes, values, concepts, themes, or competitive distinctions that the donor (or buyer) is hunting for when seeking to make a charitable gift (or purchase). Here's what's tricky: donors don't always know what their value-sought may be. It's up to the development officer to reveal it.

The process of discovering value-sought characteristics offers a wonderful opportunity to interact with your best funders in ways that you and they will enjoy. You will learn how to ask some simple, open-ended questions that have nothing to do with money. It's the open-ended probing questions that place your donors on center stage and reveal their motivations. Questions like "Why do you give to charity?" and "What are you trying to accomplish by giving to charities like ours?" are all about the donor, not about you. They reveal why your best donors give in general, why they give to the cause your nonprofit supports, and why they give to your nonprofit in particular. They provide donor perspectives and preferences in ordinary conversational language. Knowing what moves them, and being able to express it in similar terms, is as donor-centered as it gets.

Each of the three funding categories requires slightly different approaches to define their value-sought. The charitable motivations characteristic of individual donors are quite different from the motivations of grant-making organizations. And corporate contributors have yet another set of motivations. You can get every type of funder to open up and tell you what you want to hear by using three simple questions, modified slightly depending on the funding category. These simple questions encourage donors to open up and tell their story. And for reasons that I don't really understand, you, the questioner, get all kinds of brownie points for being an expert and a great listener—even though you only asked variations of these three simple questions:

- What do you want to achieve with your charitable giving?
- What do you want to avoid with your charitable giving?
- How do you know if you're choosing the charity that's right for you?

Many people are stymied when they envision asking questions of donor prospects, often because they're sure that the first question to ask is "Gimme money!" I guess that's not really a question, but you get the drift. To help you avoid that trap, I've provided some suggested probing questions to start you on the right track.

List of suggested probing questions:

- *What do you want to achieve?*
  - What inspires you to give to charity? What causes or missions are most likely to attract your attention and support? Why do you think that way?
  - What would you like your gifts to accomplish? Why is that important to you?

- If the nonprofits you support were to be completely successful, what would that mean to you? Why would that be important?
- *What do you want to avoid?*
  - When you think about charities you currently support or have supported in the past, what did you want those charities to wipe out, reduce or eliminate?
  - What is it about [the disease, social problem, environmental danger, etc.] that concerns you so much? How does that impact your charitable decisions?
  - What's at stake if your preferred charities are not able to fulfill their missions?
  - What do you think [or fear] might happen if those situations are not resolved? Why is that important to you?
- *How do you know you've chosen the right charity?*
  - How do you choose the charities you like to support? What do you like to see or hear about them to convince you?
  - What would a charity need to show you, after you have given your support, to convince you that you had made a good decision?
  - Have you ever decided not to invest in a charity, or even withdrawn your support from one? Why did that happen?

We will go into more detail about using questions like these in a later section.

Qualitative Market Research   When you analyzed your agency's value-added, you had to look at only one entity: your own nonprofit. But to clarify value-sought, you have to look at a bunch of different funders from each major funding category. The more funders you analyze in a given category, the more likely you'll be to figure out what moves them to take action. The things that motivate individuals to give may be quite different from the things that motivate foundations to make grants, or businesses to invest in sponsorships.

The value-sought analysis is conducted by means of conversations with your current funders in any particular category—individual/major gifts, foundation grants, or corporate contributions—seeking the common ideas that move those funders to give. Think of this as qualitative market research.

If you ask the same questions of 10 or 20 funders in a given category, you'll learn why they gave and expect to continue giving. It's okay if you interview more than 20 people, but once you get to about 40, you will have heard enough to describe your donor's value-sought. Then review your notes looking for common themes, words, and phrases. The ones that occur frequently are most likely to be persuasive to other funding prospects.

IMPORTANT!

The questions you use to elicit your donor's value-sought are also great questions to use when you're qualifying a new prospect. You'll see how in Chapter 3.

For Individual/Major Donors   Individual donors respond to the three simple questions in fairly straightforward ways (Table 2.1). Create variations on the standard simple questions listed earlier.

- What does the donor wish to achieve by supporting our agency? In other words, does the donor want to play a role in ending hunger, finding a cure for breast cancer, or celebrating the triumphs of amateur thespians?
- What does the donor wish to avoid by supporting our agency? In other words, would the donor be unhappy if more native plant species were lost due to home construction, if hungry children in Somalia were not fed, or if the art of silk embroidery were lost?
- What personal benefit or gain, if any, does the donor seek by supporting our agency? In other words, does the donor seek to be recognized for their giving, have a say in the direction of your charity's research agenda, or want a seat on your board in return for their large gift?

TABLE 2.1   DONOR'S VALUE-SOUGHT ANALYSIS

Donor's Value-Sought
What do they want to achieve?
What do they want to avoid?
What personal benefit or gain do they seek?

TABLE 2.2   GRANT MAKER'S VALUE-SOUGHT ANALYSIS

Grant-Maker's Value-Sought
How do they want their grantees to succeed?
What do they want their grantees to avoid
How do they measure their own success internally?

For Grant-Making Organizations   The fact that a grant-making organization publishes its granting guidelines doesn't mean you know everything you need to know about its value-sought. You need answers you won't find in the granting guidelines (Table 2.2). The three questions you'll want to answer about your best grantors include:

- How do they want their grantees to succeed?
- What do they want their grantees to avoid?
- How do they measure their own success internally?

Start this exercise with a specific grantor whom you like, and fill in the answers to the best of your ability. If (when) you discover that you can't fill in the blanks, go buy lunch for your grantor's representative and ask.

For Corporate Sponsors   Commercial, for-profit businesses can be a great asset to your funding picture, even though corporate philanthropy accounts for only about 5 to 7 percent of charitable giving in the United States. This slice of the fundraising pie could probably be larger if fundraising professionals would give it more attention. For one thing, it's easy to talk to business executives about money, since they are running their enterprises to

IMPORTANT!

Corporate sponsorship is different from corporate philanthropy. If the business is large enough, most or all of its charitable giving will come from its foundation, so if you're getting money from such a foundation, it's coming to you in the form of a grant. Corporate sponsorship dollars, however, usually come out of the company's marketing budget. The corporation invests this money to provide a business benefit, whether quantitative (more customers, more sales) or qualitative (good-corporate-citizen points).

make a profit and they talk about buying and selling all day long. If you can show executives that investing in your charity provides business benefits, you're on your way to a high-value relationship.

The executives of for-profit businesses are just as likely as other types of donors to have altruistic reasons for giving to charity, but they will also seek to obtain meaningful business benefits. Corporate gifts range from small (signing up for an exhibit space at a conference, buying a table at a gala event) to very large (acting as the title sponsor for a major event or underwriting an entire program). Corporate funders define their value-sought in terms of the business benefits they seek (Table 2.3). Find the following answers to define corporate value-sought:

TABLE 2.3   CORPORATE SPONSOR'S VALUE-SOUGHT ANALYSIS

Corporate Sponsor's Value-Sought
How/Why they want to be perceived as good corporate citizens
Business opportunities and other benefits they anticipate
Opportunities for community influence and leadership development

- How and why the company wants to be perceived as a good corporate citizen.
- What business opportunities or other business benefits the company seeks.
- What opportunities for community influence or leadership the company may seek.

What Happens after the Interviews

Take the most common themes and phrases from these interviews and organize them under headings matching the three simple questions: what donors want to achieve, what they want to avoid, and how they know they've chosen the right charity. Then shorten each of the three lists down to no more than 8 to 10 ideas. Eliminate duplicates, collapse similar themes into one, and use multivoting or other techniques for prioritizing. When you're done, you'll have one list that represents things donors wish to achieve, one for things they wish to avoid, and one for things that tell them they've chosen the right charity.

The finished product will look something like this. This list represents the value-sought characteristics of major donors for the Arboretum, the botanical garden we introduced in Chapter 1.

- What do major donors want to achieve?
  - Pass my love of gardening to future generations.
  - Extensive "botanical" world travels.
  - Keep the garden open and available to all.
  - Contribute to projects that enhance our city.
- What do they want to avoid?
  - Fear the loss of additional plant species and habitats.
  - Fear that our city's growth will harm our reputation as a great place to live and work.
  - Concern that our city's children have little contact with the natural world.
- What personal benefit do major donors seek?
  - Philanthropy is an obligation for people of wealth.
  - Want to know and work with like-minded people.
  - Appreciate the respect my philanthropy produces in the community.
  - Want public recognition for my philanthropy.

Use the same approach to clarify value-sought for each major funding category.

CASE STUDY   VALUE-SOUGHT IN THE REAL WORLD

Some people shop for groceries at the big supermarket chains because they seek certain values such as the ease of finding a local store, low prices, good service, and easy parking. For these shoppers, price plays a role even if they are well off and don't have to budget tightly; their value-sought (finding local stores, good prices, etc.) is the deciding factor. Other people prefer specialty stores promoting other values, such as organic produce and environmentally conscious cleaning supplies. While many of these shoppers may be less well off or budget conscious, low prices are not the major selling point. Their value-sought criteria (organic produce, "green" cleaning products) are more powerful or persuasive than low prices.

THE EXCHANGE OF VALUE

Now that you have developed your value-sought criteria, are you ready to engage these funders and respond properly to their values and preferences? The honest truth is a big fat *if*. You can engage them *if* your value-added intersects with their value-sought. If it doesn't, you've got two choices: fix your operation so that it does, or find donors with the value-sought characteristics that meet the way you run things today.

Value-sought and value-added criteria don't mean a lot when they stand alone and separate. The power of these two sets of criteria emerges when you compare them. The exercise of comparison produces a deep understanding of the ways in which nonprofit organizations and their funders work in partnership to achieve the mission. In simple terms, if your value-added doesn't align with the funder's value-sought, you might still win the gift, but you're not as likely to win lifetime commitment.

Comparing value-added to value-sought criteria produces the exchange of value, a way to describe this dynamic partnership. Think of it as the engine that drives your case for support.

The exchange of value is pretty straightforward. They (your funders) have to want what you (the agency) have to offer. In return, they give you what you want and need, namely, financial and nonfinancial support over the long haul. They have to want to support your mission, programs, and values, and you have to be able to respond with the mission achievement, program integrity, and levels of feedback, involvement, and recognition that they desire. Once you visualize this exchange, your ability to craft persuasive messages improves dramatically.

IMPORTANT!

How many donors have come on board because they have a connection with the CEO, founder, chief scientist, or development officer? Seems to me this is quite a common phenomenon. A few development professionals have even told me that this is a good thing.

But what happens to those donors when the big attraction—the CEO, scientist, or development officer—steps down, wins the lottery, or joins a monastery? Whether you will retain those donors is a crap shoot.

It's fairly easy to visualize the exchange of value as long as you do it in two steps. This exercise takes longer to explain than it does to execute.

In the first step, create a two-column table. In one column, write up your value-added criteria. In the other column, enter the value-sought criteria for a particular funder in a given category. Our example is a hypothetical major donor we'll call Hyacinth Gardner. Hyacinth is a retired professor of botany at the local university and has been a volunteer, board member, and supporter of the Arboretum for many years. She is a world traveler, master gardener, and enthusiastic grandmother. Hyacinth is wealthy, generous, and a delight to work with. As you see in Table 2.4, we extracted the strengths quadrant from the Arboretum's SWOT analysis, then entered the value-sought criteria for Hyacinth in the right-hand column.

TABLE 2.4   VALUE-ADDED TO VALUE-SOUGHT COMPARISON FOR THE ARBORETUM

The Arboretum—Value-Added Strengths	Major Donors—Value-Sought
• 50-year track record • Executive director well known • Interactive environment appeals to all ages • Strong research component; worldwide reputation for science • Scientists work well with volunteers, admin staff • Practical resources for gardeners • Peaceful oasis in busy city • Reputation for sound management • Known as a great place to work • Recognized for educational programs for K–12 schoolchildren	***What they want to achieve*** • Pass my love of gardening to future generations • Extensive "botanical" world travels • Keep the garden open and available to all • Contribute to projects that enhance our city ***What they want to avoid*** • Fear loss of additional plant species and habitats • Fear that city's growth will harm our reputation as a great place to live and work • Concerned that our city's children have little contact with the natural world ***Personal benefit or gain they seek*** • Philanthropy is an obligation for people of wealth • Want to know, work with like-minded people • Appreciate the respect my philanthropy produces • Want public recognition for my philanthropy

Now that you have the two lists side by side, think about where they intersect. Look for ways in which your agency's value-added strengths motivate your donors to take action or commit themselves to your support. Therefore, you want to pinpoint the value-added items with the most impact on the donor's value-sought. Only a few of your strengths will have an impact on the value-sought column, and only a few of the value-sought items will be impacted. These connections articulate the exchange of value, or dynamic partnership, that exists between your agency and its funders. Although this exchange is typically thought of in practical terms as the basis of your marketing messages, I actually see it as something more elevated. To me, the exchange of value represents fulfilling your agency's potential to achieve its mission. It tells us that the bond between the agency and its funders is sacred; without such partnerships, the mission remains out of reach, and philanthropists cannot fulfill their charitable aims.

IMPORTANT!

The exchange of value between the nonprofit and its donors represents the way your agency will fulfill its potential and achieve its mission. Isn't it a shame, then, that so many nonprofit executives view fundraising as a "necessary evil"?

The Arboretum's Value–Added to Value–Sought Comparison   Take a look at the value-exchange exercise we did for the Arboretum and our friend Hyacinth Gardner, shown in Exhibit 2.1

Notice that only four of the Arboretum's value-added strengths have made the cut. The other items, shown in gray letters, may be useful to know; they may help in recruiting employees, filling the seats at educational programs, or having an impact on public awareness. But the four items that were selected are the ones that are dear to Hyacinth's heart. This table may be visually confusing, so here's what it really tells us:

- One strength, "Strong research component; worldwide reputation for science," intersects with Hyacinth's value-sought column four times.
- Another strength, "Peaceful oasis in busy city," intersects three times.

The Arboretum—Value-Added Strengths	Hyacinth Gardner—Value-Sought
	What I want to achieve
50-year track record	Pass my love of gardening to future
Exec. Director well known	generations
Interactive environment appeals to all ages	Extensive "botanical" world travels
Strong research component; worldwide	Keep the garden open and available to all
reputation for science	Contribute to projects that enhance our city
Scientists work well with volunteers admin	*What I want to avoid*
staff	Fear loss of additional plant species and habitats
Practical resources for gardeners	Fear that city's growth will harm our reputation
Peaceful oasis in busy city	as a great place to live and work
Reputation for sound management	Concerned that our city's children have little
Known as a great place to work	contact with the natural world
Recognized for educational programs for K–12	*Personal benefit or gain I seek*
schoolchildren	Philanthropy is an obligation for people of
	wealth
	Want to know, work with like-minded people
	Appreciate the respect my philanthropy
	produces
	Want public recognition for my philanthropy

EXHIBIT 2.1   **VALUE-EXCHANGE EXERCISE**

- The remaining strengths, "Interactive environment appeals to all ages," and "Recognized for educational programs for K–12 schoolchildren," intersect twice each.

On Hyacinth's side of the table, notice that all four of the items she wants to achieve are touched or impacted by all of the Arboretum's strengths. Similarly, the three items that she wants to avoid are also impacted by all of the Arboretum's strengths. In terms of personal gain, benefit, or recognition, Hyacinth believes that people of wealth have an obligation to support charities, and she values the public recognition she is able to achieve by supporting the Arboretum. In fact, she is currently rewriting her will (we have it on good authority, since we made her up) to leave 60 percent of her estate to the institution. We're not worried about her children and grandkids; they will do just fine.

Although it is wonderful that the Arboretum has been around a long time, that employees like to work there, and that many gardeners attend its programs, those things just don't bring it home for Hyacinth. The other stuff delivers the goods.

Crafting Value Statements Once you have completed the value exchange exercise, use the results to write up your funder-selection criteria in the form of statements or value statements. These follow a certain format. You will use them later. Here are three hypothetical statements expressing value-sought criteria for the Arboretum's major donors. The highlighted words contain the value-sought expressions and those in plain type contain the value-added terms.

- Because **Donor fears the loss of additional plant species and habitats,** the Arboretum's strong research component and worldwide reputation for science are persuasive.

- Because **Donor believes philanthropy is an obligation for people of wealth,** financial support of the Arboretum's strong research component and worldwide reputation for science makes sense.

- Because **Donor has made extensive "botanical" world travels,** there is a heightened appreciation of the Arboretum's strong research component and global reputation for science.

Since other major donors may have other motivations, and since the value-added to value-sought comparison is so enlightening, we suggest that you run this exercise several times for each major category, using various current donors as your case study subjects. Once you have conducted 5 to 10 value exchange analyses for each major funding category, you will have a powerful understanding of the concepts and language that motivate funders to support your nonprofit. In fact, you can make it a habit to figure out value exchange every time you're qualifying a prospect.

We'll show you how in the next chapter.

APPLYING THE EXCHANGE OF VALUE

The most important practical application of the exchange of value is its use as a component of the ideal-funder profile. But its role in funder selection, which is where we started this chapter, is more subtle but may have much broader implications.

- It will strengthen your ability to engage and retain donors, even if their individual gifts may be modest.

- It emphasizes the partnership your agency needs to have with its funders if it is to achieve its mission. And that partnership goes beyond the financial.

- It shows how and why your nonprofit satisfies your best donors' motivations for giving, which encourages you to improve your ability to serve.

- It shows your donors how important they are to your agency, which encourages them to keep on giving, even after death, to support your good works.

Sometimes, fundraisers may lose sight of the fact that raising money for charity is a higher calling, not merely drudgery interrupted by periods of humiliation. Formalizing the ways you select funders may keep you cognizant of the reasons you seek donations.

But many nonprofit agencies—about 77 percent—lack a documented ideal-funder profile of any kind, while another 16 percent have such profiles but restrict them to quantifiable information, such as age, gender, level of education, wealth profile, and giving history. If qualifying criteria are limited to the factoids, donors themselves become interchangeable, like checkers on a checkerboard. The exchange of value articulates the synergy between donor and charity. Analyzing the exchange, and reviewing the analysis from time to time, will keep staff on its toes, dedicated to achieving the mission and willing to face the ugly truth when the agency is faced with unfavorable economic conditions or other challenges. A failure to understand and articulate this value exchange weakens your ability to select and retain high-potential prospects. It may also provoke weaknesses in your ability to serve, offer programs, build capacity, and do right by your clients.

In the next chapter, we will create the ideal-funder profile or SMART Way Scorecard. The Scorecard includes elements from the exchange of value analysis, as well as more traditional criteria. It's the practical way to build on the exchange.

WHAT WE COVERED

- The funder selection strategy is the work you do before you conduct prospect research. It articulates the qualitative characteristics of your best donors *after* the relationship has been confirmed.

- Your best funders support your nonprofit because doing so does something for them. It scratches some sort of itch that can be scratched properly only through charitable giving—preferably to your agency. If you understand the itch and know how to scratch it, your fundraising results improve.

- The value-sought analysis is the first step in developing funder selection strategies.

- Neither value-added nor value-sought criteria can be terribly effective until they work together. Compare the two criteria to see where value-added connects or intersects with value-sought.

- The exchange of value has a powerful impact on the funder selection strategy by highlighting the partnership between funding sources and your agency's ability to achieve its mission.

WHAT YOU CAN DO

- Select at least 10 or 20 current, active donors, especially those you know well and like. Ask for the opportunity to interview them in order to improve your ability to market and promote your agency's services.

- Use some version of the suggested probing questions provided in this chapter to conduct your interviews. Ask the same questions the same way and in the same order every time; otherwise it will be difficult to collate and compare responses.

- Keep notes on each interview. When you have completed your interviews, review the notes looking for common themes, motifs, phrases, and key words.

- Using templates like the ones shown in this chapter, assemble your notes into lists of no more than eight points per category.

- Conduct the exercise for each giving category—major gifts, grants, and corporate contributions.

- Complete the value-added to value-sought comparison as shown in this chapter.

CHAPTER 3

Building Your SMART Way Prospect Scorecard

A carefully analyzed funder-selection strategy provides many benefits, starting with a clear description of the exchange of value you seek from all your funders. It spells out the way your nonprofit intersects with and satisfies their charitable philosophies and motivations, regardless of their capacity to give. Thanks to the work you've done to define your funder-selection strategy, your marketing, messaging, and outreach become more targeted and effective, helping you attract funders of all categories.

What the funder selection strategy does *not* do, however, is tell you which funding prospects justify the investment of your scarce and precious development time, which, you'll remember, carries an opportunity risk factor of anywhere from $1,000 to $18,000 per hour. The SMART Way™ Prospect Scorecard is the first bulwark against wasting your time and energy and your nonprofit's money.

IMPORTANT!

Management controls are the benchmarks, guidelines, success measures, and performance indicators that enable managers to maintain transparency (insight) and accountability, and drive continuously improving productivity in a particular business function. The SMART Way Scorecard is the first such management control instrument we introduce in *Fundraising the SMART Way*.

The SMART Way Prospect Scorecard is a prospecting tool used to evaluate prospects of all categories—donors, grantors, corporate contributors—and prioritize them based on their potential for lifetime value to your agency. Once you have "scorecarded" a prospect, you will know how much development time is justified on acquiring and retaining him or her. Those prospects ranking high on this qualifying benchmark justify more time and effort than those ranking low. In fact, early signs suggest that those ranking highest will bring in larger gifts in less time than those ranking lowest. To put it a different way, your "A" prospects produce better results faster, leaving you more time to cultivate additional prospects.

The use of a documented set of qualifying criteria has been shown to improve the productivity of the development officer or salesperson. The qualifying criteria provide an objective way to measure the potential of the prospect, and thus justify the investment of more or less cultivation time. However, the Leaky Bucket study shows that only 6 percent of respondents make use of a documented set of qualifying criteria, including donor motivations. A mere 18 percent use qualifying criteria that measure only wealth profile and giving history, while about 62 percent say they have undocumented "preferences" suggesting which prospects to cultivate, but nothing documented.

Adding a documented set of qualifying criteria to the development officer's toolkit has a profound, positive impact on fundraising productivity.

The Scorecard itself is a weighted scoring matrix that includes criteria in three categories:

- The value statements you created in Chapter 2, with some embellishments.
- The fact statements, spelling out the prospect's giving capacity and wealth profile.
- The danger signs, indicators that detract from the prospect's desirability or lower the return on effort (ROE) calculation.

The Scorecard is an extremely useful tool serving at least three functions. First, it ranks each major prospect at one of four levels—A, B, C, or D—showing the funder's potential for lifetime value. Prospects ranking at A or B levels offer significantly more potential at significantly lower ROE.

DEFINITION: WEIGHTED SCORING MATRIX

The weighted scoring matrix is a decision-making tool that enables its users to narrow down a list of options to a single choice. It includes a variety of criteria, each of which is assigned an "importance weight," showing how important that criterion is to the decision. The importance weight is based on an agreed-upon scale such as 1 to 5 where 5 equals "of greatest importance" and 1 equals "not important at all."

Once the importance weights have been chosen for each criterion, the degree to which the prospect matches it is then "weighted" or evaluated based on how closely it conforms to the criterion, thus producing the prospect's score (also using the same scale, where 5 equals "matches as closely as possible," and 1 equals "doesn't match at all").

Multiply importance weight by prospect's "score" to get the weighted score for each criterion. All weighted scores are then added to calculate the prospect's final score or rank.

Second, it's a teaching tool. In order to evaluate a particular prospect, the solicitor needs to find out to what extent the prospect matches each of the criteria. Scorecard criteria state the *answers* you want to hear, not just the questions you need to ask. The more often development officers question their prospects to discover these answers, the better their skills of qualifying and cultivating become. Later in this chapter, you'll learn how to develop the prospect scale and suggested probing questions that make the *subj*ective more *obj*ective. After all, you want to be sure that everyone on your team will score the same prospects the same way.

Third, it's an analytical indicator. The Scorecard rank, expressed as a single character, is relatively easy to integrate into your donor management software platform. Your reporting methods will grow richer, more diagnostic and more meaningful. Good reporting methods, especially those that produce insightful graphs, are a huge benefit to the development team, to senior leadership, and to the board.

Okay, here's your bonus fourth method. Scorecards can produce predictive analytics. Once you've got a decent number of prospects scored, you can do some elegant analysis showing which specific criteria are most likely to influence donors to seek out your agency, become engaged, and then remain engaged over the long haul. Insights stemming from such analysis will make the messages you use to market to, select, and cultivate prospects far more persuasive.

"Predictive analytics describes a range of analytical and statistical techniques used for developing models that may be used to predict future events or behaviors. There are different forms of predictive models, which vary based on the event or behavior that is being predicted. Nearly all predictive models produce a score; a higher score indicates that a given event or behavior is very likely to occur.

Predictive analytics, along with data mining techniques and predictive models, relies on multivariate analyzing techniques, including time-series or advanced regression models. These techniques allow organizations to decide on relationships and trends and predict future behaviors or events."*

The use of predictive analytics has a profound impact on the way businesses market their current products and services. It also offers powerful insights that can produce innovation by predicting the demand for new products or services.

Source: Techopedia, www.techopedia.com/definition/180/predictive-analytics.

Nine Scorecard Principles

Before you build your Scorecards, let's review a few pertinent ideas about how to create then. Every Scorecard contains criteria in three categories: fact statements, value statements, and danger signs. The criteria, and the entire Scorecard, must comply with the following nine principles that make it robust and useful.

The effort to define a Scorecard is significant, but so is the effort to create a strategic plan. And don't forget one of the reasons that the guys on *Apollo 13* came home alive: "If you've only got 10 minutes to do something, spend the first nine *planning.*"

Principle 1: Many Minds Make Light Work

Group effort produces more and better insights, so work with others. If you are part of a large development team, get all team members engaged in the process. Don't forget to include the grant-writers. It can help to add marketing, finance, and program people to the group to get all perspectives.

If you're a one-person development shop, include other staff, board members, or even volunteers to help you brainstorm through each category. You'll get much better results, and nobody will ever say, "But you never asked me for my opinion!"

Follow strict brainstorming protocol. Everybody gets to throw out ideas in an orderly way, one person and one idea at a time; then the next person speaks. The group leader or facilitator writes them up on a flip chart or whiteboard. Keep the group focused on producing ideas while preventing those side conversations about whose ideas are better or worse. When you have exhausted all ideas and then prioritized the list, use techniques such as multivoting to whittle it down until all agree on the last 5 to 10 criteria. Multivoting is a classic method for driving collaborative decisions, and it's extremely useful to know how to do it.

DEFINITION: MULTIVOTING.

Multivoting is helpful when you end up with a large list of items. It's a way to bring that list down to a more workable number.

To multivote, count the number of items on the list and divide it in half. Each participant can vote for that number. For example, if the list has 20 items, each person has 10 votes. If it's an odd number, like 21, round the number down to the closest even number, 10 in this case. Participants may not vote multiple times for any single item.

Write down the number of votes for each item. Strike off any items that receive no votes, or only 1 or 2. Keep repeating the process until the list is down to a desirable level. Ideally the list should not exceed 7 items, but the group could go as high as 10 if there is a consensus.

Principle 2: Analyze Past Successful Relationships First

Scorecards work best when they are based on past successful relationships with funders. Remember, you're trying to clone those funders. As you set out to select Scorecard criteria, use actual funders as a source of inspiration. If you don't currently have funders in a particular category, you'll have to make educated guesses and be willing to revise your selection criteria in future based on experience.

Sort through your donor base. Seek out funding sources you have enjoyed the most, along with those that have been most generous, or the least hassle to deal with (or both). If you lack such a base of donors, use your board members, volunteers, and even clients. These constituents also demonstrate desirable exchange of value and levels of engagement.

Principle 3: Seek Answers, Not Questions

It's not enough to simply ask the question "What's your net worth?" if you haven't already decided what the answer ought to be. It's even worse to ask, "So, how do you feel about saving children's lives (ending hunger, achieving world peace, eradicating toenail fungus)?" Such blunt, pointed questions will either turn the prospect off or extract a canned or predictable answer. You don't want either of these outcomes. I mean, who's not in favor of eradicating toenail fungus?

Every statement in a Scorecard describes a sought-for answer to a qualifying question. For example, let's say your best major donors have a net worth of $10 million. Your corresponding fact statement (fact statements are always quantifiable) says, "Donor prospect has a net worth of $10 million." The prospect you're cultivating may or may not reach that level. You, however, have discovered that your most desirable major donors, the ones justifying the greatest investment of time and effort, are at the $10 million level or higher.

When it comes to assessing the value statements, questions like "What do you want to accomplish with your philanthropy?" always provoke a more nuanced, insightful conversation. Plus, the prospect ends up liking you more.

Principle 4: Choose a Few Vital Indicators

It's tempting to come up with dozens of criteria, no matter what the category. Resist the temptation. Knowing many factoids about your prospects ends up as busy-work. The Scorecard must be limited to the most diagnostic criteria only. The most valuable selection criteria are few in number. You only need to know about four or five critical things per category; knowing more can even be misleading.

Now, it might be nice to know the funder's birthday, dog's name, and favorite color, but knowing that stuff doesn't help you determine if that funder justifies a lot of cultivation effort. Don't exceed 10 criteria per category; 5 or 6 is even better. Selecting those few, diagnostic criteria works better in a group; many minds make for better choices.

As you work on defining your criteria, always ask the question, "Will it help me estimate the prospect's potential for lifetime giving if I know *this* answer?" I keep trying to figure out if knowing a funder's birthday would help me decide to pursue the prospect, and I just can't do it. If you're the kind of person who loves to send out birthday cards and holiday greetings, go for it, but remember that knowing that stuff doesn't help you uncover the exchange of value or evaluate giving capacity.

Principle 5: Create *Once,* Use Often

It may seem like a lot of work to figure out what goes into your Scorecards—in fact, it *is* a lot of work—but it's well worth the effort. Once you have defined a Scorecard, be it for donors, grantors, or corporate contributors, you'll use it dozens, hundreds, maybe even thousands of times over the years. An experienced SMART Way user can complete a Scorecard for a specific prospect in a minute or two, producing a rank and actual score automatically.

Remember the purpose of the Scorecard. It helps you get the highest possible ROE from your cultivation activities. It's designed to weed out the prospects that aren't good enough for you so you'll have more time left over to cultivate those who are. A Scorecard that's been well designed and field tested will provide substantial benefits to the productivity of the fundraising effort. It plugs a lot of leaks.

Principle 6: One Benchmark for All Solicitors

The Scorecard produces objective insights, even when the criteria themselves may be qualitative in nature. The insights are objective because everybody who's engaged in cultivation and solicitation uses the same ones. The use of specific probing questions and other tools to elicit the prospect's answers help to ensure that I'll get the same result as you. Otherwise, you might think the prospect is fantastic, and I might think the prospect is awful;

the Scorecard keeps us from duking it out in the parking lot. This objective benchmark can be particularly helpful when volunteers and board members act as peer solicitors.

The Scorecard is a serious, heavy-duty instrument for management control over the fundraising function. The Scorecard you create for major donors will be used by major gift officers. The one you build for grant-making organizations will be used by grant-seeking professionals. The one you build for corporate contributors will be used by corporate-relations people. So anyone in the organization who's prospecting for donors, grantors, or corporate givers will use that specific Scorecard.

And nothing is more fun that ruling out prospects when they're simply not good enough for you (or for my Cousin Judy).

Principle 7: All Statements Required

It's sloppy to rule prospects in or out of consideration just because they have a high net worth, or somebody else said they would make a good funder, or they are one of the "usual suspects" in your community. The usual suspects are those local, regional, or global Big Names that everybody plans to hit up for cash. Doing so will not only waste your scarce and precious development time, it will also tag you as a naïve and ineffectual fundraising professional.

The Scorecard requires you to evaluate each prospect against each criterion. Whether you choose 5, 6, or 10 criteria per category, you must score the prospect for each of those criteria. That way, you can never rule a prospect in or out based only on one criterion. Perhaps the prospect scores well on fact statements, but poorly on value statements, or vice versa. It's also possible to find a prospect who scores well on both facts and values, but racks up a high score on danger signs. Such donors should be thought of as the "donors from hell," DOAs who simply do not justify the investment of much time and effort on your part.

So make sure to evaluate the prospect against every criterion. And if you don't have the information to do so, then you'll just have to go back and ask for it, won't you?

Principle 8: Pay Attention to Rank *and* Score

The Scorecard's "output" is the prospect's rank and actual score. The Scorecard rank of A, B, C, or D tells you, at a glance, the prospect's potential for lifetime giving. The actual score shows how much potential as compared to other prospects with the same rank.

The highest possible score for any Scorecard represents the total of the weighted scores for the quantifiable information or fact statements plus the total weighted scores for the qualitative information or value statements. That total score is divided evenly into four quartiles to produce the rank of A, B, C, or D. The prospect's actual score equals the total weighted scores for facts and values, *less* the score for danger signs.

Not only will you use rank and score to evaluate potential. You will also use them to report on current levels of productivity and identify opportunities for productivity enhancement.

Principle 9: When to Scorecard, When Not to Bother

Do not scorecard a prospect unless you've got some evidence that the prospect is worth cultivating.

In simple terms, this means that you don't need to complete a Scorecard for every $25 donation or ticket to your annual event; in fact to do so would be counterproductive. However, if your preliminary research shows that the donor matches your fact profile, shows an affinity for your mission or programs, or has given regularly to yours or similar organizations over the past few years; such insights will help you justify some effort at cultivation.

Reserve the use of Scorecards for funders that fall into the "major" category. What's that? Well, you have to define it. For a small grassroots organization, a major donor may be one who gives $1,000 a year, while for others, such as big national charities, a major gift could be $25,000 (or $250,000). The same is true of grants and corporate contributors. If you know the grant ceiling is under a certain level, it might not be worth it to produce the application. If the corporation sees no business benefit to the relationship, and is just going to do you a favor by buying a table at the gala, you might not want to complete a Scorecard.

But don't forget the concept of cumulative giving. Review your donor database at least once a year looking for those donors who give year after year after year, even if the size of the gift is modest. They might just be great candidates for you to upgrade and promote to major status.

CRAFTING SCORECARD STATEMENTS

A completed Scorecard typically includes about 15 statements (five in each category) that collectively make up the weighted scoring matrix. Please note that the Scorecard examples shown here represent major donors. You can download samples for corporate sponsors and grant-making organizations from www.wiley.com/go/smartfundraising.

The Scorecard should look something like the one shown in Exhibit 3.1. Scorecard statements include four components:

- Statements, which describe the *answers* you're looking for.

- Importance weights, showing the importance of each statement to your nonprofit.

- Prospect scores, showing how well the prospect matches each statement.

- Rank and actual score, calculated by multiplying importance weight by prospect score.

Once these components have been documented, the development officer's only task is to fill in a single character in a single cell, denoting the extent to which the prospect matches the score. For every statement, that character will be 1, 2, 3, 4, or 5, where 5 equals "matches perfectly!" and 1 equals "no match worth mentioning." Then the instrument calculates the actual score per criterion and does all the math automatically to select rank and score for each scorecarded funder or prospect.

Since you figured out how to prepare value statements in Chapter 2, let's start building your Scorecard with them. Then we'll work out fact statements and danger signs.

Value Statements

Value statements represent the qualitative characteristics of your best funders. This information is the most important of the three categories, but it's also more difficult to uncover, and more likely to require a personal encounter with the prospect. But by the time you interview a sufficient number of donor prospects, you'll get better at discovering how well the prospect in question matches your ideal profile.

Scorecard for the Arboretum

Major Donor, Grant, Sponsor?

Donor Name	Key Contact:
Opportunity Within Account:	Source:
Account Exec:	Phone:
Estimated Revenue:	E-mail:
Date Created:	Category:

	Rank	Ideal Score	Actual Score
			0
RANK = A, Justifies MAXIMUM Effort			
RANK = B, Justifies REASONABLE Effort			
RANK = C, Justifies MODEST Effort	D	285	
RANK = D, Justifies LITTLE Effort			

	Weight	Prospect Score	Weighted Score
FACTS, SPECIFICS STATEMENTS - ENTER 1 (LOW) – 5 (HIGH)			
Donor has capacity to give at least $100,000 per year	5		0
Donor resides in our city at least part of every year	3		0
Donor has a net worth of over $10,000,000	5		0
Donor ranks at top level in peer-support review	4		0
Donor has been a member continuously for more than 10 years	5		0
Donor has volunteered, taught classes, or written articles for our membership magazine	5		0
Subtotal this category	135		0
VALUE STATEMENTS - ENTER 1 (LOW) – 5 (HIGH)			
Donor is passionate about gardening and wants to inspire younger people to feel the same way	5		0
Donor has traveled extensively, often focusing on "botany" trips	5		0
Donor wants to ensure the Arboretum will remain open and available to all residents and visitors for many years to come	5		0
Donor is concerned about loss of plant species and habitats	5		0
Donor is motivated to share wealth through philanthropy	5		0
Donor is concerned that children have little contact with the natural world	5		0
Subtotal this category	150		0
DANGER SIGNS - ENTER 0 (NOT AN ISSUE) – 5 (HIGH)			
Donor has a reputation as a "pot stirrer"	5		0
All contact must go through attorney or financial adviser	5		0
Big talk, no action	5		0
Overcommitted to too many organizations	5		0
Donor expects a level of recognition we can't support	4		0
Subtotal this category	120		0
IDEAL SCORE	285		
ACTUAL SCORE THIS PROSPECT			0

EXHIBIT 3.1   SAMPLE MAJOR-DONOR SCORECARD FOR THE ARBORETUM

The exchange of value—how your value-added connects with donors' value-sought—is powerful. When you can identify funders whose value-sought is a good match to your value-added, those prospects are more likely to engage, invest, and become your ambassadors and advocates. But as we saw in Chapter 2, figuring out how "theirs" fits with "yours" requires thoughtful effort and analysis. Users of the SMART Way method often find it more difficult to develop these statements—after all, information about the prospect's wealth profile is (relatively) easy to find, and the danger signs are easy to spot.

That's why I want you to spend so much time defining these statements. Spend time with the current donors, board members, volunteers, and clients you like the most, the ones that are most committed to you. Extract the reasons they are so enthusiastic about your charity. Carve those reasons into your value statements, especially the ones that connect strongly with your nonprofit's value-added strengths. Try your best to develop at least four or five such statements if possible. Four is the absolute smallest number you can afford to use, and I strongly suggest you find five instead.

I said earlier that the Scorecard turns the subjective—"I think I like this prospect"—into the objective—"based on these considerations, this prospect offers only modest potential." But value statements seem subjective, don't they? You can make them much more objective by collaborating with other members of your team to come to consensus on the statement itself and on its importance.

Think of it this way. As long as you and your team have selected these statements based on mutual agreement, then those qualitative statements or yardsticks will act *as if* they were quantifiable. Make the statements even more objective by agreeing on the prospect scale, the way you will measure the extent to which the prospect meets the statement, as described in Chapter 2. This work converts these subjective-seeming characteristics into statements that can be managed as if they were, in fact, quantifiable. It also means that you will have to learn some sophisticated questioning techniques in order to discover what makes the prospect tick, which we discuss further in Chapter 4.

The Vital, Few Value Statements   Keep the number of value statements somewhere between 5 and 10. Fewer than 5 may be too few to be diagnostic, while more than 10 is simply unmanageable. You may have

---

DEFINITION: THE PROSPECT SCALE

Before you start scorecarding your prospects and current funders, figure out how to assign the score you will give to the prospect for each criterion. For example, let's say your ideal major donor has the capacity to give you $100,000 per year. If you discover that this particular donor has the capacity to give $250,000 per year (more than $100,000 last time I checked), then you'd assign a score of 5 points. But what score do you give to a prospect whose capacity is only $50,000 a year? Maybe it's only 3.

---

to experiment for a while to be sure that you've chosen the most diagnostic or insightful statements, but that's all right. Don't be surprised if your first Scorecard goes through a few revisions until you get it right, especially if you can agree on only three or four statements at first. If that's the case, start using the Scorecard anyway. Just remember to get together and review your Scorecard with your team on a regular basis, and enhance it based on the feedback you'll be getting.

Assign Importance Weights   The importance weight shows how important it is *to your nonprofit* that a funder embodies the criterion. Importance weights are assigned on a scale of 1 to 5, where 5 equals "most important," and 1 equals "not important," as shown in Exhibit 3.2. It's essential that value statements always carry an importance weight of 3, 4, or 5. Criteria of lower importance are simply not important enough to make it to the Scorecard.

VALUE STATEMENTS - ENTER 1 (LOW)–5 (HIGH)	Weight	Score	Score
Donor is passionate about gardening and wants to inspire younger people to feel the same way	5		0
Donor has traveled extensively, often focusing on "botany" trips	5		0
Donor wants to ensure the Arboretum will remain open and available to all residents and visitors for many years to come	5		0
Donor is concerned about loss of plant species and habitats	5		0
Donor is motivated to share wealth through philanthropy	5		0
Donor is concerned that children have little contact with the natural world	5		0
Subtotal this category	150		0

EXHIBIT 3.2   **THE ARBORETUM: VALUE STATEMENTS AND IMPORTANCE WEIGHTS**

Value statements make the most sense and work best when they are stated as whole sentences:

- Funder prefers . . .
- Funder is committed to . . .
- Funder is passionate about . . .

Follow this protocol and it becomes easier to ask questions that reveal the prospect's thoughts, views, and feelings.

Fact Statements   Fact statements are quantifiable criteria such as net worth, gender, age, giving history, and the like. Gather some of your best, favorite, and most prolific funding sources, and analyze the factual characteristics they have in common.

Fact statements may include conventional qualifying criteria such as age, gender, net worth, giving history, and zip code, all of which are factors you can usually find somewhere in the public record. Those are the same criteria you might choose as your search filter when searching a public database. There are other fact statements that may be difficult to find in the public record, but not so tough to discover in a conversation. Remember that your task is to select the *answers* you want to hear, not just the questions you want to ask. Here are a few examples:

- Prospect is 65 years of age or older.
- Prospect has a net worth of $100 million or more.
- Prospect has given gifts of more than $250,000 to us or a charity in our sector within the past 10 years.

Note that what's most important here is the specific number. If you're thinking of choosing a range such as "should be somewhere between 59 and 72 years old," slap yourself on the wrist and try again. The only time you should use a range is when the lower limit is defined—$100 million— and the upper limit is simply "or more." Among other things, explicit criteria are easier to score. Let's say your ideal prospect is "65 or older." So if you meet a 73-year-old prospect, what do you do? You say, "This prospect matches the age criterion at a 5." What if the prospect is only 39 years old? You say, "This prospect matches the age criterion at a 3." In both cases, you then say, "Let's see how well the prospect scores on the rest of the criteria."

Some fact statements cannot be uncovered in the public record and require that you have an encounter of some kind with the prospect. A good example is "Prospect likes to volunteer for the nonprofits he/she supports." This is a factual statement—the prospect likes to volunteer or doesn't—but you might not know it until the two of you have a conversation.

Fact statements will differ depending on the funding category, although the principles for selecting these criteria are virtually identical. Obviously, the fact statements appropriate for major individual donors will be very different from those for corporate relationships or grant-making organizations.

Weighting the Fact Statements   Assign importance weights to fact statements following the same protocol you used for value statements, showing how important it is to your organization that the funder matches the criterion. You need to decide if the criterion is extremely important, only moderately important, or not important whatsoever. Use the same 5-point scale used for weighting value statements, where 5 equals "most desirable" and 1 equals "not desirable at all." Make sure that everyone in your group comes to consensus on the importance weight. If you disagree with one another, keep talking until your group comes to a decision that everyone can live with.

If all of the criteria you selected have the same importance weight, that could be all right—especially if all of the weights are 5s. But if no criterion is a 5, something is wrong; you have not yet identified the criteria of greatest importance. Keep on working at it. For fact statements, just like value statements, any criterion with an importance weight of only 1 or 2 is probably not important enough to include in your Scorecard (see Exhibit 3.3).

Danger Signs

Of the three Scorecard categories, danger signs are usually the easiest and the most fun to create. Everybody loves to trash their least favorite donors, and here's a nice, socially acceptable way to do so, without ever insulting an actual person! What could be better than that? Danger signs are fairly likely to be repeated in all funding streams, and even from one nonprofit to another.

Since people are more likely to remember what went wrong, who annoyed us, and how the other guy is a loser, this Scorecard category could

	Importance Weight
FACTS, SPECIFICS STATEMENTS - ENTER 1 (LOW)–5 (HIGH)	
Donor has capacity to give at least $100,000 per year	5
Donor resides in our city at least part of every year	3
Donor has a net worth of over $10 million	5
Donor ranks at top level in peer-support review	4
Donor has been a member continuously for more than 10 years	5
Donor has volunteered, taught classes, or written articles for our membership magazine	5
Subtotal this category	135
VALUE STATEMENTS - ENTER 1 (LOW)–5 (HIGH)	
Donor is passionate about gardening and wants to inspire younger people to feel the same way	5
Donor has traveled extensively, often focusing on "botany" trips	5
Donor wants to ensure the Arboretum will remain open and available to all residents and visitors for many years to come	5
Donor is concerned about loss of plant species and habitats	5
Donor is motivated to share wealth through philanthropy	5
Donor is concerned that children have little contact with the natural world	5
Subtotal this category	150

EXHIBIT 3.3   **THE ARBORETUM: FACT STATEMENTS, VALUE STATE-MENTS AND THEIR IMPORTANCE WEIGHTS**

almost be developed with a pull-down menu. Please resist the temptation to rely only on the following examples of classic danger signs:

- Prospect talks big but never takes any action.
- Prospect shuts down when the conversation turns to money.
- Prospect is a "pot stirrer" and inclined to litigate.
- Prospect wants more recognition than his/her level of support warrants.
- Grantor wants a level of matching funds that we can't afford.
- Grantor's reporting requirements are too onerous for us to support.

We're sure you can think of plenty more. Write them down until you've run out of ideas. Now, once you've gotten all that evil glee out of your system, go over your list and select the 5 or 6 danger signs that really make a difference to you. If your Scorecard has 3 fact statements, 4 value statements, and 14 danger signs, you either need to do more analysis or start taking antidepressant medication.

In spite of all the wisecracking, danger signs are very important. They help you discover—quickly—if a prospect is really worth pursuing. It's possible that a prospect could be a very good match to your fact and value statements but be so difficult to work with that winning the gift turns out to be a bad idea. We call these funding sources DOA—"dead on arrival." Once you discover that a particular prospect will end up being more work than it's worth, you'll really value your danger signs. Often, your danger signs will reveal that a member of your team (or board) is pursuing one of the infamous "usual suspects" without doing the due diligence required.

Danger signs are often revealed in "water-cooler" conversations or after hours, as if it were shameful to acknowledge that some of our donors drive us crazy, push us away from the mission, or otherwise end up costing more to live with than their gifts may be worth. We really should acknowledge these important characteristics, rather than making light of them or reserving them for gossip. Knowing whether the prospect matches any danger signs helps the fund-development team discriminate between great donors, donors that are just so-so, and donors that are DOAs—dead on arrival and more work than you can justify.

Weighting Your Danger Signs   Danger signs must be weighted, just like the other two categories. Be aware that the Scorecard will *subtract* the danger sign score from the fact and value scores. Danger signs reduce the prospect's actual score. Use the same 5-point scale, but in this case an importance weight of 5 means that it's *extremely important to avoid that criterion!* An importance weight of only 1 suggests that you need to be aware of the criterion and work around it.

Unlike fact and value statements, danger signs are still useful even if their importance weights are as low as 1 or 2 (see Exhibit 3.4).

Develop the habit of seeking evidence that danger signs exist. Awareness of these negative criteria can raise your productivity dramatically, simply by encouraging you to lose the phone numbers of those funding prospects who are more trouble than they'll be worth in the long run.

By the way, we're finding that danger signs are relatively common to many—if not—most nonprofits, while fact and value statements are more specific to a particular agency.

DANGER SIGNS - ENTER **0** (NOT AN ISSUE)–5 (HIGH)			
Donor has a reputation as a "pot stirrer"	5		0
Can't contact donor directly; must go through attorney/financial adviser	5		0
Big talk, no action	5		0
Overcommitted to too many organizations	5		0
Donor expects a level of recognition we can't support	4		0
Subtotal this category	120		0

EXHIBIT 3.4   **THE ARBORETUM: DANGER SIGNS AND THEIR IMPORTANCE WEIGHTS**

SCORING THE PROSPECT

The prospect score is the third component of the Scorecard. Once you've selected the criteria and importance weights that make up your Scorecard, you'll need to figure out how to score your funders. Do this using a similar 5-point scale. If the prospect is a close match, then enter a 5 for that score, 3 or 4 if it's just a moderate match, or 1 or 2 if it's a poor match.

Then simply multiply the importance weight by the prospect score. The result is the weighted score.

IMPORTANT!

The ideal score represents the total of all fact and value statements multiplied by 5. The prospect's actual score represents the total of all fact and value statements multiplied by the score you assigned per criterion, *less* the total danger signs score.*

*To obtain a copy of a spreadsheet template you may use for your Scorecard, visit www.wiley.com/go/smartfundraising.

Add up the total actual score for facts and values, which represents the ideal (highest possible) score. Divide that ideal score into four even quartiles to obtain the rank. The highest quartile gets an A, and the lowest a D. Once you have completed your Scorecard for a particular prospect, you will have obtained an objective reading of the prospect's potential for lifetime value. This data can be captured in your donor management or constituent relationship management (CRM) platform for analytical purposes.

The Prospect Scale

At this point, you've defined the criteria against which you'll measure the potential of the next funding prospect. However, you don't want the prospect to be scored in a subjective manner. Remember, the prospect should get the same score whether I scorecard her or you do. Since we want your Scorecards to be objective and accurate, it's important to figure out how to assign a prospect score for each criterion. We call this the *prospect scale*.

Let's use a fact statement from the Arboretum as an example. This says that the ideal major donor will have a net worth of $10 million. But Hyacinth Gardner, the major-donor prospect we're cultivating, has a net worth of only $5 million. How do you ensure that everyone on the team would give her the same score for this criterion? You look at the prospect scale for this statement, which should be fairly simple to calculate. Here's an example:

- 5 = Prospect's net worth is $10 million or above
- 4 = Prospect's net worth is $5 to $9.9 million
- 3 = Prospect's net worth is $3 to $4.9 million
- 2 = Prospect's net worth is $1 to $2.9 million
- 1 = Prospect's net worth is less than $1 million

Hyacinth has a net worth of only $5 million, so she gets a 4 for this statement. Since we gave the $10 million level an importance weight of 5, then Hyacinth's actual score for that criterion is 20. Importance score of 5 times prospect score of 4 equals weighted score of 20. That's pretty straightforward.

The prospect scale for value statements is typically qualitative, just like the value statements themselves, and Hyacinth gets a score of 5 for each item. How do we know she gets 5 points? Again, we came up with a mutually agreed upon way to score these qualitative statements. Let's use the first value statement as our example, which reads "Donor is passionate about gardening and wants to inspire younger people to feel the same way." The prospect scale for this statement reads like this:

- 5 = Donor is a lifelong gardener, is certified as a master gardener or holds other gardening credentials, hosts annual tours of his/her garden, and/or demonstrates his/her fascination with gardening in other ways.

- 4 = Donor belongs to garden clubs, attends garden tours, or spends a few hours gardening every week.
- 3 = Donor has a small garden, subscribes to a gardening magazine, has expressed an interest in learning more.
- 2 = Donor has visited our gardens on numerous occasions over the years.
- 1 = Donor visits our garden only to entertain out-of-town visitors.

In Hyacinth's case, her passion for gardening is well known; the Arboretum even carries the book she wrote about gardening in the gift shop.

Now there is one thing to think about regarding Hyacinth's score. She is involved with three other garden clubs and is a member of the Climbing Rose Association and the Peony Society. She just might be a little bit overcommitted to other organizations. So Hyacinth's score will go down a few points; we gave her a score of 1 for the danger sign "Donor is overcommitted to other organizations," dropping her actual score by 5 points.

But Hyacinth's rank is still an A. The Scorecard makes it impossible to rule a prospect either in *or* out based on a single criterion.

Hyacinth Gardner's Scorecard is shown in Exhibit 3.5.

SCORECARD AS MANAGEMENT CONTROL

The Scorecard provides mechanisms that help to "control"—that is, to maintain accountability and drive continuous improvement—in several ways. The first and most obvious is to sort out high-potential funders from those offering lower (or no) potential for lifetime giving. This form of control is pertinent to every level of the fundraising hierarchy. It certainly helps the individual development officer to use time more wisely, concentrating effort on higher-potential funders, and freeing up time that would otherwise be spent (lost?) pursuing those with low potential. In the next chapter, we demonstrate how any development officer can use the Scorecard to focus attention and time on the right candidates, and hand off those with low potential to less costly cultivation mechanisms.

But there are other forms of management control. For one thing, it's simple to analyze and report on the distribution of funding prospects or current donors based on their rank. If, for example, the monthly graph in

Scorecard for The Arboretum		Major Donor, Grant, Sponsor?	Major Donor	
Donor Name	**Hyacinth Gardner**	Key Contact:	Ms. Linden	
Opportunity Within Account:	Naming Opportunity	Source:	Trustee Circle	
Account Exec:	Marjorie Willows	Phone:	234-567-8901	
Estimated Revenue:	$250,000	E-mail:	hyacinth@blooms.com	
Date Created:	3/15/2014	Category:		

		Rank	Ideal Score	Actual Score
RANK = A, Justifies MAXIMUM Effort				
RANK = B, Justifies REASONABLE Effort		A	285	275
RANK = C, Justifies MODEST Effort				
RANK = D, Justifies LITTLE Effort			Prospect Score	Weighted Score
		Weight		
FACTS, SPECIFICS STATEMENTS - ENTER 1 (LOW) - 5 (HIGH)				
Donor has capacity to give at least $100,000 per year		5	5	25
Donor resides in our city at least part of every year		3	5	15
Donor has a net worth of over $10,000,000		5	4	20
Donor ranks at top level in peer-support review		4	5	20
Donor has been a member continuously for more than ten years		5	5	25
Donor has volunteered, taught classes, or written articles for our membership magazine		5	5	25
Subtotal this category		135		130
VALUE STATEMENTS - ENTER 1 (LOW) - 5 (HIGH)				
Donor is passionate about gardening and wants to inspire younger people to feel the same way		5	5	25
Donor has travelled extensively, often focusing on "botany" trips		5	5	25
Donor wants to ensure the Arboretum will remain open and available to all residents and visitors for many years to come		5	5	25
Donor is concerned about loss of plant species and habitats		5	5	25
Donor is motivated to share wealth through philanthropy		5	5	25
Donor is concerned that children have little contact with the natural world		5	5	25
Subtotal this category		150		150
DANGER SIGNS - ENTER 0 (NOT AN ISSUE) - 5 (HIGH)				
Donor has a reputation as a "pot stirrer"		5	0	0
All contact must go through attorney or financial advisor		5	0	0
Big talk, no action		5	0	0
Overcommitted to too many organizations		5	1	5
Donor expects a level of recognition we can't support		4	0	0
Subtotal this category		120		5
IDEAL SCORE		285		
ACTUAL SCORE THIS PROSPECT				275

EXHIBIT 3.5   **HYACINTH GARDNER'S SCORECARD**

Exhibit 3.6 shows a high proportion of C- and D-ranked prospects, the chief development officer (or executive director or board chair) can intervene and ask why. The answer could be that the development team is not using their Scorecards carefully or consistently (or at all). However, it might also mean that the Scorecard needs refining; it's not accurate enough.

Management's contribution to the success of the fundraising effort includes guiding your development team to focus on higher-potential donors

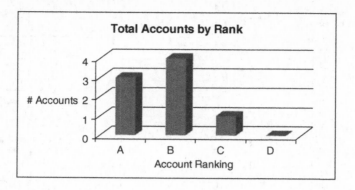

EXHIBIT 3.6   TOTAL ACCOUNTS BY RANK

and offload lower-potential contributors to less costly cultivation methods, including everything from direct-appeal campaigns to online giving.

WHAT WE COVERED

- The SMART Way Scorecard enhances the funder selection strategy by providing an objective method for ruling prospects in or out based on their potential for lifetime donor value.

- Scorecards help development officers free up their time so they can concentrate on best-qualified prospects and delegate less well-qualified candidates to methods of cultivation and acquisition that offer a higher cost-benefit ratio.

- Creating a Scorecard demands group effort, but once it's complete, it can be used repeatedly. It takes only a minute or two to complete a Scorecard for an individual donor or prospect, as long as you know the questions to ask that will reveal the answers you seek.

- Management controls are mechanisms that produce transparency and accountability and are especially useful for functions such as fundraising, which are difficult to manage.

- The SMART Way Prospect Scorecard is the first of the management controls that comprise Fundraising the SMART Way.

WHAT YOU CAN DO

- Review the nine principles for developing a Scorecard.
- Review the value statements you developed in Chapter 2 and assign importance weights to each statement. It's desirable to have at least five value statements and no more than ten.
- Prepare fact statements the same way. Be sure to assign importance weights to each statement. Again, it's desirable to have at least five fact statements and no more than ten.
- Prepare danger signs as well. Make sure to keep the number of danger signs around five or six; less is more.
- Assign prospect scales to each statement where they are required.
- If at all possible, do this work in collaboration with other members of staff, board, and/or volunteers. Mutual agreement among a diverse group produces a stronger scorecard.
- Download the SMART Way Scorecard template from www.wiley .com/go/smartfundraising. It's a live spreadsheet containing all the formulas needed to calculate the prospect's rank and actual score

CHAPTER 4

The Scorecard as a Management Control Device

When I began to develop Fundraising the SMART Way™, the first element of management control that came into focus was the opportunity pipeline. The critical importance of funder selection and ideal-funder profiles emerged only later, as we worked with more and more nonprofits. Without being consciously aware of it, I was using the proverbial LAI approach as a qualifying technique—you know, finding out if the prospect has the right Linkage (connection to the agency's staff or board), Ability (money), and Interest (in the mission and programs). It sounded an awful lot like the simplistic qualifying tactics I had learned in corporate sales where they called it MAN—does the prospect have the Money, Authority to spend the money, and the Need that justifies spending the money.

But over the years, I've become convinced that neither LAI nor MAN has the power to drive prospect/funder selection in any beneficial manner. LAI tells us only if the prospect has a connection to the agency and so on; it *doesn't* tell us if time invested in cultivating that prospect will produce a desirable return on effort (ROE). It also doesn't tell us what motivates the donor to take action, what kinds and frequency of recognition the donor prefers, or how likely it is that the donor will become and remain deeply engaged with our mission or programs. In fact, there's a risk in the LAI model that usually goes unspoken: if the donor is "linked" to the agency because of the executive director, the development officer, or the board member who recruited him, then once that individual leaves the organization, the funder is very likely to go along for the ride.

However, the SMART Way model provides a powerful method of assessing the potential for long-term engagement—the SMART Way Prospect Scorecard. The Scorecard is more than a qualifying benchmark. It is a highly effective, powerful tool for management control.

DEFINITION: MANAGEMENT CONTROL SYSTEM

"A **management control system** (MCS) is a system which gathers and uses information to evaluate the performance of different organizational resources like human, physical, financial and also the organization as a whole considering the organizational strategies. Finally, MCS influences the behavior of organizational resources to implement organizational strategies. MCS might be formal or informal." Fundraising the SMART Way is a management control system for maintaining and continuously improving the performance of the fund development function.

* www.managementexchange.com/sites/default/files/media/posts/documents/ Management%20Control%20System.pdf

---

USING THE SCORECARD TO MANAGE THE FUNDRAISING PROCESS

Before I show you how to create your Scorecards, I'd like to tell you why they justify the effort you'll put into them, and there is some effort, no question about it. The use of the Scorecard offers the following six benefits to its users:

1. The development officer is able to figure out if a specific prospect justifies additional effort, based on an objective set of criteria which rank funders based on their potential for lifetime value.

2. The Scorecard buys back time that development people might otherwise waste cultivating prospects whose potential for lifetime value is modest or worse.

3. It's simple to report on the distribution of donors and prospects by rank, and thus to pinpoint necessary initiatives to improve the cultivation or retention of more donors offering higher potential.

4. Fully developed Scorecards contain clear instructions that produce consistent responses regardless of which development officer is doing the qualifying, reducing subjectivity and improving accountability.

5. The consistent use of the Scorecard, with its accompanying prospect scale and probing questions (more on this later) escalates the learning curve of junior development staff.

6. Scorecard data can be analyzed from time to time to correlate the phrases, keywords, and other elements most likely to improve identification, attraction, and conversion of potential prospects (or "suspects") through the use of low-cost inbound marketing techniques.

There are several additional ways in which Scorecard data provide robust levels of management control, but since these methods involve cross-referencing these data with data from the opportunity pipeline, I'll save that until Part 2.

VALIDATING THE SCORECARD

The first draft of your Scorecards is like any first draft, just begging to be revised, which is a good thing. Like any first draft, you discover upon review that what seemed to make sense in the "laboratory" no longer makes as much sense. (The "laboratory" is the work you did with your group to select Scorecard components.) In fact, people who go back to review that original Scorecard, even if it's just a couple of days old, often say, "Hey, who came up with *this* statement, *that* importance weight, *this* prospect scale? They must have been nuts."

Well, no, they weren't nuts, they were *you*. So relish the fact that the statements, weights, and prospect scales made sense at the time but don't make as much sense now, when you have a better understanding of their purpose. Now, you've got a context to work with. The best way to validate your Scorecards is to use them under controlled conditions and modify them as you go along. The process of using the tools at the same time you're improving them is called *concurrent engineering,* a term you'll often hear among those who develop software applications for a living, as well as from me. In practical terms, concurrent engineering means "don't wait until it's perfect because it will never be perfect. Use it now to bring it *closer* to perfection."

The first time you use your Scorecard to evaluate a known funding source, I can almost guarantee that it will take at least 10 or 15 minutes to complete. Don't be discouraged. It takes so much time because you will challenge the statements and importance weights and argue, no doubt in a polite manner, about how to score the prospect for each criterion. After you've completed a few Scorecards and gotten the hang of it, you'll be able to finish them in a minute or two.

A cautionary word here: Before you start the validation process, consider the capacity of your development team. Larger development shops may have specialists dedicated to major gift work, grant seeking, or corporate relations. If that's the case, each team can validate the relevant Scorecard. For small shops, however, you're better off validating one Scorecard profile at a time. Tackle the profile you built for the category of funder that's most interesting, important, or familiar to you right now. If you want to tackle major donors first, work on that Scorecard. Ditto if it's grant-seeking or corporate relations. Don't fall prey to the notion that you have to perfect all of your Scorecard profiles immediately.

The Scorecard Sanity Check

The more accurate your Scorecards become, the greater the amount of fundraising productivity is possible. Since the Scorecard is a key component of the fundraising process, and since all business processes by definition can be improved through careful metrics used in an iterative manner, then validating the Scorecard is a good, low-cost way to improve results. Decent validation is a two-step process.

Do a sanity check first. Get your team together to review the Scorecard draft and revise it based on discussion. Go over it with a magnifying glass. For every component, ask questions like these:

- Does this statement/importance weight/prospect scale make sense?
- Will it help us determine the funder's potential?
- If we capture data based on these components, will they provide good reports or other meaningful insights?

Don't simply answer yes or no. Find reasons that the component in question makes sense ("This component makes sense because it shows, tells, demonstrates, blah blah blah"). Challenge yourselves to articulate why or how it provides insights into the funder's potential or fails to do so. Consider why reports based on Scorecard data might help improve productivity and in what ways. Revise the Scorecard once your group has come to consensus on everything.

Next, select some current funders and run them through the Scorecard. It's best if you use funders you know reasonably well. A couple of things are likely to happen:

- You may find you can't assign a prospect score for some of the criteria, especially the value statements. If that's the case, it means you don't actually know the funder as well as you thought and you should go back and ask some more questions.

- You may discover that a funder you formerly considered to offer high potential actually ranks at a low potential—sometimes *really* low. If that's the case, it may mean that your funder-selection strategy needs clarification. It may also mean that it's time to diversify your funding sources.

In either case, learning how to ask effective probing questions will provide significant benefits, both to the accuracy of the Scorecard profile, and to your team's skills of discovery and cultivation.

CASE STUDY   THE WAR STORY

We worked with a large social services agency whose primary funder, since inception, was a single government agency, accounting for about 85 to 90 percent of the budget. The balance was made up of small grants from private foundations. In their desire to reduce vulnerability, senior leadership decided to build a Scorecard profile to help select additional grants from private foundations first, and tackle major donors later. During the validation process for the grant-maker profile, they discovered that their primary funder exhibited many danger signs and scored low on several value statements.

When all was said and done, the agency realized that its primary funding source was merely a "B-minus" candidate. What a wake-up call!

THE SUGGESTED PROBING QUESTIONS

In preceding chapters, we introduced the Scorecard concept and developed its three sets of criteria, namely the statements (facts, values, and danger signs), their assigned importance weights, and the prospect scales that show how to score each statement. You still are missing a piece—the suggested probing questions. These are carefully designed, open-ended questions that elicit the answers you're hoping to hear from the prospect, even if they're answers telling you the prospect is not qualified. Most Scorecard statements, regardless of category, produce more reliable answers when such questions have been predefined and "baked" into the Scorecard template.

Scorecards containing such suggested questions have several benefits. They show all of your solicitors how to determine if the prospect fits the profile using one consistent yardstick. It doesn't matter which development officer is assessing the prospect's potential; if they all asked the same questions the same way, they should all get the same result.

These are the kinds of questions that invite donors and prospects to build relationships, revealing their deeper charitable motivations, philosophies, and other expectations, and preventing canned answers. They engage the prospect more rapidly so you can rule out the ones that don't fit a lot faster, improving ROE and keeping your opportunity risk factor at a manageable level. The questions themselves are "softballs," easy to ask even if you're not an expert or even know all the details of your agency's history, programs, and credentials. An added bonus is that using this questioning technique does a great job of reducing "ask reluctance."

Conventional wisdom reminds us to listen more than we talk when we're out there cultivating donors. But unless you know the answers you're listening for, it's easy to lose your way. Most people who make a living cultivating donors (or customers, for that matter) are fairly gregarious and enjoy the schmoozing and making-friends part of fundraising a lot. While these are desirable traits, they can also be dangerous. It's easy to fall in love with your prospect, especially if the prospect is accessible and loves to spend time with you (especially if you're buying lunch). The link between time spent and gifts received is not only weak, it's deceptive.

Yes, I'm well aware of the extended cycle time it may take to win over a major donor. If the gift is sizable, it takes longer, as any capital campaign expert can attest. A philanthropist who intends to underwrite the new oncology wing and get it named after himself doesn't usually write that multi-zillion-dollar check without thinking it over (and putting his lawyers and financial advisers to work on it, too). I just want to make sure you've decided to wait him out because you have some *evidence* that waiting will produce reasonable financial results.

But, Ellen, how do I know if I'm waiting for the right prospect? Simple answer: you *ask* them. Please do not confuse the verb *to ask* with the phrase *making the ask,* a term I personally find abhorrent. It always sounds slightly scatological to me. Plus, we English majors don't like it when verbs are converted into nouns, especially when there are equally meaningful and far more euphonious verbs available that already mean the same thing. Verbs like *solicit, invite,* and *invest* come to mind.

Asking the right questions leads to establishing trust with the prospect or donor, thus gaining the right to invite or solicit the donor's support. You will be happy to know that the right questions are a lot easier to ask than you might think. The right questions are even easier for your board members to ask, if your board members have agreed to engage in peer solicitation. If you're asking the right questions and getting the right answers, then waiting for the prospect to act may well be justified—because you'll have evidence that it will be.

IMPORTANT!

If you're going to lose the gift anyway, you might as well lose it early.

Three Simple Questions that Establish Donor Trust

Turns out there are three simple questions that can be asked in an almost infinite variety of ways to extract the answers you seek. These are open-ended questions, meaning that the respondent can't answer with a simple yes or no. They require more thoughtful responses. They are "softball" questions—you don't have to be much of an expert to ask them—but because they invite the respondent to think and then talk about their own desires, wishes, needs, preferences, and pet peeves about philanthropy in general and their own experiences in particular, you end up sounding like an expert.

The three simple questions are:

1. *The success question:* "What do you want to achieve with your charitable giving?"

2. *The frustration question:* "What do you want to avoid by giving to charity?"

3. *The "right-charity" question:* "What helps you decide which charities to support?"

Prepare questions based on this model, and add them to the statements in your Scorecard profile. They will help the inexperienced or junior development officer to gain confidence and learn quickly. They'll also help the experienced, senior people maintain focus on the objective nature of the Scorecard and avoid making assumptions about the prospect's true potential.

It's easy and tempting to assume that the current prospect is quickly going to turn into a great donor just because you trust your intuition. I sincerely hope your intuition is more reliable than mine, and I've been acquiring funders and clients for the past 40-odd years. (It only took about the first 10 to *stop* trusting my intuition.)

There's another reason to integrate such questions into your Scorecard profile. The questions themselves add to the degree of management control afforded by the Scorecard. The questions become an element of the benchmark. You can experiment with suggested probing questions to select those that produce good insights, delete those that have little impact, and so on.

Why These Questions Work   Questions like these are easy to ask because they don't have anything to do with asking for money. They also work because they put the emphasis directly on the donor—what do *you* think, want to achieve, avoid, prefer?—and almost none of it on your charity's financial needs. Ask questions like these, and your funding prospects will want to find out if they're interested in supporting your organization. Rather than *pitching,* a polite term for "beating the prospect over the head," you invite the prospect into a relationship, or at least into a state of rapport, in which both parties learn about the other and assess the potential of working together in some way or other, to be determined by continued dialogue.

Questions like these, which can be framed in an almost endless variety, remove or at least reduce what we call *ask reluctance,* the nonprofit version of a corporate malady called *sales reluctance.* Ask reluctance means "fear of making the ask" (and you already know how much I love that term). What usually happens is that the asker—development officer, board member, volunteer— knows he's supposed to raise money, but he hates raising money so much, and he's so conflicted about it, that before he even opens his mouth to say good morning, he feels under pressure to ask for a gift *right now this second!!!* And if he doesn't, the fundraising police will take him away in handcuffs.

Phew. Who wouldn't have ask reluctance?

So instead, he doesn't ask anything. He pitches. He tells. He sells. He lectures. He twists his friends' arms and asks them for favors. He alienates his friends and acquaintances. But he doesn't find out what prospective funders want to achieve or avoid with their philanthropy. Ask reluctance just might be one reason why donors leave your nonprofit after their personal solicitor does. It could be because somebody asked the prospect to "do me a favor" rather than engaging the prospect for the greater good of mankind. Once the obligation has been fulfilled, it's bye-bye donor.

Develop good questioning skills based on questions like the ones here and you will interrupt the pattern. You'll interrupt your own pattern as a solicitor, which might include a moderate dose of "ask reluctance," by adopting a questioning technique that invites the funder to share insights and motivations with you. Interrupt the prospect's pattern, too. The prospect may well be bracing himself to resist the battering-ram solicitation that he currently fears, thus giving rise to "I gave at the office," "I can't afford it right now," and "Call me another time." Many such responses translate to "just go away and stop bothering me," and it can be difficult to get past them. They are not rejections; they are *ob*jections. Many fund-development people, just like salespeople, have been trained to "overcome" such objections. From my perspective, overcoming objections is like kicking the dog. If you've already alienated the prospect by asking for money too soon, or whatever else you did, arm-wrestling to overcome the so-called objection is not likely to produce better results. Rather, it reinforces the reluctance experienced by both parties, the asker and the askee.

Reframing Your Agency's Value

Your organization is justifiably proud of its mission, programs, and outcomes, and so are you if you're raising money for it. If you're not proud, committed, or motivated to support your organization and achieve its mission, you might not be in the right job. Funders can sniff out an uncommitted fundraising person a mile away. So let's assume that you're a huge fan and booster of your agency and its mission and programs. Now ask yourself these two questions:

- Are we spending enough money to achieve our mission?
- How much more do we need?

Increase the income. Don't cut the budget.

Once the financial or economic value of achieving your mission is firmly in place, you've shifted over to the Cousin Judy approach, and your task now is to find out if the next funder or prospect is "good enough," or offers sufficient potential, for you to invest time in cultivation. Watch the anxiety level go way down. Not just yours—the prospect's also.

Remember that work you did in Chapter 2 to define exchange of value? All that work produced the answers you want to hear. You want to hear donors tell you if their charitable motivations are the value-sought that matches your nonprofit's value-added. Those that match are worth cultivating. Those that don't aren't. The exercise enabled you to develop value statements that represent criteria your best donors should meet. Now learn how to ask donor-centered questions.

A quick note here concerning the famous "elevator pitch," that short statement that is supposed to sum up the reasons your nonprofit deserves money. Personally, I find it counterproductive to start a prospect relationship with a brain dump like the elevator pitch. Instead, use the three simple questions to invite the prospect to learn your story. The elevator pitch is far more effective later in the arc of cultivation. At the earliest cultivation stages, starting with identification and discovery, you don't really need to say much about your agency other than to repeat your mission and add a sentence or two about programs offered and population served.

DEVELOPING YOUR QUESTIONS

Review your Scorecard statements and choose one or two that would benefit from adding such questions. Some statements simply don't need them. For example, if you found the donor's wealth profile and giving history on Wealth Engine or some other database, you don't need probing questions to elicit those details. You've got the information you need and can score those fact statements on your own.

Statements that benefit from the use of the three simple questions tend to be more qualitative in nature. If we use the Arboretum as our case study, and we want to find out if the prospect shares the idea that supporting the Arboretum will maintain its status as a "peaceful oasis in our busy city," you're not going to say, "So how much would you give me to maintain the Arboretum as a peaceful oasis?" I hope not. Instead, you're better off asking, "What life experiences have you had that have made you such a fervent supporter of our gardens?" And now you're off to the races.

Question 1: The Success Question, to Elicit the Donor's Positive Motivators

The first question is very simple: "What do you want to achieve by giving to charity?" Like all three questions, these few words offer enough variations and options to keep your prospect talking for hours. Here are some variations and elaborations on the success theme:

- What inspires you to give to charity? What causes or missions are most likely to draw your attention? Why?
- What personal/life experiences have you had that led you to becoming the person you are today?
- What do you want to accomplish through your charitable giving?
- Why is that important to you?
- If the nonprofit that you support were to be completely successful, what would that do for you (the community, the world)? Why would *that* be important to you?

IMPORTANT!

Don't ask "Why do you give your money to *us*?" unless you're conversing with a current donor. It's okay to ask questions like that of your current funding sources, so you can understand donor motivations more clearly, but not to prospects.

As you can see, the success question alone will open up enormous amounts of back-and-forth discussions with prospects as well as current funders. There is no limit to the number of times you can use it and no limit to variations on the theme you can devise.

IMPORTANT!

So you ask the question, "What do you want to achieve by giving to charity?" The prospect gives you a blank look, thinks for a few moments, and then says, usually slowly, "Say, that's a really great question. Let me think about it."

You've just hit a home run.

Question 2: The "Avoid" Question, to Elicit the Donor's Negative Motivators

The second question on our list is the avoid question: "What do you want to avoid by giving your money to charity?" This question elicits answers that are the flip side of the success questions. An answer like "I want to *achieve* world peace"(the success answer) can be paired with " . . . and *avoid* additional warfare" (the avoid answer). But avoid questions may also be the "psychological opposite" of success, revealing a completely unexpected perspective. So maybe it's "I want to achieve world peace" paired with "It's time to take action to *prevent* further sea-level rise and *reduce* threats posed by bio-engineering." Answers as disparate as these just might describe your ideal donor!

IMPORTANT!

The avoid question is designed to discover what prospects want their charitable investments to *avoid or eliminate* by wiping out the problem addressed by your mission, rather than whether they will like or dislike the way you treat them after they become donors. That perspective is revealed by the right-charity question.

There's another important reason to use the avoid questions, and that has to do with human psychology. Some people are more likely to open up when you ask positive questions, while others are easier to reach when you approach them from the negative point of view. In our long experience cultivating prospects, we find this dichotomy to be true, and since we simply don't know which approach will be more successful with any new prospect, we always try to use both.

Major funders, such as those who provide extremely large gifts, grants, or sponsorships, have been asked why they want to give so often they have developed "canned" answers—answers that sound like they were written by the marketing department, all that predictable stuff about "giving back" and "caring about our community." Even if those sentiments are true, they have been overused to the point that they have no meaning. If you can break through the canned language and get to the more deeply felt, intimate thoughts and ideas, you will have established a much higher degree of rapport. And the language you'll hear will make future outreach and messaging much more impactful.

Classic variations on the avoid question include:

- When you think of charities you have supported (or currently support), what do you want those charities to fix, wipe out, or resolve?
- What is it about the [issue, problem, disease, social condition] that bothers or concerns you so much; how does that affect your charitable decisions?
- What's at stake if your preferred charities are not able to achieve their mission?
- What do you think/fear might happen, if [this social or medical, etc., issue] is not resolved?
- Why is that important to you?

Question 3: The "Right-Charity" Question, to Elicit Donor Expectations about Service and Recognition

The right-charity question asks: "What helps you decide which charities to support?" Like the first two simple questions, this one can be presented in many variations, but its purpose is to learn what prospects expect from the charities they support and what will turn them off. You need to understand their expectations regarding recognition, but it might be even more important to learn how they expect you to use their gifts, to what purpose their money is being put, and whether you are getting the results they want you to get in return for their contributions. Some variations:

- How do you choose the charities you want to support? What would you have to see or hear from a nonprofit in order for you to make a significant commitment?

- What would a charity need to show you, after you've made your gift, to convince you that you had made a wise investment?

- When selecting a charity, what is uppermost in your mind?

- Have you ever decided not to invest in a charity, or even withdrawn your support from one? Why did that happen?

- When you think about other charities that you have supported or currently support, what did you like best about them? Why was that important to you?

- What about charities that disappointed you, or that you would be reluctant to invest in, other than their mission or cause? Why did they disappoint you, what were you trying to avoid?

Always remember that most prospective major funding sources have already given support to other charities. Major philanthropists are skilled at selecting their beneficiaries and clear about the standards those beneficiaries have to meet before they decide to give. Remember, therefore, that when you solicit such philanthropists you are most likely asking them to *add* your nonprofit to their philanthropic portfolio, or even to transfer their support away from another charity and over to yours. In the world of supermarkets and other retail establishments, this is called the "shelf-space battle." Whenever you want to add a new "product" to the "shelf," the supermarket executive has to consider the potential harm or loss of profitability such an addition might pose.

You must be as diplomatic as possible when asking the right-charity question, in order to engage the trust of prospects and donors, to convince them to add your organization to their roster of charitable beneficiaries.

Avoid, at all costs, anything that could sound remotely disparaging of any other charity the prospect might support in the future or has supported in the past. You risk the loss of rapport and mutual respect, even if the other charity is in the headlines for fraud, mismanagement or malfeasance. In fact, that would be the worst situation; the funder probably feels like a sucker already.

DEFINITION: THE SHELF-SPACE BATTLE

Supermarkets only have so much "shelf space" for displaying their products. There are so many shelf inches to display brands of toothpaste, for example, and each bit of space is supposed to produce a predictable amount of turnover (sales) and margin (profit). If you want that supermarket chain to carry your new brand of toothpaste, you've got to convince the supermarket executives that your unproven brand will make them enough money to justify reducing the shelf space and anticipated turnover and margin they currently accrue from other, proven brands. And don't think the established brands won't fight back.

It costs a lot of up-front money, time, and effort to win the shelf-space battle. So you had better know ahead of time if that's the battle you want to fight.

Assume that you're the new brand of toothpaste and your donor's current portfolio of nonprofits is the shelf. Now you know what you're up against.

FIELD-TEST THE SCORECARD

You began adopting your Scorecards by simply reviewing all the components and revising them where appropriate. Now you have prepared and integrated some suggested probing questions, or at least you've got the concept down. A good place to start is by using the questions presented in Chapter 2. Add to that list by including questions oriented to the particular statements you've included in your Scorecard.

Now take your Scorecard out for a test drive. Schedule meetings with current donors and board members (get permission where warranted). Have conversations with them where you ask those famous probing questions. Then sit down immediately afterward and fill out a Scorecard for each individual to see how well they scored. Please use the spreadsheet version of the Scorecard so it will calculate the donor's rank and actual score. Otherwise, you have to do the math by hand.

CALCULATING RANK AND SCORE BY HAND

Our Scorecard template already has the calculations built in, but you can also calculate them yourself.

First, calculate the ideal score. To do so multiply by 5 the importance weight for each criterion in the facts and values categories, then add up the two scores. Since 5 is the highest possible 'match,' this number represents the ideal score. Divide the ideal score into four equal quartiles. The highest quartile gets a rank of A; the lowest, a rank of D.

Now, calculate the prospect's actual scores for facts and values the same way.

Finally, calculate the weighted scores for danger-sign criteria. Add up the total weighted score for danger signs. Subtract it from the total facts and values scores.

Compare the total actual score to the ideal score, and choose the quartile to which it belongs.

Spend plenty of time with these donors. Consider these conversations as a particularly effective means of stewardship. When you meet with donors about their personal giving motivations, it's more likely that you'll retain and even upgrade them—not to mention getting some referrals.

It's perfectly acceptable to let the individual know that you're trying something new, seeking more insights to improve your outreach, and so on. It's even okay if you let on that you feel a bit awkward about the process, but only if you actually do; such an admission can enhance rapport.

Keep track of your results. At the very least, set up a file folder on your system to hold each Scorecard as you produce it. You can also set up another spreadsheet that captures the donor's or prospect's name, rank, and actual score. In Part 2, I'll review ways you can integrate your SMART Way Scorecards and other management controls with your donor management platform, but to start with just keep track of the Scorecards, ranks, and actual scores.

Fine-Tuning Your Scorecards

After a couple of weeks of field-testing, you will probably have a decent number of completed Scorecards to compare. Review the notes you took.

Find out what you learned by having all those conversations. Modify the Scorecard appropriately based on what you learned. The more closely your statements match the way donors and prospects express themselves, the more persuasive those statements will become. Such changes will enable your development officers to be more persuasive since they begin to mirror those expressions and emotions. It can also have a powerful positive impact on your marketing messages and outreach campaigns. The more persuasive your language, the better your results.

The local affiliate of a national organization devoted to women's reproductive health participated in a collaborative exercise to build their major-donor Scorecard. The value statements they came up with in their workshop seemed to be accurate:

- Donor demonstrates a commitment to social justice issues.
- Donor believes that philanthropy is a moral obligation for people of wealth.
- Donor values and seeks a financially sound charity as a repository for their philanthropy.
- Donor supports preventing teen pregnancy.

On the face of it, these criteria make sense, but they don't necessarily make the heart beat faster. As meaningful as it might be to recognize the value of philanthropy, those statements had no impact and in fact several donors disagreed with them. Their reasons for giving to charity, especially this charity, were much more personal. So the vice president of development went out and interviewed 40 of their long-term major donors, some of whom served on the affiliate's governing board. She listened to what her donors actually said. They told her they were motivated to give because:

- They (the donors) were strongly committed to supporting women, children, and families.
- They were grateful to the organization because it had been there for them (the women donors), a relative, or a dear friend.
- They wanted to have a beneficial impact on another woman's or girl's life, just like the positive impact they (or their relatives or friends) had received.

Language like this is lively, accessible, and motivating. Plus, it's a whole lot easier to say, "Mrs. Jones, you've often told me that the experience you [or your sister, cousin, granddaughter, best friend] had back then made a big difference in your life. Can you tell me more?" It's not so easy, and sounds positively deadly, to say, "How do you feel about philanthropy? Do you think it's an obligation for wealthy people like you?"

Ask good questions. You'll get better answers.

Test Your Scorecard   You have already interviewed lots of current funders, and revised your Scorecards accordingly. Now test their accuracy by "scorecarding" some of those same funders, as well as others who didn't make the interview list. Compare the funder in question to each statement at a time, and enter the prospect score, a number from 1 (a low or poor match) to 5 (a terrific, positive, couldn't-be-better match).

Scorecard some of your current funders to see how they rank. Their scores should jibe with what you already know of them. Funders you like, and who provide significant financial benefit, should score high; those whom you don't like, who are difficult (therefore more costly) to work with, or who promise much but deliver little should score low. If they don't, especially if you've compared more than one or two current funders, you should remain open to the idea that your statements are not as well-honed as you would like them to be, and consider modifying the Scorecard accordingly.

For example, let's say a fact statement reads "Donor has a net worth of $20 million," and its importance weight is 5. Donor X has a net worth of $100 million, which gets a prospect score of 5, while Donor Y has a net worth of only $1 million, poor soul, which merits a prospect score of 1. Since the Scorecard multiplies the importance weight by the prospect score, Donor X gets 25 points on this statement, and Donor Y gets 5 points. Now let's say a value statement reads "Donor is dedicated to organic gardening and never uses chemical fertilizers or pesticides," and its importance weight is 5. Donor A is a dyed-in-the-wool "greenie," and no petrochemical has ever darkened the shelves of her garage; she gets a 5 on this one, for a total score of 25 points. Donor B, however, is somewhat more flexible and simply can't handle the fire ants on his property without man-made chemicals, though he's organically orthodox in other regards; let's score him at a 3, for a total score of 15 points.

Remember that danger signs are calculated differently; the Scorecard subtracts danger sign scores, which means that, if they exist, they lower the total actual score. If the danger sign doesn't exist, score the funder at zero; if it does exist, score it from 1 to 5. Since the Scorecard does the same multiplication here, a prospect score of 5 multiplied by an Importance Weight of 3 means an actual score, for that danger sign, of *minus* 15. All danger sign scores are subtracted from the total scores for fact statements and value statements, giving the actual score.

The Scorecard compares the actual score to the ideal ("highest possible") score and assigns a rank of A to D, with A being best or highest.

You have by this point fine-tuned your Scorecards so that they represent the characteristics of your best funders. It took a lot of effort to get to this point, so let's make sure you get a great return on all that work.

Publish them. Here's how:

- Announce that you have completed the creation of the Scorecards, benchmarks for qualifying prospects for major gift work, major corporate giving, or major grant seeking. That means you tell every-body on the development team, in senior leadership (including programs and administration), and members of the board.

- Give all relevant parties copies of the Scorecard.

- Make sure the Scorecards are filed securely somewhere in your information technology, where they can be accessed easily. The Scorecards you will file should be considered "masters" or templates. You and your development team will fill out a Scorecard for every major prospect (and current major funder) and keep it filed with the prospect's or funder's contact information, cultivation, and donation records.

THE CONTROL PART

Every element of the Prospect Scorecard provides controls. The Scorecard has its origin in your funder selection strategy. The value statements evaluate the extent to which prospects match or fail to match your agency's values. The fact statements reveal the prospect's capacity for giving or lack thereof. The danger signs lay out early warnings indicating that the prospect might end up costing more than you're willing to spend.

Taken together, now development officers know how to invest their time. And development directors, CEOs, and other senior executives have methods for keeping their talent pool, those costly development officers, focused and on track. Even better, the data reveal when they're on track, when they're not, and what can be done to improve results for the next cycle.

WHAT WE COVERED

- Your Scorecards provide a significant element of management control, useful to the individual solicitor, the chief development officer, senior management, and the governing board.

- Field-testing your Scorecards through a sanity-check review and then using them to score existing donors will contribute to their accuracy.

- Mastering the use of the three simple questions, which are heavily donor focused, will improve your team's ability to gain rapport and establish trust with prospects and donors. Board members, even those who are skittish about raising money, will like them, too.

- Because the Scorecard is filled with meaningful data, it's easy to capture, collate, and report on those data to provide clarity and accountability.

- Don't wait until your Scorecard profiles are perfect. Put them to work right away and improve them over time, based on evidence.

WHAT YOU CAN DO

- Gather your group together, preferably the same people who helped you develop the first draft of your Scorecard.

- Do a sanity check by scrutinizing all statements, importance weights, and prospect scales. Challenge each one. Collaborate on any improvements you decide to make.

- Prepare suggested probing questions for each statement needing them. Some statements are easy to score, while others require sophisticated questioning in order to find out how well the prospect matches the criterion. If you're having trouble formulating your questions, use the sample questions from Chapter 2 as a starting point.

- Now take your Scorecards for a test drive. Use them to score some of your current funders and board members. The feedback you receive may prompt further modifications to the profile.
- Set up a special file folder on your own computer or your nonprofit's shared drive (or both), where you'll store all of your Scorecards. Later on, we'll discuss steps you may choose to take to integrate the Scorecard with your donor management platform.

PART II

Defining the Fund Development Process

According to contemporary management theory, it's difficult—if not impossible—to manage or improve a process if you look only at what happens at the tail-end of the process. Management theory geeks call this the *inspection model,* by which they mean you look at the teddy bear, disk drive, or washing machine only after it falls off the end of the assembly line, and if it doesn't pass inspection, you throw it away. Or maybe you eat it. How many of you get a mental image of Lucy (*I Love Lucy,* not the *Peanuts* character) in the candy factory?

Bye-bye, all that wasted time, money, raw material, effort, profit margin, and cost of lost opportunity.

The cultivation process simply cries out for better management controls, which is what Part II is all about. If the funder-selection strategy and its product, the Prospect Scorecard, represent one of the bookends that control productivity, then the other bookend is opportunity management.

Unfortunately, the most common way nonprofit professionals "manage" the fund-development process is by counting up the bucks that come in at the end. Money is invariably a trailing indicator; it doesn't show until after the work to get it has been done. It's a truly important and meaningful trailing indicator for sure, but if you just keep track of the dough you raise by counting it up at the end of the year, quarter, or month, you really have no way to learn how much you might have *lost* through poorly targeted cultivation tactics or pursuing under-qualified prospects, especially when you pursue them for too long just because they're "nice" to you.

You must keep track of income, and you must compare the income you raised to the targets set for that income. But if that's all you're tracking, you're not learning much.

IMPORTANT!

The Leaky Bucket study tells us that only about 63 percent of participants establish targets for total income, while only 52 percent set targets for income by funding category. Scary.

We already know that productivity improves when the development officer selects prospects using agreed-upon criteria. Opportunity management adds another arsenal to the battle for continuous improvement because you can hook data from the Scorecard to additional data arising from the arc of cultivation, from identification through cultivation to fulfillment. Without that ability, you're seeing only half the picture.

The Moves Management^{TM} model, introduced by G. T. Smith in the 1970s, was an early entry in the effort to manage nonprofit opportunity. Although the model has many fans and I respect it, it hasn't evolved to the point where its use provides specific insights into ways to gain productivity. And that's not altogether surprising.

Compare the Moves Management discipline with the field of quality management. The earliest entry came toward the end of the nineteenth century, when Frederick Taylor became the world's first efficiency expert. Efficiency was a great place to start, but it wasn't very well targeted, and sometimes the cure was worse than the disease. For example, one route to efficiency for stoking coal-fired furnaces was to give the coal shovelers bigger shovels—more coal per scoop, but a corresponding cost in fatigue and stress injuries.

Taylor's work was eventually superseded by the work of W. Edwards Deming, with the introduction of Total Quality Management (post World War II), which shifted attention away from pure efficiency and toward the concept of quality, which combines productivity and reliability using methods of statistical analysis. TQM was later superseded by Six Sigma, which raised the productivity ante to the level of only one "defect" per million. Six Sigma was subsequently supplanted or enhanced by newer models such as Lean, Information Technology Infrastructure Library (ITIL), Lean–Six Sigma and who-knows-what new acronyms coming on board. Standards such as the Malcolm Baldridge Criteria for Performance Excellence are now known and used all over the world. Every one of these new entries has demonstrated improvements in the ways we select, measure, and analyze business processes with the aim of producing increasingly innovative products at ever more affordable costs. While Moves Management has the potential to drive better results, it has not spawned the same sort of evolution we have seen in the field of productivity improvement—at least until now.

I'll discuss the Moves Management model in more detail in Chapter 5.

The opportunity-management aspect of Fundraising the SMART Way™ takes the Moves Management concept to the next level. The SMART Way model is streamlined, stripped down, more measurable, more dynamic. Data from opportunity-management controls can easily be cross-referenced with data from Scorecard rankings, producing breakthroughs in clarity and accountability. They point the way to innovation. And they do it with less work and effort.

The Association of Fundraising Professionals' (AFP's) Fundraising Effectiveness Project shows some disturbing statistics reinforcing our Leaky Bucket findings. As we said in the Introduction, gains in gifts were virtually flat from 2010 to 2012, with new gifts offset by reduced gifts and lapsed donors, along with unquestionably significant declines in donor retention. The use of carefully analyzed qualifying benchmarks such as the SMART Way Scorecard will have a beneficial impact on these statistics, yet an even more powerful contribution will come from controls over opportunity management.

Although the Cousin Judy approach applies only to funder selection and not the process of cultivation, there's another "kissin' cousin" approach that does—namely, the sales process. If you were to examine the hundreds of sales-force automation software products on the market, or scan the thousands of books and training courses on the subject, you would find lots of attention paid to the "sales funnel" or opportunity pipeline, two interchangeable names for the same thing. As far as I can tell, the pipeline concept is not nearly so widely used among fundraising people. When such guideposts exist, they tend to be variable or situational, especially as compared to the standard steps (first do this, then that, then the next thing) you'd find salespeople using. I aim to solve that problem with Fundraising the SMART Way, where opportunity management leads to enhanced productivity in direct, observable ways. In the SMART Way model, the opportunity pipeline gets the attention it deserves.

In Chapter 5, we'll explore the underlying concept of process management and apply it to gift cultivation. We'll also introduce robust performance indicators based on the stages of opportunity management, which we call Donor Moves in honor of Moves Management. Data gathered from Donor Moves determine where your productivity bucket might be leaking.

Chapter 6 shows how to make use of those performance indicators by establishing targets for each one. Performance indicators are far more meaningful when the user has documented targets associated with them. Please read this chapter with care. Remember, if you can't measure it, you can't manage or improve it. Without performance targets, your performance indicators only tell you what to do next; they don't give you insight into efficiency or productivity. We'll show you how to set meaningful and reliable targets quickly, without the need to mull them over for hours and hours. When I studied statistical analysis, one of my favorite discoveries was that *inexact* measurements of the right things are more valuable than exacting measurements of the wrong things. Some of the things you'll measure in this approach are somewhat inexact—but they give tremendous insight into progress or the lack of it.

Finally, Chapter 7 takes us through the validation process, using techniques similar to the ones used in validating your Scorecards. This chapter also gets you into the world of continuous improvement. Even though to this day I can't handle basic arithmetic without a calculator, I've discovered that statistics are easy for me, and using them to drive continuous improvement is downright exciting (well, for me anyway, but I'm turning into a statistics nerd). Chapter 8 will introduce you to some of the most venerable and reliable methods you'll rely on once you move into full-blown implementation.

CHAPTER 5

The Fund Development Pipeline

The fund development pipeline is that useful checklist of opportunities currently being cultivated, from which we forecast the gifts and grants we expect to come in, and when. The pipeline concept is ubiquitous in the for-profit world, but I've met quite a few nonprofit executives who aren't familiar with it. What's worse, it hasn't gotten a whole lot of attention from providers of donor-management software, which tends on the whole to pay more attention to managing donors after acquisition and to be weak on the cultivation process. Virtually every corporate sales-force automation platform has a module dedicated to opportunity management, and it would be advantageous if all nonprofit platforms did so as well.

It's easy to tell when development officers lack effective automated ways to report on their fundraising pipelines. Instead of simple reports with tables, charts, and graphs, they deliver anecdotes, short stories about gifts, grants, or sponsorships that haven't come to fruition yet. Often, such anecdotes are heavy on details of a particular situation, such as why your donor canceled the meeting, but light on the evidence of progress.

Human psychology is predictable, unfortunately. Too many stories with too much distracting detail doesn't always lead to applause. More likely your audience will remember your screw-ups and failures, and forget about stuff that's going well. They may jump in with off-the-cuff suggestions out of context. If you're reporting to the board of directors, those suggestions seem to take on the force of authority. As the CEO of a major nonprofit once told me, such presentations easily convert positive conversations into negative ones.

Let's hit the reset button here and discuss how to create a fundraising pipeline and get enormous value out of it. The pipeline issue has poked dozens of leaky holes in many fundraising buckets, so let's figure out how to plug them.

PIPELINE BASICS

The standard fundraising pipeline should include the following data:

- The name of the individual, business, or foundation that you're pursuing, plus a way to show which are new and which are retained.
- The category of the donation (gift, grant, or sponsorship).
- The size of the anticipated donation.
- When you started working on the donation or opportunity.
- How close the donation has come to fruition, defined by specific "opportunity stages."
- The date you think the donation will close.

Most often, we use the pipeline for forecasting, one of its most pertinent functions. You and your boss need to know which funders are going to say yes and when. The ability to forecast accurately is the basis of the organization's financial stability. Faithful understanding and use of opportunity stages improve your ability to predict when the money will move from their bank accounts to yours.

One of the most appealing and effective elements of pipeline management is the use of those opportunity stages mentioned earlier. Those opportunity stages represent key points in the process, based on the assumption that every new deal or opportunity will evolve through roughly the same steps, milestones, and plateaus. Thus, a pipeline user can determine the location of the opportunity, using this mutually agreed upon set of standards. The SMART Way™ pipeline approach brings in some innovative tools discussed later in this chapter.

However, though pipelines are primarily used for forecasting purposes, the way they're currently set up makes it difficult to forecast with a high degree of accuracy. Major gift officers may fall into the "hope" trap and state that the gift has evolved much closer to the point of closing than is really so. Sometimes they try to make themselves look good, by failing to document the progress of the gift until it's already trembling on the brink of closing. In both instances, the wrong information is being used the wrong way.

Here's the problem. Hope, as the estimable Rick Page of the Complex Sale, has noted, is not a strategy.[1] The *evidence* that a gift or grant is about to appear may be hard to find in the conventional pipeline. While the pipeline invariably includes opportunity stages or milestones, these typically describe the activity of the development officer. So does the Moves Management model.

But when you measure activity, you find out only about the amount of activity you've produced. The statistical link between activity and results is weak.

Activity measures tend to move us right back to management by anecdote. They fail to provide evidence regarding the progress of the potential gift. What data exist tend to be anecdotes about what you did, such as "met Mrs. Jones," "had another conversation with Jim from the foundation; their CEO just had a heart attack and everything is all messed up," or "Mr. Smith canceled our meeting and I don't know when he'll reschedule."

The fact that you held a meeting or delivered a proposal is no guarantee that the prospect will decide to give. These actions are merely mechanisms for delivering your ideas and recommendations.

Despite the many other desirable contributions provided by contemporary nonprofit constituent relationship management (CRM) systems, few of these systems offer useful opportunity-management modules. Either the module simply doesn't exist or it's constructed using opportunity stages describing actions taken by development officers.

To make matters worse, however, the Leaky Bucket data show that only 29 percent of participants use any form of donor-management technology, including a simple homegrown spreadsheet. Combine this lack of automation with opportunity stages based on activity, and it's no surprise that the Fundraising Effectiveness Project shows such disquieting results. If you can't track the progress of active opportunities, if you base your forecasts on guesses and intuition, and if you can't pull useful reports that show where you need to fix shortcomings in the process, the ability of your development shop to produce desired results is compromised.

We seem to be asking our development officers to scale Mt. Everest without bottled oxygen, ice axes or safety ropes. Enough already. If there was ever a nonprofit business function crying out for some management controls, fundraising is it.

---

[1] Rick Page, *Hope Is Not a Strategy: The 6 Keys to Winning the Complex Sale* (New York: McGraw-Hill, 2003).

The SMART Way Pipeline Revolution

Having used, managed, and reported on the performance of pipelines for many decades, I eventually realized why they didn't give me or my salespeople particularly useful information. Pipelines are designed upside down. To fix the problem, I turned them right side up.

Conventional opportunity management divides the pipeline into stages. Invariably, those stages describe the activities of the gift officer or salesperson. Remember, what you measure is what you get, so if you decide to measure activity, that's what you'll get, often in large quantities. Measure phone calls? Get lots of phone calls. Measure demonstrations of your product? Get lots of demonstrations. Measure proposals out the door? Ditto.

Standard pipeline stages describe actions and outputs performed by your development officers. SMART Way pipeline stages describe actions taken by your funders and funding prospects. When the gift officer takes a prescribed action, you can measure that it was taken. When the funder takes one of the documented actions, that's the *result* of the gift officer's actions. And since what you measure is what you get, measuring results now tells you some important things. Here are some examples:

- Prospects tell you enough about themselves for you to determine how well they match your Scorecard, so you can decide if they justify additional effort.

- Prospects show or tell you that they are sufficiently interested in your organization to consider making a gift or obtaining a proposal.

- Prospects willingly review your proposal and negotiate the details.

- Prospects tell you they have decided to make the gift.

You certainly have to make yourself known to the prospect, schedule the initial meeting, find out if she likes cats better than dogs, discover her major charitable motivations, take her to the ball game, invite him to the dedication ceremony, ask her to buy a brick in the memorial walk. You take these actions, at least in part, in order to persuade prospects to reveal their motivations, accept proposals, and make larger gifts.

SMART Way pipeline management is straightforward. There are only nine opportunity stages, and they occur in an unvarying sequence. They apply to all types of funding, including major gifts, corporate contributions, and grants.

But unlike more conventional pipeline-management techniques, we organize opportunity-stage definitions so they can provide statistical insights into performance. Each opportunity stage is a key performance indicator. As such, it's not only possible but proper to document specific, quantifiable performance targets and assign them to individual gift officers and to the development shop overall. These metrics can be cross-referenced with Scorecard rank information, so everyone from the gift officer to the chairman of the board gains unprecedented levels of clarity, insight, and accountability regarding the fund-development process.

PROCESS MANAGEMENT FOR NONPROFITS: A PRIMER

We introduced the Four Simple Laws of Process Management in Chapter 1, but let's review them again here:

- Law 1: You can't manage or improve it if you can't measure it.
- Law 2: What you measure is what you get.
- Law 3: You can't figure out much by using a single measurement.
- Law 4: If the only thing you measure happens after the process is complete, you haven't learned much about the process.

In other words, measuring; measuring things that are diagnostic; using a range of measurements that complement one another; and making sure that you measure things at the beginning, middle, *and* end of a process all combine to provide management controls over the fundraising function. At the present time, such levels of control are practiced by only a small number of nonprofits, primarily the largest universities, major museums, and other cultural icons. For the rest of the nonprofit world, many such controls are MIA—missing in action. For those charities, no matter how hard they may work at it, and no matter the size of the development officer's contact list, raising enough money year after year is pretty tough. A lot of it is guesswork.

IMPORTANT!

Measure the same things the same way every time, and you'll gain meaningful insights into the health and effectiveness of your fundraising pipeline. Measure different things different ways every time, and you'll get a lot of information, but it might not tell you much.

The SMART Way Prospect Scorecard reduces a lot of guesswork by providing an objective, mutually agreed upon standard against which to measure the next prospect's potential. Careful and consistent use of the Scorecard reduces time wasted and effort lost pursuing the wrong prospects. But that's only part of the equation. If we look at the Scorecard through the lens of formal process-management theory, it can be described as a set of specifications for the raw materials of your fundraising process. In order to convert these raw materials—your prospects—into donors that remain engaged and giving for years, we now need to figure in the methods that add value, that facilitate the transformation from prospect to donor.

The SMART Way pipeline model, Donor Moves, complements the Scorecard, further reducing guesswork and offering insights into the health, effectiveness, size, shape, and velocity of your pipeline. This approach uses performance metrics effectively to drive productivity. Let's see how it compares to the Moves Management model.

MOVES MANAGEMENT VERSUS THE SMART WAY

Moves Management was conceived to help major gift officers map out a strategy for winning the next large gift. When used properly, it can be very effective. But the model was not designed to support business analytics, so it doesn't. Instead, it has a *situational* application, meaning that every major gift opportunity requires a unique Moves Management map to get the job done right.

Each development shop defines its own moves, usually between 7 and 10 in number. Then each major gift officer develops a campaign strategy *per major donor*. There are foreground moves, background moves, and complex ways to show relationships between the donor being cultivated for the next gift and all the links or connections that exist between that donor and other donors, community influencers, board members, staff members, clients, and so on. Such an approach can drive larger gifts, and it's a useful teaching tool for less experienced gift officers. It certainly encourages a donor-centered point of view and helps to support an agency-wide mind-set of philanthropy. So far, so good.

Here's what it doesn't do. It doesn't provide the metrics needed to produce useful business analytics. Thus, it doesn't enhance the agency's funder selection strategies or identify gaps or leaks in the productivity of the fundraising effort. That's why I like to compare Moves Management with the evolution of process management starting from the efficiency experts of the late 1900s, to Total Quality Management in mid-twentieth century, Six Sigma in the 1990s, and Lean and so on in the twenty-first century. Think of Moves Management as an early entry for improving fund development. The SMART Way pipeline model provides the next generation of systems, or systems thinking, for fundraising effectiveness, taking up from where Moves Management leaves off. If you, the reader, are already a proponent of Moves Management, the SMART Way approach will make all kinds of sense to you. Here's how it complements what you already know:

- Funder-selection strategies are based on a collaborative effort including deeper analysis and a higher level of academic rigor that goes beyond giving capacity and a connection with a key executive or director.
- Opportunity stages are standardized, not situational, to support data capture, analysis, and reporting.
- Opportunity stages describe the donor's giving process, rather than the major gifts officer's (MGO's) cultivation process.
- It's simple to keep track of the number of times each opportunity stage has been achieved in a given period of time, thus providing statistical insights about conversion ratios, which measure progress moving from one Donor Move to the next.
- Cross-referencing data from Scorecards with data from opportunity stages produces powerful business and predictive analytics.

Finally, there's the issue of staffing. Some Moves Management experts recommend that the agency designate someone on staff to be the Moves manager. This individual is accountable for ensuring that the right data are entered into the donor-management platform the right way, and for making sure that each MGO, donor, and campaign has its own set of reports. In my not-so-humble opinion, this position looks like a special fundraising-only data entry clerk, which adds to the headcount and is likely to be available only in larger organizations. If the model is so complicated that it requires a dedicated administrative person just to keep track of the data, it's hard to see how this adds to productivity.

In the SMART Way, no "SMART" manager is required, largely because it's so simple for the user to update the progress of each campaign, usually by selecting an option from a pull-down menu built into the donor-management platform. Automation handles all data capture, collating, and reporting. Since pipeline progress is reviewed frequently, development officers and their managers and leaders can observe progress or the lack of it and use these insights to coach team members "to the model," as they say.

SMART Way opportunity-stage definitions and related metrics provide early-warning signs showing at which points in the process productivity may currently be leaking. You then use classic process-management techniques such as root-cause analysis to find the source (the root cause) of the problem somewhere upstream that's affecting results downstream. Glitches, wasted effort, and opportunity cost are typically easier and cheaper to repair back at their source, before too much time or money has been lost.

ELIMINATE PROCESS BOUNDARIES OR ADD THEM?

Henry Ford's most important contribution to society wasn't the Model T, it was the assembly line. Before Ford figured it out, automobiles were ruinously expensive largely because each component part was custom-made by specialists who had to lug the various parts of the embryonic auto from here to there to get the darned thing finished. If one of the specialists goofed and destroyed a component, not only did he waste time and materials, he had to do it over again. We call that *rework*.

Ford standardized the parts and laid out the steps required to assemble them in a line. Workers had a handy supply of standard-sized parts at each stage, thus reducing wasted time and materials. The workers didn't have to move from place to place; the line did that by carrying the evolving car from Point A to Point B—significantly less waste of raw materials and significantly less rework. Ford's truly brilliant insight showed him things would work better if he *eliminated* the boundaries between one stage and the next of the auto-building process.

Process-management disciplines have come a long way since Ford's day, of course, but one of their defining principles remains the notion of removing or reducing boundaries between chunks of a business process, since that's where most of the "waste" crops up. In most "hard" business functions such as manufacturing and distribution, productivity can be lost because of disconnects, obstacles, or bottlenecks that crop up between stages and within any given stage. Some proponents of early process-management techniques thought of the whole concept as "reducing waste." Deming's work to restore the Japanese economy after World War II raised the bar by introducing the notion of quality, which means improving the reliability of the finished product, not just the efficiency with which it was made. These days, management experts have been able to find ways to improve productivity of "soft" or front-office processes, as well as the more traditional manufacturing and distribution functions.

Contemporary disciplines continue to measure, manage, and improve levels of waste, rework, and so on in many areas, and now they employ more sophisticated statistical tools and automated processes. As long as you can observe and measure waste and rework, any business process can be improved with pinpoint accuracy.

Here's an example: "Reduce wasted materials at Machine B by 37.8 percent by March 1." This performance indicator states *what's* to be achieved, *where* the improvement should take place, *how big* the outcome should be, and *when* you want it to be completed. Kind of looks like a SMART objective—it's specific, measurable, assignable (somebody's in charge), realistic, and time defined. Similar applications have brought about improvements in other business functions from distribution to order processing. As long as you can measure or track something observable, it becomes prime fodder for an improvement initiative.

Boundaries in Fundraising?

In the fundraising world, however, there are few if any visible stages. The "building" of the gift is invisible. It takes place between the donor's ears. Without some clear boundaries, it's tough to figure out if wasted effort or rework might occur.

Neil Rackham, a guru of sales-force productivity, has likened the sales process to a long, dark tunnel where "the company puts in sales resources at one end and *hopes* a contract comes out at the other."[2] Substitute the words

---

[2] Neil Rackham and John De Vincentis, *Rethinking the Sales Force* (New York: McGraw-Hill, 1999), 205. Emphasis added. I owe a real debt of gratitude to Rackham and De Vincentis; this single sentence inspired me to develop Fundraising the SMART Way™.

nonprofit for *company, development resources* for *sales resources,* and *gift* for *contract,* and this insight applies perfectly to the nonprofit fund-development process. Rackham, who also recognizes that hope is not a strategy, suggests *imposing* logical boundaries on the fund development process, to make the glitches, missteps, wasted motion, and rework visible. Otherwise, they slip through—they "leak"—in ways we might not notice, where costs go up, time goes wasted, and frustration goes sky-high. "Waste" means you invested too much in the wrong prospects, or you ran an event at a loss. Rework takes place when the qualified donor decides not to give after all and you have to go out and find another one, but your pipeline is empty.

CRM systems designed for corporate sales, containing opportunity management modules, take advantage of Rackham's insight. They impose the missing boundaries by providing defined opportunity stages. Standard opportunity stages are expected to reveal the progress of the sale (gift opportunity) from identification to depositing the check. Unfortunately, because they tend to describe the activities of development officers, they don't provide as much insight into productivity as they could.

Activities Are Not Results

Development-shop activities may influence results, but they don't measure your ability to achieve them. You certainly need to send marketing materials, schedule initial meetings, and conduct discovery calls, but doing such things doesn't tell you if you've got the right prospect or what you want your prospect to do next. With enough years in the saddle, experienced development pros might gain a pretty good sense of what's going to happen next, but such intuitions are unreliable; they don't provide evidence. And anyway, there's little evidence here to help you waste less time qualifying the prospect or get to yes more quickly. When opportunity stages are defined by development-shop activities, they might even lock the officers into tactics or behaviors that might not be efficient or beneficial. Does every single prospect require a facility tour? Or even a birthday card?

To make matters worse, if you only track and measure activity, all you'll know is how much activity you produced. What's more important—sending out invitations or getting people to attend the event? Putting a pledge card at each place setting, or obtaining completed pledge forms? That's why I'm so insistent on defining opportunity stages that describe results. When donors attend events and make pledges, they produce the *results* of all those invitations and pledge cards.

With gratitude to the Moves Management model, we came up with a simplified approach to opportunity management based on the donor's giving process, where each stage describes the *result* of development activity. We call it the *Donor Moves*. Donor Moves dissect the cultivation process into a series of stages defined by donor behavior. What a simple change, but how impactful.

The Donor Moves

Donor Moves are actions performed by donors and prospects representing the results of your efforts at cultivation and solicitation. They occur in a fixed sequence. Every opportunity achieves every move, at least to the point where the opportunity may be lost. Even if some of those moves happen in a compressed period of time, such as a single meeting with the prospect, we can assume the prospect advanced through the entire series, at least mentally. They are:

- *Move One:* Prospect shares charitable motivations, needs and preferences.
- *Move Two:* Prospect "validates" our claims that we can fulfill expectations, deliver on our mission, and serve our clients as we said we could.
- *Move Three:* Prospect asks for a gift proposal or indicates willingness to accept one.
- *Move Four:* Prospect reviews our proposal with us, and discusses terms, scope, payment schedules, and the like.
- *Move Five:* Prospect/donor accepts the proposal or makes the gift.
- *Move Six:* Donor expresses feedback on satisfaction (we met his expectations).
- *Move Seven:* Donor gives again.
- *Move Eight:* Donor refers us to other like-minded people.

There is also a ninth stage of great importance, Move Zero, which I'll discuss below. Move Zero is the point at which you identify leads or suspects, people who seem to justify some more effort to see if they're reasonably well qualified. It's the only portion of the cultivation process that describes the actions of the development officer.

Donor Moves are unambiguous and unvarying in sequence. Ask yourself if the donor took Move Two and the answer will be yes or no. Move Two always comes before Move Three and after Move One, reducing the agonizing question of "what do I do *now*?" The answer is always "persuade the prospect to achieve the next move."

Furthermore, the Donor Moves sequence lacks the complexity of the Moves Management model, with its foreground/background and direct/indirect complications. While Donor Moves are carefully documented, the tactics employed by each development officer may differ based on what works for the officer and what works for that particular prospect. Donor Moves represent the science of fundraising, while development officer tactics and activities represent the art.

You don't really care which tactics your people used, as long as they delivered desired results and, naturally, they didn't do anything illegal, immoral, or otherwise unacceptable. Thus, this model empowers development officers to use their talents, brains, and experience—the art of fundraising—within the context of a documented framework—the science of fundraising.

IMPORTANT!

Don't assess your development officers' performance based on how many hours they put in. They're all sleep-deprived anyway, and you don't want to make it worse. Assess it based on their results. If they can produce desired results in 30 hours a week, then encourage them do so.

Plenty of experienced fundraisers are convinced that fundraising is all art, no science. Here's the problem. A lot of those development professionals learned their trade when times were good and we could afford the years of practice needed to become proficient and get to know everybody in town. Such luxury has gone extinct, like the dodo bird. Your new hires have to show results pretty quickly.

The Most Important Move When I ask which move is the most important, people often say Move 5 because that's where the money shows up. They are wrong.

The single most important Donor Move is *Move One: Prospect shares charitable motivations, needs, and preferences.* Move One means the prospect has given you enough insight for you to decide if it's justifiable to invest more time and effort. Getting the prospect to achieve Move One means you figured out the donor's potential for lifetime giving based on your Scorecard, using those helpful suggested probing questions from Chapter 5. If you can't complete the Scorecard based on what you've heard, then the prospect has not achieved Move One yet and you need to ask more questions.

If you have completed the Scorecard and ranked the prospect, then you will know enough to make an informed decision. Donor's rank is an A? Great, persuade him to achieve Move Two. Donor's rank is a D? Forget it; be nice but push that donor back to the marketing team and make sure they send him the newsletter and direct-appeal postcards.

Development officers with lots of seniority may have some trouble with this, because they're more likely to have the habit of assessing the prospect based on intuition and experience. Such officers may assign desirable characteristics to the prospect based on the officer's assumptions rather than the prospect's answers. Try to discourage this practice. It can be a source of considerable wasted effort. Remind them—and teach this to the newbies—tracking Donor Moves, which means entering the information that the next move was achieved, provides the statistical insights that power continuous improvement. They're not just tracking stuff for the sake of tracking it. They're finding ways to earn more income with less effort, make their jobs easier, and move the agency ever closer to achieving its mission.

Move Zero

Where all eight Donor Moves describe actions or behaviors executed by prospects and donors, Move Zero refers to work done by the development team. It refers to your target market, your following, the list of subscribers to your newsletter, the people who like your Facebook business page and follow your executive director's tweets. People (and businesses) like these have already raised their hands and said, "Tell me more." They can certainly include clients, clients' families, directors on your governing board, volunteers, friends or relatives of your staff, and others whom you and your development officers have tripped over. Everyone whose name is on your contact list has already, in some minor or major way, told you that your agency's work has piqued their interest.

It's a good idea to make sure this list is as big as you can make it. This is the pool in which you'll fish for your next minnow—a qualified lead.

Expanding the Move Zero pool is yet another reason for devoting all that time to funder-selection strategies and Scorecard statements. Thanks to the miracles of inbound marketing technology, once you've developed your funder-selection strategy and Scorecards, you have identified the keywords, phrases, and descriptions likely to attract strangers to your nonprofit's electronic presence and convert them to visitors. (In marketing-speak, a "visitor" is anyone who visits your web site.) If your web site, blog, or newsletter is sufficiently interesting, some of those visitors will convert themselves into prospects (again in marketing-speak, a prospect is any visitor who fills out a form or downloads something you've offered, often simply for the cost of their e-mail address).

Pulling together such a list of interested persons used to be difficult and expensive. It usually meant buying or renting a list from a list broker, typically a big expense followed by the discovery that the list was out of date based on the number of returned letters marked "no forwarding address." But interactive technology has revolutionized the process of attracting interested parties. Keep this in mind when you're worried about your marketing expenses. As long as your web site is up to snuff, attracting visitors, and converting them into prospects, you're getting your money's worth. Take advantage of these visitors and prospects. If you don't have the knowledge, skill, or time to fine-tune your web site and e-mail content to attract the right people in sufficient quantities, find someone who does and spend the money.

This stuff is truly, deeply, and excruciatingly important so let me repeat it.

- Use your Scorecard research to identify the keywords, phrases, descriptions used by your best, most valuable donors.

- Sprinkle those keywords and phrases liberally throughout all electronic communications, including web site content, e-newsletters, e-blasts, blog postings, landing pages, lead nurturing schemes, and the like.

- Keep track of all visitor or prospect contact information and use it— frequently! Everyone whose name is on that list has told you they are interested in your nonprofit and willing to learn more.

I've worked with many fundraising rookies over the years, people thrust into fundraising for young, untried nonprofit organizations with no track record. The thing that worries them the most is how to identify leads. There are hundreds of techniques for doing so, but the easiest, fastest, and least expensive way to do so is to leverage your agency's electronic presence by using the language of your best donors, board members, volunteers, clients, or any others who are fans of your nonprofits. Their words will attract more people to your Move Zero list.

What do you do with those on that nice, big, fat list of Move Zero entries? You filter them through your Scorecard's fact profile. Then you convert the ones who match to Move One.

DEVELOPMENT DRIVERS

What Moves Management simply calls moves, I call *development drivers*. These comprise a short list of actions taken by members of the development team that have proven themselves to contribute to higher fundraising productivity. Like Donor Moves, they should be few in number; any more than seven or eight and you'll be overwhelmed. Unlike Donor Moves, they don't occur in sequence, and your team is not necessarily going to execute them in every situation.

As important as Donor Moves are, development drivers balance the situation. They are not used to map out the campaign strategy for Donor X, laying out the steps of that particular dance. No, what they do is to make sure that development officers execute certain activities that have proven to be diagnostic. Think of development drivers as a set of best practices that have been shown to persuade your ideal funders to take desirable action. Again unlike Donor Moves, it may be useful to select development drivers based on the category of the gift or grant. Actions taken by your development shop to win additional grants will likely be quite different from those to win major gifts.

Some development moves come right out of the standard Moves Management checklist, for example:

- Conduct annual or biannual meetings with major donors (where you do *not* ask for money).
- Ask for referrals from current donors or board members.
- Follow up with new prospects after an event.

- After submitting a gift proposal, follow up within a certain number of days.

Development drivers such as these help to reveal insights into your team's opportunity risk factor and other areas where improvement initiatives might be pertinent.

To select development drivers, take stock of outreach and follow-up activities that have proven most successful in your development shop. Select a few of them. Track those few things along with your Donor Moves, and you've got a powerful framework in place for continuous improvement of fundraising productivity and effectiveness.

Do I Know What's Expected of Me?

Marcus Buckingham has written extensively about what distinguishes great managers from those that are merely "good." In his groundbreaking book *First Break All the Rules,* Buckingham notes that one way to evaluate the manager's skills is to ask the people who report to him or her 12 revealing questions, the first of which is this: Do I know what is expected of me at work?[3]

If we asked that question of the development staff, I think most people would say, "Sure, of course, I'm expected to raise money. Duh." If only things were so simple. A more honest answer might well be "Sure, of course, I'm expected to raise money—but I don't always know what to do *next.*" The Donor Moves model, including Move Zero, tells the development officer what to do next: persuade the donor to achieve the next move. At Move Three, prospect asks for a proposal, then you've got to "move" her to Move Four—review and negotiate the details.

Using Donor Moves is less complex than Moves Management, so it's easier to implement and adopt. But Moves Management was specifically designed to help the development officer know what to do next. If that's the only way to use Donor Moves, what's the difference?

The difference, it turns out, is huge. Donor Moves create the framework for continuous improvement. Getting them to do so, however, means using them as key performance indicators (KPIs). And performance indicators need a bit more explanation, which I'll share with you in Chapter 6.

---

[3] Marcus Buckingham and Curt Coffman, *First, Break All the Rules: What the World's Greatest Managers Do Differently* (New York: Simon & Schuster, 1999), 33.

WHAT WE COVERED

- While the Scorecard represents the first "bookend" of the SMART Way model, SMART Way pipeline management techniques or Donor Moves represent the other bookend.

- Pipelines use so-called "opportunity stages" to show progress. Traditionally, these stages describe actions taken by the development team; thus, they track activities. But activities are not results.

- Our opportunity stages describe actions taken by the donor and thus are called Donor Moves. Such actions are the *result* of actions taken by the development shop.

- Donor Moves simplify the Moves Management concept. They are standardized, making them easier to track. They are unambiguous and unvarying in sequence.

- Development drivers complement Donor Moves. They represent a small number of development activities, the ones that are most effective at persuading donors to move along the arc of Donor Moves. They do not occur in sequence and may not be necessary for every gift opportunity, but when we track them, they provide additional insights demonstrating the "health" and effectiveness of your cultivation pipeline.

WHAT YOU CAN DO

- Take a look at the way you keep track of gift and grant opportunities today. Identify the milestones you use to locate a particular gift. Does your list of milestones provide good predictive indicators?

- Select two or three gifts currently in the process of cultivation. Figure out which Donor Move was achieved last by the prospect or donor. Refer to the list of Donor Moves above. What actions would be most appropriate for you to take, in order to move each of those gifts to the next Donor Move?

- Make a list of your most important activities or tactics, the ones most likely to have an influence on donor/prospect behavior. Select no more than six of them.

CHAPTER 6

Setting Performance Targets

O kay, now you've got ways to impose those desirable boundaries or milestones on your pipeline, so it's easy to figure out what to do next with any particular opportunity. If the opportunity is *here,* then you want to push it to *there,* the next stage. Both Moves Management and our Donor Moves model can do that for you beautifully. But there's still something missing. Using the moves to manage a particular opportunity (i.e., to remember what to do next) is tactical or situational. It doesn't necessarily impact the health, speed, size, or shape of the pipeline.

The "situational" use of Donor Moves does not help you manage the process for continuous improvement. To gain continuous improvement, breakthroughs, and innovations, you must measure the frequency by which these opportunity stages are achieved and the lapsed time between stages. Measuring the data requires that you establish specific targets stating the results you're seeking.

The strategic use of Donor Moves provides the raw material for continuous improvement, largely by uncoupling Donor Moves *data* from Donor Moves *anecdotes.* Once the data has been separated from the anecdote or situation, we can work with the statistics produced by the data. Let me elaborate by drawing another comparison with the classic moves management model.

In Moves Management, every "map" is vertical. In other words, you sit down and create a map describing the moves to take to move Mrs. Moneybags' potential major gift from point A to point B to point C, and voila, the gift shows up. Meanwhile, you're also paying attention to your other 43 prospects. In the meantime, I'm doing the same thing with my 52 prospects. The great thing about this approach is that you or I can pluck any individual donor out of the pile, figure out what's working and what to do next, and get some coaching from our director or another gift officer. Where Moves Management fails us, however, is that we can't uncouple the data from the individual prospect.

The Donor Moves model allows us to manage the individual prospect the same way—the vertical view of each particular prospect. But it also allows us to take a "horizontal" view of staff performance, by collating the number of occurrences per Donor Move at no fewer than two levels: the level being achieved by the individual officer, and the level being achieved by all officers. We simply keep track of the number of times donor prospects reach each move. By collating the numerical data separately from the situational information (information about a specific donor), we reveal such vital information as:

- How long it really takes to advance donors from one opportunity stage to the next.
- The conversion ratios we're able to achieve, or how many opportunities at one stage will "convert" to the next stage.
- Where we can anticipate a slowdown in the velocity at which opportunities move through the pipeline. If we know that it takes more time to move from Donor Move Four, where the donor negotiates the details, to Donor Move Five, where the donor makes the gift, then we can deploy our resources more effectively during such downtime.

These insights are needed in order to engage in the practices of continuous improvement. When we evaluate the development process one prospect at a time, the insights disappear, or at least become more obscure. By separating the story of individual gift opportunity from the data about all gift opportunities, we gain fresh insights into productivity.

EVERYTHING YOU EVER WANTED TO KNOW ABOUT CONTINUOUS IMPROVEMENT

Continuous improvement, as I've said before, means something quite specific. The phrase describes one of the most valuable elements of process management, namely, the ability to keep track of performance based on statistical insights, pinpoint the need for improvement initiatives, execute them, and see if they change your desired results. You simply can't produce continuous improvement unless you can assign performance targets properly for each item you measure, capture the "actuals" data, and compare actual performance to targeted performance. In this chapter, I discuss how to wring more value out of the Donor Moves model, by adding performance targets.

A performance indicator is made up of three components:

1. What you're measuring.
2. The way you measure it.
3. The desired result or target you aim to reach.

A performance indicator lacking either the means of measurement or the documented performance target fails to provide management control. Once you have decided what to measure, and specified the desired result, you have management control. Not only does this set meaningful expectations for the worker, it also provides feedback for workers and managers showing whether the desired result is being met. Think of the performance indicator as a thermostat. The thermostat shows two things: what you *want* the temperature to be, and what it actually *is*. Oh, and by the way, this measurement also tells you how to "improve" the situation. Too hot? Too cold? Raise or lower the *target* temperature to the desired level.

Donor Moves make great performance indicators. They include all three components. They tell the user what is being measured, which is the frequency with which each move is achieved. The way to measure them is straightforward: count up the number of times the move has been achieved in a given period of time. The desired result? The number of times you think the move should be achieved in order to be successful. Now the Donor Move is not simply a guideline about what to do next; it has become a true performance indicator: "Achieve Move X 168 times this year or 14 times each month."

Such carefully constructed performance indicators are not only the answer to the questions "do I know what is expected of me at work?" and "what do I do next?"; they also answer another question of even greater importance: how well am I performing as compared to those expectations?

In fact, they answer that question at several levels:

- The development officer's level: How well am *I* doing as compared to the expectations I've been given?

- The development director's level: How well is *my team* doing as compared to the collective expectations we've been given?
- The CEO's level: How well is *the agency* doing as compared to the overall expectations we've agreed to?
- The board's level: How well is *our employee, the CEO,* doing as compared to *our* expectations?

When you can answer these questions with reasonable accuracy, you have a system of management controls in place, one that is relevant at every level of the organizational hierarchy.

IMPORTANT!

When you use opportunity stages to figure out how to manage a particular opportunity from a particular prospect, you're using them "vertically." You keep track of what that donor did last and map out what you need to do to move him to the next level.

When you use them as performance indicators, you're using them "horizontally," to demonstrate the collective health of the pipeline, collating the data from all your opportunities or all of the team's, to demonstrate where your pipeline is moving, where it's stuck, and what you can do about it.

Leading Indicators; Trailing Indicators

Performance indicators rarely exist in a vacuum. Not only do they need to include the thing being measured, the way it's measured, and the desired outcome; they also need to be designed in a sequence, pointing out (indicating) various points of the process. Leading indicators describe the early stages of the process, while trailing or lagging indicators tell you what happens after the process is complete. Each indicator can be measured and compared to the target result. Invariably, it is less expensive, less wasteful, to change something "upstream"—something that takes place earlier in the process—to get better results "downstream."

The old inspection model produces a lot of waste. Remember, that's the model where you complete the process, look at the output, and then decide if it's good enough to use or needs to be thrown away. If the trailing indicator is unsatisfactory, you've wasted all the time, energy, and money it took to get to an undesirable result. Process management, however, can "speak" to you by helping you find the point where the problem first arose, so you can fix it there, where it's a lot cheaper.

For example, if you have invested 50 of your $1,000 hours to cultivate a prospect who turns out to be a DOA, you just wasted $50,000 of opportunity risk, and the hours that are left now carry a correspondingly higher opportunity risk. However, if you were able to assess the prospect as undesirable in only two hours, you've saved a considerable amount of time and energy by lowering your opportunity risk factor.

In the fundraising process, the first five Donor Moves, Moves Zero through Four, are leading indicators. Move Five is a trailing indicator; that's where cultivation converts to gift acquisition.

Moves Six through Eight, interestingly enough are also leading indicators, even if they show up *after* the trailing indicator of Move Five. They now describe the process of stewardship, which in its turn rotates back to the process of cultivating of the *next* gift.

ASSIGNING TARGETS

Some people will do anything to get out of setting a target. I can understand that; it's not too tough to say "do this," but it's a little tougher to say "do this 15 times by Monday at 4:30," even though you set a deadline target every time you decide to get dinner on the table by 7:15 P.M. Dinnertime is a performance target. I don't actually care when you eat your dinner, but I do care about the value and importance of setting performance targets.

Unfortunately, our Leaky Bucket study data suggest that more nonprofits *lack* such targets than enjoy them, and I think I might know why. They don't know which number, percentage, or deadline is the right one to choose. So they end up not setting any targets. Even that easiest-to-measure item—income—may lack performance targets. Income is easy to measure, for obvious reasons. But as we have seen, about 37 percent of our respondents don't even measure their total income, and 48 percent don't track their income by funding category, so there's obviously room for improvement.

It's easy to measure Donor Moves. You count up the number of times each move has been achieved. But how do you know which target is the "correct" one? You might not know which target is right since you lack a baseline, a historical track record. Fortunately, since it's more valuable to get

TABLE 6.1   ESTABLISHING PERFORMANCE TARGETS FOR DONOR MOVES

Establishing Performance Targets for Donor Moves—Example

Total Income Target	$1,200,000
"Ideal" Size of Gift	$50,000
Total Number of Gifts to Achieve Target	24

Donor Move	Annual Target in Number of Occurrences	Monthly Target
Move Five: Approves Gift	24	2
Move Four: Negotiates Terms, Scope, Details of Application	36	3
Move Three: Agrees to Consider Application	54	4 or 5
Move Two: Validates Your Mission, Offer	81	6 or 7
Move One: Explains Charitable Philosophy, Expectations	120	10

inexact measurements of the right thing than to get exacting measurements of the wrong things, it's worth it to establish targets for Donor Moves based on an educated guess.

You may already have a target in mind for the total amount of income you need to raise for the current fiscal year, which gives you a starting point. Next, you choose the size of donation you'll use as your common scale. Let's assume that you plan to raise $1,200,000 in major gifts in the next 12 months. Let's further assume that the size of your "ideal" or "typical" gift is $50,000. Yes, you'll accept donations that are larger or smaller, but for you and your agency at this time, a $50,000 gift would be just right (Table 6.1).

Now divide your target income by the size of that "ideal" gift, and you see that you'll need to obtain 24 gifts: $1,200,000/$50,000 = 24. Thus, your target for Donor Move Five is "24 occurrences of Donor Move Five this year," and "2 occurrences of Donor Move Five each month." Then work backwards from Move Five to establish targets for Moves Four, Three, Two, and One, as shown in Table 6.1.

Assigning Donor Moves Targets

Note that the annual and monthly targets for each Move from Four back to One increase by a factor of 1.5. In other words, we assume that Donor

Move One needs to be achieved about one-and-a-half times more often than Donor Move Two, and so on down the line. The conversion ratio between leading Donor Moves in this example is 1.5. Now, a ratio of 1.5 to 1 is pretty tight and rather difficult to achieve. Yours may end up being looser, maybe 3 to 1 (or worse).

The Vital Few Indicators

There are many things you can do in fundraising that can be measured, but not all of them are particularly useful. What you measure is what you get, so if you measure things that are not particularly diagnostic, your team will do those things, even if doing so slows down the flow of income. Measure phone calls and you'll get lots of phone calls. Measure my all-time favorite activity, birthday cards, and your team will send out tons of birthday cards. I know that sending out birthday cards can be a useful way to stay in touch with your donors. But keeping track of how often you send them isn't likely to tell you much about your fundraising pipeline.

One of the main reasons Donor Moves make great performance indicators is that they describe the *results* of outbound efforts. It's helpful to know that you've been able to move 20 new donor prospects to Move One and 15 of those donors to Move Two. It's even better when the number of moves achieved matches or exceeds the target for those moves. However, it might not be particularly helpful to know that you made 75 phone calls last week, except to understand why your ears are tired.

The SMART Way^{TM} model uses a wide range of measurable indicators, both leading and trailing in nature.

- The trailing indicators are:
  - Total income.
  - Income by funding category.
  - Income from newly acquired donors.
  - Income from retained donors.
- The leading indicators are:
  - Number of contacts in your target database ("Move Zero").
  - Number of prospects ranked A or B that you have decided to pursue.

- Number of times prospects moved from the current Donor Move to the next in the sequence.
- Number of times development officers executed development drivers.

Donor Moves, development drivers, and income obtained make for a rich mix of indicators and measurements. This is a "goldilocks" list—not too big, not too small, but just right. Each indicator is diagnostic; it helps to diagnose the health, efficiency, and effectiveness of your fundraising process. There is a relatively small number of indicators, but each one is vital. Each one sharpens insights into the health of the fundraising process.

If you decide to measure too many things, the picture gets muddier, not sharper. That's one reason we restrict the number of Donor Moves to a total of nine, and the number of development drivers down to six or seven. Tracking information against these vital, few indicators once a month provides a desirable level of management control.

The Art of Measurement

In process management, not only do you need to decide what to measure, you also need to select the way you'll measure it. You can:

- Count it.
- Calculate a percentage or ratio (also called a conversion ratio).
- Measure by Yes/No/Always/Never.
- Measure by assigning a deadline.
- Measure by an assigned turn-around time.

Some things simply can't be measured. Robert Mager, an expert on instructional design, calls these things "fuzzies."[1] Some classic "fuzzies" include such things as team spirit, friendliness, being a "self-starter," and being "safety-conscious." All too often, the employee's annual performance review is just chock-full of such un-measurable abstractions. Are these elements undesirable? No, by no means; we want our people to be safety-conscious self-starters who love the team spirit shown in our organization. But we can't measure degrees of friendliness, percentages of safety consciousness, or ratios of team spirit.

---

[1] Robert Mager, *Goal Analysis: How to Clarify Your Goals So You Can Actually Achieve Them*, 3rd ed. (Atlanta, GA: Center for Effective Performance, 1997), 23.

The things that you can measure produce observable evidence, in the form of data, showing results that prove the level of team spirit or whatever it is. That's one reason Donor Moves are so powerful. They measure something that can be observed. You can count up the number of times the move has been achieved in a defined period of time.

GOOD TARGETS, BAD TARGETS

While all three components of a performance indicator are important, the performance target itself may be the most motivating—as long as you know how to use it to track performance. It's all too easy to use targets as a way of punishing your development officers, who might just be the most important and strategic members of your staff. No money, no mission.

I suspect that many nonprofit executives shy away from establishing explicit targets because of a misconception. They see the term *target* and think "uh-oh—if I miss the target, I'll be in trouble." Leaders and managers can misuse targets by beating development officers over the head with them. "Reach this target," says the mean boss, "or we'll fire you." This is pretty much like saying "flog the crew until morale improves." The reason we call it a performance indicator is that it *indicates* where performance is desirable or undesirable so you can figure out how to make it better. Targets focus the lens of continuous improvement, so you know where to adjust your process.

If the team is not reaching its income targets, compare the actual performance of Donor Moves to their targets to see where the process has gone off the rails. If the team is not reaching the target for Donor Move Four, take a look at actual performance for Moves Three, Two and One. If the team reaches the target for Move Five (number of times Move Five occurs) but still does not reach the income target, reassess all upstream moves, and scrutinize your Scorecard. Or recalculate the number of Move Fives based on changing the size of your ideal gift. If you've set targets based on an estimated gift of $50,000, but your typical gift is more like $25,000, all your Donor Moves targets may be too low to sustain desired performance.

Insights gained from analyzing actual performance may result in something as simple as changing the target. Let's say you decided it would take 300 people to Move Three in order to get 150 people to Move Four, but it turns out you only need 200 at Move Three to get 175 to Move Four. You assumed incorrect targets. Change them! You're free to change Donor Move targets in either direction (up or down) depending on the evidence. Actual perform-ance data are the navigational instruments, the diagnostic tools that put you back on track, or suggest an even more efficient track altogether.[2]

Reframe the way you think about targets, and use them as guidelines to measure capacity. Think about asking questions like these as you evaluate the data:

- Is there enough capacity (i.e., enough forecast-able income) in our pipeline to achieve the desired level of new gifts?

- Is there enough capacity (i.e., enough retained donors) to keep the level of recurring income at the desired level?

- Is there enough capacity (i.e., enough funding opportunities from new major-gift prospects) at Donor Move Three—ask for gift proposal—to convert to the desired level at Donor Move Four—negotiate scope and terms?

- Do we have enough resources (people, time, money, technology) to ex-pand our capacity for acquiring sufficient new donors and new income?

- Do we have the right resources (people, time, money, technology, skill) to expand our capacity for retaining, stewarding, and upgrading our current donors?

- Do these data suggest breakthroughs or innovations that could be used to build capacity and design our own future?

- Do we have the capacity to identify over 1,000 new prospects capable of giving at the level of $5,000?

And don't forget the magic question: *what would we have to do differently to get better results?*

Until you develop pertinent, complete performance indicators including targets, you simply will not have the data—the evidence—to know if you're making the right decisions. You're guessing at the answers.

Web Analytics as a Metaphor   The use of electronic tools such as Web analytics has transformed marketing and outreach. Every web site, no matter how amateurish, can produce detailed analytics, statistical measurements that are scientifically valid, to help the marketer decide which words and

---

[2] If simply changing the target doesn't solve the problem, use techniques such as root-cause analysis and the Plan-Do-Check-Act cycle described in Chapter 8.

phrases are most likely to attract visitors to the web site, which ones are most likely to persuade those visitors to engage with the web site ("just give us your e-mail address and we'll send you this white paper"), and persuade those visitors to give money, to volunteer, to come to an event.

Twenty or thirty years ago, most advertising and marketing specialists would have committed murder to get such data, but it simply wasn't possible. In those days, the science of marketing could be applied only to mass marketing such as newspaper, TV, or radio advertising. Few nonprofits or small businesses could afford such exposure.

These days, anyone with a web site or Facebook page has access to the scientific tools of marketing. Web analytics can tell you how your website is performing and suggest ways to make it better. Anyone can use search-term suggestion tools to choose words and phrases already proven to be effective at motivating Web visitors to take action. Most likely, you're already using your own Web data to select keywords, design lead-nurturing campaigns, and do other sophisticated marketing tactics simply because you have the statistical evidence that this phrase works better than that. And your results show it. Here's a very simple example: your very first online donations page said simply, "Click here to give." Bet you didn't get a lot of donations. But when you enhanced the page to say "$25 pays for one child to get vaccinated this year; $250 pays for one child to get vaccinated and have three well-baby checkups this year," specifying what the gift will deliver to a client produces better results from online giving.

If statistical insights can improve the performance of marketing tactics, they can—and will—improve the performance of fundraising.

MOVE ZERO TARGETS

When it comes to Move Zero, the bigger the better. Just take a look at the conversion ratio. The typical conversion ratio for moving a prospect from Move One to Move Two is about 1.5 to 1. The typical conversion ratio for moving a lead or so-called "suspect" from Move Zero to Move One is more like 10 to 1. Follow the math here and you'll realize that if you need to get 120 prospects to achieve Donor Move One, then you'll probably need at least 1,200 at Move Zero, which may be why, whenever I run a SMART Way workshop, somebody always says, "But where do we find all those people for Move One?"

Move Zero represents your target-market database, the list of followers who know your nonprofit exists and have shown interest in learning more about it. The contacts on this list have come from a variety of sources. They are people you and your development team may know. Your board members may have referred them to you. They attended an event. They subscribe to your newsletters and blogs; they visit your website and download white papers; they like your Facebook business page, follow you on Twitter, connected with you on LinkedIn, hang out with you on Google+.

Without a large following or target list, it's more difficult to attract the right candidates to achieve the first Donor Move. Conventional methods for expanding the Move Zero pool of candidates may include renting or buying a list from a list broker, and subscribing to databases such as WealthEngine and LexisNexis. These investments can pay off handsomely, as long as you have well-honed mechanisms for outbound marketing. These include such classic techniques as direct-mail campaigns, media advertising and even cold calling. Such techniques are of great value, but may be too costly in terms of money and elbow grease for smaller organizations.

Inbound marketing techniques, most of which are automated, may be even more valuable in the long run, whether the agency is a global powerhouse or a neighborhood grassroots outfit. Inbound marketing refers to the wide variety of electronic techniques that attract people to you. These include blogs, podcasts, videos, e-books, e-newsletters, search-engine optimization, marketing through social media such as Twitter and Face-book, and other forms of content marketing. These are "pull" mechanisms. You pull interested individuals to your cause, mission, or programs. The individuals signal their interest to you by giving you their email addresses, signing petitions, making online donations, volunteering for something, or answering some other call to action. Individuals attracted this way have taken some action that shows their interest. They have already been "warmed up" by automated means.

To make your inbound marketing successful, you must have engaging content. The content must include language that appeals to the funders you want to reach and persuades those funders to seek you out. If you have no presence on social media, you're missing out on a prime source of prospective donors. If your website is out of date, static, or lacking ways for visitors to interact, you're also missing out. That's why it's so important to adopt inbound marketing techniques, and to stay informed about their ongoing evolution. New tools and techniques come into the market every day.

Age Diversity

There's another reason to master inbound marketing as a way to build your Move Zero following. It's the primary way to attract younger candidates. For one thing, all of these tools and techniques are the native language of anyone who graduated from college after the year 2000. If you can't reach the Millennials, your donor base will die off, and then what will you do? You'll be in a pickle. Donors who can make major gifts (i.e., gifts greater than $25,000) do, in fact, tend to be older. However, the habits and benefits of philanthropy start young.

Who's Right for Move Zero?

If you master all the ways you can build your Move Zero database, eventually you will have contact information for a large number of people, with insights into how they want to be involved with your nonprofit. The database will most likely include:

- Individuals who may give much smaller gifts. For example, millions of dollars were raised to deal with the 2010 earthquake in Haiti, through donations from $2 to $5 solicited by text messaging.
- Individuals who may not give any gift but are interested in the cause; may wish to volunteer; may wish to enroll a relative in one of your programs, and so on.
- Corporate executives who may be interested in your mission or cause, or because they're searching for a way to demonstrate their willingness to support local nonprofits, or because they're seeking a way to develop the leadership skills of their junior executives.
- Past or current clients and their relatives because they are grateful to you.
- Anyone who has ever attended your event, visited your facility, participated in one of your community activities, or signed up for your newsletter.

- Foundation executives, who might become interested in inviting you to apply for a grant.

- People referred to your nonprofit by staff or members of your board.

- Anyone else you can think of who has some sort of interest in what you do.

Since you wisely prepared an ideal-funder profile or Scorecard for each funding category, and you have some clarity about your best donors' value-sought, you are now able to fine-tune your marketing messages and case for support so they appeal to all of these constituents. And, of course, you're actively engaged in communicating with this universe on a regular basis, with e-newsletters, blogs, web site updates, and other state-of-the-art outreach efforts.

Aren't you?

You are responsible for gathering these names and their contact information. The list doesn't simply appear out of thin air. Pull all this contact information together in a central location, preferably in a donor management software application designed for the purpose or at least a home-grown spreadsheet or database. It's deadly to have prospect contact information scattered all over the place.

Pick the Low-Hanging Fruit

Your Move Zero database becomes the orchard from which you'll pick the ripest plums. Which prospective fruit is hanging lowest? Typically, it's a suspect or lead with whom you or members of your team have some prior connection. Maybe that individual has already become a donor at a modest level. Or maybe the individual has not given but has subscribed to your newsletter, attended the roof-raising ceremony, liked you on Facebook, or commented on a blog posting. Any such connection makes it easier to start a conversation.

The techniques of lead nurturing can also help to get some of those plums hanging a little lower on the branch. Let's say the individual joined your Move Zero database because she signed up for your e-newsletter. Then let's say she also clicked on a link in your newsletter to take a look at the dogs available for adoption at your no-kill animal shelter. Well, you already know this person has some interest in your organization, and has even demonstrated her interest in dog adoption. She's a perfect candidate for the e-mail blast about the Doggy Adoption Fair you're holding next Saturday. If she in fact shows up at the fair, she has shown you enough interest in the cause to justify a phone call. Use the phone call to learn more about her potential match to your major-donor Scorecard. Just remember that this first phone call has to be about thanking her, not about demanding more money.

What do you do with all the other prospects who are not qualified to become major donors? You turn them into *minor* donors! If your target list is composed of contacts that have already demonstrated some affinity for your cause, they are candidates to give at a modest level.

Many major donors start out as minor donors.

IMPORTANT!

According to Giving USA, about 72 percent of all philanthropic income comes from individual donors, with only about 15 percent from grants and about 6 percent from corporations. The remainder, about 7 percent, comes from bequests, another form of individual giving.

PERFORMANCE TARGETS AND THE SMART WAY SCORECARD

The prospect scorecard is also a potential wealth of useful data, as discussed in Part 1. The process of validating your Scorecards produces reliable marketing messages, keywords and key phrases likely to attract individuals predisposed to support your mission, to take action.

Scorecards also provide two additional areas revealing productivity. One is simply to know how many prospects your team has scorecarded. The other is the correlation between Scorecard rank and Donor Moves data. This correlation answers at least three important questions:

- How many "A" prospects are currently active in my pipeline? How many B's, C's, and D's?
- How much "A" income is currently being tracked by my pipeline? How much B, C, and D income?
- How many A, B, C, and D prospects are currently located at each opportunity stage?

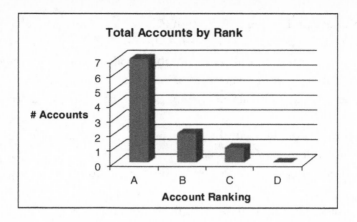

EXHIBIT 6.1   **GREG HANSON'S ACTIVE GIFT OPPORTUNITIES BY SCORECARD RANK**

Imagine the degree of management control such correlations could provide. A simple graph can easily show the distribution of active prospects by rank, by amount of forecast-able income in the pipeline, and by cross-referencing income, rank, and Donor Move.

In Exhibit 6.1, we see that Development Officer Greg Hanson has done a nice job of cultivating prospects so far. Most of his prospects are A-listers. He has a couple of B's, only one C, and No D's. So far, so good, Greg, keep it up.

As shown in Exhibit 6.2, Greg also has an apparently attractive forecast. His A-listers offer a potential of more than $400,000, while his B and C prospects offer very little income. That might be a good thing. Let's assume that in Greg's nonprofit, C prospects tend to be poor investments, and it also takes a lot of time to close the B's. Maybe Greg's doing the right thing by concentrating on his A's.

Based on Exhibits 6.1 and 6.2, we might have been very enthusiastic about Greg's overall performance, but Exhibit 6.3 shows some troubling insights.

First, the positive news: Notice that most of Greg's individual prospect campaigns are stuck at Move Three, ask for proposal, and the number that have converted to Move Four, negotiate details, is less than half. The curve picks up again at Move Five, makes gift, which is pretty terrific, and the number and amount of money that reach Move Six is great.

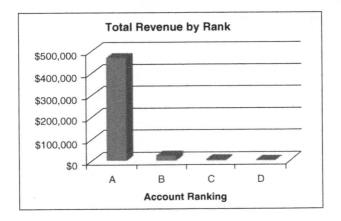

EXHIBIT 6.2   **GREG HANSON'S ACTIVE GIFT OPPORTUNITIES BY AMOUNT OF REVENUE**

However, there is reason to be concerned about Greg's performance. Notice that there are almost *no* prospects at Moves One or Two. This graph suggests that Greg hasn't been paying attention to bringing more opportunities into the pipeline. Greg, find some time to start cultivating new opportunities—even if they're opportunities from current donors.

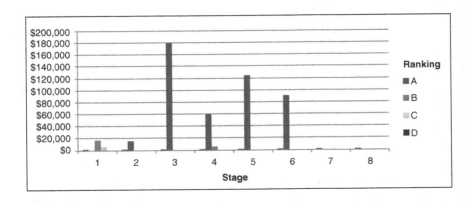

EXHIBIT 6.3   **GREG HANSON'S ACTIVE OPPORTUNITIES BY SCORECARD RANK, AMOUNT OF INCOME AND LAST DONOR MOVE ACHIEVED**

Reviewing Performance

No matter where you stand in the corporate hierarchy, a review of these graphs can guide your improvement initiatives. Graphs are easy to read and understand. A quick glance can tell you where your development officers are wasting time with low-ranked prospects. Since it usually takes less time to close larger gifts from A-ranked candidates, at least based on what other SMART Way users tell us, then you can guide and coach development officers who invest too much effort in the C- and D-ranked prospects.

Take their money, by all means, as long as taking it doesn't jeopardize your ethics or pull you off mission. But don't waste your most expensive resources—the time and effort of your development staff—on the DOAs.

Less Is More When It Comes to the Pipeline

Track the progress of individual donors only when their prospective gifts are large enough to justify the effort. It's not practical to trace the progress of every small gift through the Donor Moves; it's probably not even possible. Most small gifts come in as a result of a direct-marketing campaign such as the annual appeal, and without the intervention of a development officer.

Establish a firm standard for major gifts, grants, and sponsorships. Direct your development officers to ignore donations that don't meet this standard; there are other ways of tracking performance for smaller gifts. A good way to decide what the standard should be is to look at the donations you received last year. If the largest gifts you obtained were around $1,000, that's the standard for major gifts this coming year. In other words, if you've never gotten a gift larger than $1,000, it doesn't make much sense for you to seek gifts whose average size is $25,000. You won't have candidates with that level of giving capacity.

Major gifts justify considerably more handholding than minor gifts. If you've ever cultivated a larger gift, then you know how much depends on your ability to establish rapport with your prospect and influence the outcome. And you also know that it can take a long time, sometimes even several years, before a major gift closes. Although we don't have the data on this yet, it surely seems that the larger the gift, the longer it will take to close the deal.

But something interesting happens when you're tracking the progress of your major gifts: successful growth in major-gift income tends to be reflected in the growth of minor-gift income. We think that's because the marketing messages, relationship-building efforts, and recognition techniques you master to win such major gifts are also highly likely to reach the eyeballs of midlevel and minor donors and influence them as well.

TARGETS FOR DEVELOPMENT DRIVERS

Although development drivers do not occur in unvarying sequence as do Donor Moves, they deserve performance targets as well. The big challenge here, however, is choosing the development drivers that are worth tracking.

You could probably draw up a list of development activities several pages long. Some development activities work for some development officers but not all. For example, you already know about my aversion to sending birthday cards. I don't even give my grandchildren birthday cards, so don't expect me to send them to my prospects. My friend Susan, however, keeps a constant supply of birthday cards, holiday cards (for every religion by the way), and other celebrations; she's a genius at the discipline of card sending.

Some development activities work for all donors, while others work only for some donors. Keeping track of all the cultivation activities *you* like with the activities your *donors* like could conceivably drive you crazy.

And to add insult to injury, you can't set up one way to track Susan's activities, another way to track mine, and a third way to track the way Frank does it. Not only will such profligate tracking make you nuts, it's unreliable. You've got to measure the same things the same way every time for everybody, or the data will be meaningless.

Choosing the Drivers Worth Tracking

The best way to choose which drivers to track is through collaborative effort. Sit down with your team and brainstorm a list of development activities. A longer list is desirable at this point. Once you've all run out of ideas, prioritize them to bring the list down to somewhere between five and eight options. You can do so by discussion, talking it out until you come to consensus, but if that technique doesn't work, use multivoting, described in Chapter 3. The final short list comprises the development drivers worth tracking.

Once you have chosen the few, vital drivers you'll track in the future, assign performance targets to each one. You're doing this to discover which drivers correlate with obtaining desired amounts of income, and with key

Donor Moves, even though the drivers themselves do not necessarily occur in any sequence. At the outset, your driver targets may be entirely arbitrary, which means it will take you some time to develop a reliable baseline.

Examples of beneficial development drivers—I mean they are beneficial because they correlate so well with achieving desired numbers of Donor Moves and/or income—include the following:

- Attend [a particular number of] networking events where I can meet potential advocates, ambassadors or investors. (Useful in communities that hold lots of networking events for groups that might become useful donors. For example, if your agency provides pediatric health services for poor families, you would want to network with pediatricians.)

- Conduct at least one meeting per year with each major donor to report on our progress; not to ask for money. Here the target depends on the number of major donors in the gift officer's portfolio.

- Follow up with every major-gift proposal within [five?] business days of submitting the proposal.

And not a birthday card in sight!

Development drivers you track must be diagnostic and easy to measure, and they must also be relevant for every gift officer. Drivers meeting these standards are worth tracking; those that don't aren't. This doesn't mean that your development officers should avoid the other activities; it just means that you don't plan to track them.

WHAT WE COVERED

- Design performance indicators that include three components: what you're measuring, how you're measuring it, and the quantifiable target you'd like to achieve.

- Donor Moves and Moves Management are both effective at helping the development officer "move" the prospect along the arc of cultivation to the point of solicitation. When used only in this way, neither model offers much insight into the health, effectiveness or productivity of the fundraising effort.

- Donor Moves make excellent performance indicators. They include all three components. It's easy to assign performance targets to them, based on the number of times you want your donors and prospects to achieve each move in a given period of time. Thus, they provide great insight into the productivity of the fundraising process.

- Assign targets to the Donor Moves, and you now have a pipeline based on documented standards, which supports continuous improvement.
- Donor Moves describe leading indicators—Moves Zero through Four—and a critical trailing indicator—Move Five. The remaining Moves, Six through Eight, are also leading indicators describing stewardship and retention, leading to the next gift.
- Correlating Scorecard rank data with Donor Moves data provides deep insights into the performance of development officers, showing their ability to invest development hours in the right candidates and avoid the wrong candidates (those with lower ranks).
- Tracking development drivers can complement the insights you'll derive from tracking Scorecard and Donor Moves data. Over time, you'll begin to identify drivers most likely to propel the fundraising process and build improvement initiatives around them.

What You Can Do

- Establish Donor Moves targets for yourself, using the table in Chapter 5 as your template.
- Rethink the way you use these targets. If possible, ask yourself how many Donor Moves you achieved with your prospects over the last month or week. Once you see how many (or few) you've achieved, go back to the suggested probing questions introduced in Chapter 4.
- Choose the development drivers that seem to offer the greatest insights into fundraising performance. Set targets for each driver.
- Establish targets based on two time frames: for the year and for the month. Dividing your targets into months, manageable chunks of time, gives you better feedback from the process and early warnings that you've gone off the rails.

PART III

Implementing Fundraising the SMART Way

The fundraising revolution relies on leadership. It requires strong, thoughtful, consistent leadership to implement Fundraising the SMART Way™. Remember, the SMART Way is not the latest, greatest set of cool tricks and campaign tactics; it's a way to manage the business of the fundraising department for continuous improvement. If you expect your development officers to adopt this new approach but don't change your leadership skills or style, things are likely to get worse, not better. You will have heightened your team's expectations but then failed to deliver on the implied promise.

Guess what *that* causes? Disaffection, distress, cynicism, and eventually distrust of you as the manager or leader. Don't go there.

In Part III, we discuss what it takes to translate Fundraising the SMART Way from theory to practice, turning it into your team's business-as-usual, and "the way we do things around here." To accomplish this transition requires the ability to capture data on the key performance indicators we've identified, the technology to report on them easily, and the leadership skills and talents to guide the staff to better performance.

There are many hidden challenges on the road to the future, starting with human nature. If your development officers have done things a certain way for a period of time, it's difficult to change those habits—*even if you all agree with the needed change*. This is where good, informed leadership, management, and reporting methods make all the difference. Good leadership is not merely having a charismatic personality, nor using the "pep rally" approach.

The pep rally approach—"Go team go! I know you can do it!!"—has been known to backfire, sometimes spectacularly.

The revolution of managing the performance of the development shop will take place not because somebody said "do this or else," but because that same somebody facilitated the adoption process using purposeful methods. After all, we're trying to improve accountability, and that means a duet: doing the work and maintaining the accountability.

Let's say that the SMART Way model has made all kinds of sense up to now, in the "classroom" of reading this book. But once you're out in the so-called real world, you will just plain forget and do it, whatever it is, the old, familiar way. Changing the way you think and behave means you have to rewire your brain, literally. Current brain science shows us that when we learn new stuff we're actually laying down new neural pathways inside the brain. It's easier for children to do so. For us grown-ups who conduct fundraising activities, we need all the help we can get. The best people to provide the coaching and other kinds of support we need are your non-profit's leaders and managers.

Up to now, our focus has been on theoretical concepts: the ideal-funder profiles or Scorecards; opportunity-stage definitions or Donor Moves; what to measure, how to measure it, and how much of "it" you want to achieve. And if we've done our job right, these concepts have made sense. In Part III, the focus is on leading the process of adoption and implementation. If you're a development officer, you may feel uncomfortable, even awkward. If you're the team leader, the chief development officer, or the CEO, your job will be to help your people slide over the awkwardness and create new habits and new neural pathways. That might make you feel a little awkward as well. You too will learn new things: new ways to assess the work, interpret the reports, and guide the team to improvement initiatives. Sometimes you may feel like you're working without a net. But if you stick with it, you, your role as leader will be rewarded with a high-performance team and the satisfaction of your own personal growth. The new model gives leaders and officers alike meaningful evidence—data—providing clarity and accountability. Such insights call on a more enlightened, engaged style of leadership. Leaders and managers are no longer passive recipients of reports showing how busy the officers were last month. Now they become active partners by facilitating analysis, identifying and approving improvement initiatives, coaching to obtain better results while maintaining morale, and evaluating the unanticipated breakthroughs that drive innovation.

However, if leaders are *not* engaged in the process or fail to exercise their unique roles in it, you probably won't get much out of your investment. Introducing a major change, such as moving the management of the fundraising function from tactical to strategic as we're describing here, requires care and thought when it comes to implementation. The components of the methodology— including funder selection strategies, Scorecards, the Donor Moves process, and the like—are only the foundation of the change. If you stop now, your people will have a few new buzzwords and tactics, but they might not be able to revolutionize the development function.

Chapter 7 addresses two components of the methodology that operate in tandem, namely, the reporting methods that reveal evidence of progress and the leadership skills required to facilitate adoption, integration and continuous improvement. If either of these is missing, it becomes difficult, if not impossible, to move beyond seeing the SMART Way model as a bunch of "stand-alone" piece-parts. Effective adoption of the methodology integrates information to provide meaningful intelligence about the business. The reports themselves reveal everything from the health of the pipeline and the accuracy of the Scorecard to the ways development officers deploy their time and effort. And leadership skills, some of which may seem new or unfamiliar to you, maintain accountability, drive collaboration, and coach for continuous learning.

Chapter 8 introduces the skills, tools, and methods that produce continuous improvement such as root-cause analysis and use of the Plan-Do-Check-Act cycle. These elegant tools deliver the greatest benefits of the SMART Way approach, and distinguish it from more tactical fundraising schemes.

Chapter 9 discusses ways to apply the SMART Way concepts to mass-market fundraising, such as direct appeal and online giving campaigns. Even though it would not be practical or affordable to use the SMART Way model to track small gifts through every Donor Move, there is no question that mass-market techniques can benefit from the rigorous analysis, funder-selection strategies, and use of metrics you have reviewed. After all, smaller donors provide significant levels of unrestricted, sustainable income. Plus, smaller donors tend to become the major donors of the future.

CHAPTER 7

Reporting and Leading for Better Results

Everything we've covered up to now is the appetizer before the main course, which is continuous improvement of fundraising results. Yes, it's necessary to create funder selection strategies and all the other components of the SMART Way™ model. If you don't transform the way your development team works, and move them from tactical to strategic, nothing new will happen. The implementation phase transforms the SMART Way from an academic exercise into a different way of working that provides better results year after year.

Fundraising the SMART Way, as I've said before, is not merely a set of clever tactics to obtain this particular gift from that particular prospect. That's not the point. The point is to manage the slippery business of fund development for continuous improvement, as measured by the predictability and consistency of income growth. The higher the productivity, the more gifts at lower cost of time and effort.

Predictable, consistent income growth does not come about simply by trying harder, staying up later, working more hours, or showing more enthusiasm. At the end of the day, those practices can even hurt growth. To make consistent gains over the long haul, we need the kinds of guidelines, performance metrics, and reporting methods I discuss in this book, and we need them to be deployed properly. It takes the combination of good reporting methods and enlightened leadership skills to make this work come alive.

Moving the development shop from theory to practice requires two "dances": the dance of doing the work and capturing the data, and the dance of interpreting the data and selecting improvement initiatives. Often, the dancers are the same people, especially in smaller organizations, but just as often they are different people: those who *do* the work, and the leaders, managers, and coaches who *guide* the work and hold the "do-ers" accountable for results. It doesn't matter if some of your dancers dance both roles. What matters is that you understand the way those dances differ.

In the dance of doing the work, the dancer—i.e., the development person—makes the appointments, uses the Scorecard to assess the prospect's potential, and shepherds the gift opportunity from Donor Move to Donor Move, while keeping track of the data. In the dance of interpreting results and guiding improvements, the dancer—the development officer, director, or higher-level executive—collates the data, analyzes it, and interprets it to draw insights and suggest changes for the next cycle of work. Up to now, we have focused largely on defining the elements of the first dance, by developing your Scorecards and Donor Moves. Now we move into the second dance.

LEADERSHIP 101

My dear friend and sometime business partner, Rebecca Staton-Reinstein, who has a PhD in organizational psychology, likes to say, "Great managers *do* nothing." Sign me up! Here's what she really means:

- Workers *do* the work, whether it's the work of cultivating donors or the work of mowing the lawn.

- Managers *convince others* (workers) to do the work, make sure the work is done to desired standards, and keep the work and the workers on task and on track.

- Leaders *set direction* and inspire everybody to follow that direction.

Ergo, great managers—and great leaders—"do" nothing. Instead, they manage and they lead. They set direction, assess performance against plan, and provide guidance and coaching to get better results next time around. Doing so effectively requires skills you may not have learned or have learned in a different context. These skills become invaluable once the SMART Way components have been crafted because without them it's likely that the methodology will remain academic. It won't become business as usual, and thus if you get better results, it's a crapshoot, a game of chance.

In Parts 1 and 2, we focused on building the Scorecards, understanding Donor Moves, and selecting development drivers. We also showed how to establish performance targets associated with each of these components. Finally, we urged you to validate your Scorecards and Donor Move targets by interview and experimentation. By now, your SMART Way components are mature enough to be put into play.

This is the point at which the real, deep, and transformative value of Fundraising the SMART Way comes to fruition. Everything up to now is prologue.

First, There is a Mountain . . .

There's a Zen riddle that explains the adoption process beautifully. In case you were thinking that I study Zen Buddhism, you would unfortunately be wrong; this particular riddle was brought to us back in 1967 by the British pop singer Donovan. The riddle goes, "First there is a mountain. Then there is no mountain. Then there is a mountain."

Adopting the SMART Way model is a lot like that riddle. At first, it's easy to see the "mountain"—the methodology and its component parts. They're unfamiliar. It takes mental effort to make sense of them. Then you start to use the components, capture the data, pull the reports, use leadership skills to guide adoption, and identify improvement initiatives. At first, it's clumsy and awkward, but it gets easier with practice. Pretty soon, there's "no mountain."

Finally, you start to see the "mountain" again. But this time, it's not your enemy; it's home base, your navigational instruments, your best friend. Now you see how using the instruments, reporting on them, and interpreting the reports delivers improved fundraising results. In due course, that same "mountain" can even deliver guidance on program outcomes, volunteer recruitment and deployment, all sorts of things.

"Vertical" versus "Horizontal" Reporting

Over the years, I've observed literally thousands of reports and reporting methods in the fundraising and corporate-sales games. The most common of these to date has been "vertical" reporting, my term for reporting on the status and progress, or lack thereof, of a particular gift or sale opportunity. When you're reporting vertically, you describe pertinent information about an individual situation, such as which donor's potential gift is under cultivation, where it is in the cultivation process, how big it is, and when you think it's going to close. You use vertical reporting to forecast the point at which you expect that opportunity to come to fruition so you can collect the money. The vertical approach to reporting—drilling down into a specific donor prospect and a particular gift—isn't just common, it's valuable, even if the report itself contains extraneous information, such as details on where, with whom, and when you ate lunch.

> ### DEFINITION: VERTICAL REPORTING
>
> The "vertical report" is situational by its nature. A vertical report captures information about a particular situation, and only that situation. We use it to describe what's going on with a single donor, prospect, or gift opportunity.

Many constituent relationship management (CRM) or donor management software applications are pretty good at vertical reporting. If they have any kind of opportunity management module, it will be fairly simple to keep track of each gift in the pipeline. These systems also let you keep notes on the progress of the gift, the relationship, and any other information striking your fancy. Of course, most of these ad hoc comments are listed by date only. If you don't remember exactly when you made that note about the prospect's motivations, it can be tough to find. And because the notes and comments are "unformatted," which in techno-speak means they are not predefined, you get to make them up as you go along. That's convenient for you, but you can't pull a report from a bunch of unformatted notes describing lots of different things. To make matters worse, your gift officers record notes relevant to them at that moment, so *his* are different from *hers* or yours or mine.

Development officers are usually pretty good at keeping track of each individual gift or prospect opportunity. They have mastered the concept of vertical record keeping and reporting. These skills might make you pretty comfortable about the way you keep your development activities under control, but if your only way to report is vertically, you end up doing "management by anecdote." You tell the story of your progress one gift and one prospect at a time. While the story might make sense to you, your audience will probably get frustrated, bored, or impatient. If you're reporting at the development team meeting, your fellow gift officers are probably paying more attention to making their reports sound good compared to yours; they're not learning anything from you. If you're reporting to the CEO or the board, your audience might just tune out after the third or fourth anecdote. The only things they're likely to remember are your failures, lost opportunities, delayed projects, or that you're carrying around some perennial pipeline fillers that never, ever close. Even if your report is positive overall, your audience may hear only the bad news. Presto! They've turned your positive report into a negative one.

"Horizontal" reporting, however, is definitely *un*common. Horizontal reporting is my term for gathering data across a range of users, activities, or situations, where the data have been predefined or "formatted," information in the report has been measured the same way at the same time, and the "actuals" data captured show insights into performance. Some of the data or evidence in horizontal reports may be desirable, some undesirable, and some neutral, but overall you, your fellow development officers, your manager, the CEO, and the board get to see what's really going on. They learn.

Even if your report is mostly negative, your audience will take the news in balanced, unemotional fashion, turning a negative experience into a positive one. The data help to create the "emotionally neutral zone," thus providing a safe environment in which to confront the truth, or as Jim Collins says in *Good to Great*,[1] "face the brutal facts" because if you can't see or confront them, you can't resolve or improve them.

DEFINITION: HORIZONTAL REPORTING

"Horizontal" reporting collates data across a range of situations. A horizontal report describes the distribution of agreed-upon metrics from all sources or by segments of sources. It's "decoupled" from information about which donors did what when.

Horizontal reporting brings insights, business intelligence, and analytics that help you do what you might not have been able to do before: figure out

---

[1] Jim Collins, *Good to Great: Why Some Companies Make the Leap . . . and Others Don't* (New York: HarperCollins, 2001).

what it takes to get better results. It allows you to observe where your fundraising pipeline encounters bottlenecks or obstacles, then points out ways to release or eliminate them. It reveals the accuracy of your funder-selection and prospecting strategies, and the effectiveness of your inbound marketing efforts. It calculates the return on effort your team is capable of delivering. And it does all this because the raw data can be measured separately from the stories about each opportunity.

If our Leaky Bucket study data tell us anything, it's that the majority of nonprofits lack the metrics and reporting methods needed to deliver such improvements.

This reporting philosophy has been embraced by leading corporate organizations for decades. Every business that has implemented Total Quality Management (TQM), Six Sigma, or the Baldrige Criteria for Performance Excellence has done so because they knew that, otherwise, they risked losing their competitive advantages. The best of those organizations have profited in significant ways, from improving margins to creating innovative products and services.

The nonprofit sector is late to the performance excellence party. Nonprofit executives have either failed to embrace the body of knowledge related to performance excellence or simply are not aware it exists. Or even worse, they know it exists, but refuse to invest the time and money, on the mistaken assumption that investing in organizational improvements would cost too much, and therefore would be frowned upon by funders, the board, or the community.

Good Reporting and the Emotionally Neutral Zone

Organizational psychology tells us that the use of quantifiable metrics can have a beneficial impact on performance because they create what is called the "emotionally neutral zone." We all know the difference. If I were to ask you, "How come you haven't brought in any decent gifts? What's wrong with you?" I would have effectively moved you into an emotionally *loaded* zone. I would sound angry even if I weren't, and you would be ready to punch me in the nose or burst into tears, so neither of us would be in a good position to evaluate your actual performance or find ways to improve it.

However, if we both agreed that you needed to paint exactly 100 purple polka dots on the wall next week, and you painted only 73, we could have a much more enlightened conversation. We could discuss what kept you from reaching the polka-dot target. It might have been that 73 polka dots filled up the wall nicely; you didn't see the need for more. Maybe you ran out of paint. Maybe the carpet installers arrived before you could finish your job. I start with the assumption that you did the best you could, and ask for further enlightenment rather than jumping down your throat. We could discuss whether we set the right target, obtained the correct amount of materials, or need to revisit the way we schedule the carpet installers. There's no need to punish *or* to celebrate. The information is "neutral"; it comes without emotional overtones. Because it's neutral, we can learn something from it.

Those of us who are veterans of the school of management by intimidation will find this approach very refreshing,[2] as will those individuals who suffer from "ask reluctance." And for those who have never quite been able to figure out what facts or numbers to measure, this approach will revolutionize their ability to lead and manage. It takes the pressure off.

When implementing performance management disciplines, great leaders lead through collaborative discovery, not exhortation. They direct attention toward the information itself, guiding the "dancers" to evaluate their own performance, seeking their insights into what worked and what didn't. This work may seem challenging to some people in leadership positions. They may assume that "leadership" is synonymous with "do it my way," "do it because I said so," or "do it or you're fired."

Do I need to tell you that none of these is particularly useful?

SMART WAY REPORTS

The Donor Moves process can certainly provide effective "vertical" reporting for any particular donation or donor, and from time to time the gift officer and department director will find it useful. After all, each opportunity needs to be moved through the process expeditiously or dumped out of the process if it's dead. If the particular opportunity is stalled, the manager has lots of opportunities to coach the officer about that situation. This can be especially helpful when the opportunity in question is one of those perennial nongifts that seem to pop up in everyone's pipeline from time to time. These are apparent gift opportunities that won't ever really close, but for some reason the gift officer (and sometimes the donor) just can't seem to let them die their otherwise

---

[2] Regrettably, management by intimidation is all too common in for-profit sales organizations, where sales managers are notorious for flogging the crew until morale improves. I hope it's not as common in development shops.

natural deaths. Maybe it's because keeping it in the pipeline makes the officer feel better, or maybe the donor is too nice to come out and say "forget it." If the gift officer's boss can help declare "time of death," and get the "body" off to the morgue, everybody's better off.

So, yes, SMART Way reports can do "vertical" as well as any other approach. But they shine when it comes to the horizontal stuff. The horizontal reporting built into the model provides insights that simply cannot be derived from those conventional vertical reports. The reports themselves range from simple tables, where pipeline data are collated by account, rank, amount, category, gift size, and Donor Move, to considerably more complex. Many reports show distributions: donor prospects by funding stream and rank (potential for lifetime giving); by funding stream, rank, and potential income; or by funding stream, rank, potential income, and move (location in the Donor Moves pipeline), like the figures shown in Chapter 5. These are standard reports; because of the richness of data collected, all sorts of analysis, including predictive, can be performed.

The simplest report of all is a table that lists your opportunities including the funder's name, Scorecard rank, type of gift (gift, grant, corporate contribution), estimated size of gift, and latest Donor Move achieved. This table can also, if desired, note the name of the development officer who "owns" it, the campaign the gift is associated with, and the source of the gift (whether the opportunity came about from a referral or some marketing effort or other). Plus, if you publish it in spreadsheet form, you can sort it many different ways, depending on what you want to find out.

The spreadsheet in Exhibit 7.1 shows us that Greg carries an income target of $250,000, and thus a pipeline target three times that size, working

Pipeline Target (3X Actual Income Target):			$750,000				
Total Est. Pipeline:			$407,500				

Account	Opportunity	Source	Rank	Est. Revenue	Stage	Line of Business
Meineke Auto	Community Relations	Board Member	B	$5,000	6	Corporate Giving
Frank Meineke	Naming Opportunity	Annual Campaign	A	$60,000	4	Donors
Jane Benson	Annual Campaign	Past donor	A	$10,000	4	Donors
Brett Hanson	Naming Opportunity	Direct mail	A	$125,000	3	Donors
Sam Bernstein	Naming Opportunity	Donor referral Meinek	A	$125,000	5	Donors
Helen Mann	Annual Campaign	Past donor	A	$45,000	3	Donors
Jen Kaplan	Annual Campaign	Board referral	A	$15,000	3	Donors
Kaplan & Shore PA	Community Relations	Direct mail	B	$17,500	2	Corporate Giving
Nerds.net	Community Relations	Direct mail	C	$5,000	1	Corporate Giving

EXHIBIT 7.1 **GREG HANSON PIPELINE**

on the assumption that Greg will have to cultivate three gifts to bring in one. He's at nearly two-thirds of his pipeline target, which could be good, depending on how close Greg is to the end of the fundraising year.

The first time I showed a report like this to a nonprofit leader, I was honestly taken aback by her reaction. After all, this report is about as basic as you can get. Yet that executive director, and many others since her, said, "OMG, this is great! We can't do this today! We've never done this! Oh boy, would our board love to see this!!!!" It was the first time in her 20 years of nonprofit work, she told me, that she had ever seen a report on fundraising progress that *wasn't* based on management by anecdote.

There are many other reports you can obtain. As you put your SMART Way "toolkit" together, you selected lots of performance indicators or metrics that can be captured and collated to give insights into fundraising performance. See Table 7.1 for suggested reports derived from the various metrics.

TABLE 7.1   SMART WAY METRICS AND THEIR USES

The SMART Way Data Field	Use in Reports
Scorecard rank and actual score	Distribution of donors and prospects by rank and score; by giving category or overall; by individual officer, group, or entire department. Purpose: pinpoint needs for improvement.
Weighted scores of various Scorecard statements	Distribution of statements in descending order of importance; correlation between statements of one category and another category; correlation of statement (s) with gifts won. *Purpose*: predictive analysis.
Forecasted revenue and Scorecard rank	Distribution of opportunities by rank and potential income. *Purpose*: pinpoint need for improvement.
Forecasted revenue, Scorecard rank, and Donor Move	Distribution of opportunities by gift category, rank, potential income, and Donor Move. *Purpose*s: pinpoint need for improvement; predictive analysis.
Donor Moves targets compared to actuals	Tracks progress of gifts through Donor Moves process, by category, officer, or all. Creates baseline for improved targets. Correlates Donor Move speed, cycle time, etc. with income. Validates cycle times per size of gift. *Purpose*s: pinpoint needs for improvement; market analysis; predictive analysis.
Development driver targets and actuals	Shows target versus actual performance; correlates with Donor Moves data, pipeline and income targets, and actual. *Purpose*: pinpoint needs for improvement; predictive analysis; market analysis.

TABLE 7.1 **(CONTINUED)**

The SMART Way Data Field	Use in Reports
Pipeline target compared to pipeline actual	Shows gap between actual size of pipeline and targeted (ideal) size, typically a multiplier between 1.5 and 3X. *Purpose*: pinpoint need for improved number and size of forecasted opportunities.
Actual income compared to target income	Shows gap between actual income (donations received) and income target, by gift category, by all gifts across categories, by individual officer, by all officers, by accounting period, year-to-date, or total year. *Purpose*: pinpoint need for improvement; predictive analysis; market analysis.
Targeted donor acquisition or retention compared to actual acquisition or retention	Shows gap between actual and targeted; brings attention to donor retention as well as donor acquisition. *Purpose:* pinpoint need for improvement.

Insights such as these are hard to come by in many development shops. But just imagine their usefulness! By capturing only a few new data fields—primarily Scorecard rank and last Donor Move achieved—and collating them properly, you now have a set of powerful management controls. You have moved your fundraising productivity from catch-as-catch-can to predictable, consistent, and improving continuously.

ENLIGHTENED LEADERSHIP PRACTICES

Leadership development is an enormous topic covering many facets and practices. The whole area has spawned an entire industry including hundreds of books, training courses, and executive coaching practices, most of which is beyond the scope of this book. But there are some fundamental leadership practices you must learn if you want to get the most out of the SMART Way methodology.

Effective leaders facilitate the adoption of SMART Way management controls by setting performance targets, then reviewing performance against plan regularly and coaching their team to improve. I like to start the adoption process by setting a simple, short-term target for only one SMART Way component at a time. As a leader, I have to remember that adult learning is more likely to stick if we offer it in small chunks, send the "learners" out into the field to use the new learning, and then bring them back again to review, before introducing the next new bit. By doing it this way, I accomplish several objectives simultaneously. My team validates and refines the component—for example, their Scorecard statements, importance weights, prospect scales, probing questions—by using it. They begin to memorize or internalize it so they don't have to follow the instructions quite so carefully next time. After a while there is "no mountain" and they're ready to tackle the next piece.

Managing the Review Meeting

Implementation begins by setting up a schedule for performance reviews. The performance review meeting is a very special, predictable animal with a standard agenda. It has only one purpose: to review progress against plan, interpret findings, and select improvement initiatives when necessary. In order to hold such meetings, you must have the following ingredients at your command:

- Data demonstrating the performance under review, in report form. Do *not* use the meeting to report or gather data. Use your technology to capture the data ahead of time.
- One hour of time. Ideally the time should be set and immutable. If some individuals can't make it go ahead anyway. Everybody needs to schedule their other work around this meeting.
- The ability to facilitate effectively, and to avoid getting caught up in emotions, arguments, or anything else that distracts attention from the data.

There. You've already begun to exercise leadership.

The meeting agenda starts with a few minutes of review. Ask attendees to review the data, to "read the story the numbers tell you." Then ask them to discuss what they have observed, what questions they would like answered, and what recommendations, if any, they would like to suggest.

Even though this may sound like the most ordinary meeting format imaginable, you have to know that most people can't manage a meeting this way the first time out. One reason is the temptation to judge the results yourself and declare them to be bad (or good). By doing so, you inject blame into the dialog, a highly undesirable experience. If you're running the meeting, it's your leadership skills that are on the table, so master the art of asking open-ended probing questions that relate directly to the data in front of you. Great questioning skills are paramount for demonstrating the kind of collegial leadership you need to manage performance. Here are some examples:

- "I see we met our targets for [whatever you're measuring this week]. Was it difficult to do so? Why or why not?"
- "What did you learn by reaching your targets?"
- "I see we did not meet our targets for [whatever]. What stood in your way?"
- "What could we suggest that might prevent this obstacle in the future?"
- "What could we learn from this situation?"
- "What changes could we make that would make it easier to meet our targets?"

You may have to prompt people to get them engaged in the collaborative effort and to neutralize their prior assumptions that, since performance is being reviewed, some people are about to get their faces ripped off. Since you want to avoid such a distressing outcome at all costs, learn to use neutral, nonjudgmental questions. Stop blame or self-justification as soon as it rears its ugly head. If somebody has not done the work, or has not satisfied all aspects of the assignment, any excuse is acceptable, even if the dog ate his homework. Your question would then be, "What might you do to prevent the dog from eating your homework in the future?" If no suggestions are forthcoming, *you* start the ball rolling: "Would it help if you [locked the dog in the doghouse, distracted the dog with a doggy treat, finished your assignment online so there's nothing for the dog to eat and so on and so forth]"?

You will, without question, hear your people tell you that they just didn't do the work, with or without further justifications. Your reply? "What would you need to do differently so you could complete the assignment?"

See how easy that was? If your personal rage-o-meter is going into the red zone, count to 10.

As long as you stick with this leadership approach, focusing on collaborative learning and refusing to punish failure to perform, your team will eventually stop trying to "game" the system or find excuses for their actual performance. In due course, they'll welcome these meetings. Honest, I promise.

Where to Start

Start somewhere simple. My favorite technique for launching implementation is to set a simple target for completing a number of Scorecards. Set a very low target that will be easy to achieve, and include the deadline for achievement, which should always be immediately before the next performance review meeting. Here's one that has worked very well for many SMART Way users: "Complete at least *one* Scorecard for a current donor or prospect by the end of the week. By Friday, send me an e-mail telling me how many Scorecards you completed. Bring printed copies to the meeting. We'll review progress next Monday at 9 A.M., during our regular performance-review meeting."

The team's not ready yet to improve proportions of funding diversification, expand the pipeline target to three times actual, or figure out why the process encounters a bottleneck at Donor Move Three. Right now, it's enough for them to complete some Scorecards—at least one—by the end of the week.

The first leadership skill, therefore, is that of establishing targets. Since these are targets for adopting new skills or methods, the target must include the level of execution (in this case, the number of Scorecards to be completed), and the date by which the target is to be completed. The second skill, which follows immediately after the first one, is reviewing performance. I think that knowing how to review performance is one of the most valuable of all leadership skills.

Reviewing Performance the Right Way

Since you wisely scheduled your meeting so soon after the completion of the assignment, the information is fresh in the minds of the team. Last week you told them to complete at least one Scorecard, to inform you of the number completed by the end of the week, and to bring printed copies of those Scorecards with them to the next meeting.

Start the meeting by reviewing the total number of Scorecards completed by all parties and then by each. If you can, summarize the information in a table that you've set up before the meeting.

Now what? Focus on the data. Do *not* say anything about who did a good job, who didn't, or who completed more Scorecards. Use those same questions above, now modified for this particular measurement:

- "I see you all met your targets for completing so many Scorecards. Was it difficult to do so? Why or why not? "

- "What did you learn by reaching your Scorecards-completed targets?"
- "I see some of you did not meet your targets for completing Scorecards. What prevented you from doing so?"
- "What did you learn by failing to reach your Scorecards-completed targets?"
- "How could you change the way you work, so it would be easier to meet such targets?"
- "What could you personally, or all of you collectively, do differently next time to get better results?"

Notice that you're completely focused, at this point, on your team's ability to complete a certain number of Scorecards, and nothing else. Completing Scorecards is a necessary skill your people must learn.

If there's enough time, and the dialog about Scorecard completion targets has been exhausted, then you can turn to discussions about what the Scorecard revealed, whether the statements were accurate, or if the development officers found it difficult to get the information that would allow completing the Prospect Score. Try framing such questions this way:

- "So, value statement 4 doesn't make much sense to you, Fritz. What do you think would make more sense? Do others agree with Fritz? How do you think we should change the statement? Or do we need it at all?"
- "If the value statement is basically okay with you guys, would it help if you used better probing questions? What questions would be more revealing?"
- "If we were to change the value statement, what should it say instead? How important should it be?"

When it comes to reviewing performance, the leader's job is to keep the team focused on effective collaboration to improve accuracy of components, metrics, and targets; reveal insights; and consider improvements.

IMPORTANT!

Results are just results. They are neither inherently good nor inherently bad.

TRACKING DONOR MOVE TARGETS

You're probably accustomed to being asked, "How much income will you deliver this month/week/day/minute?" The underlying message, though usually unstated, is punitive: if you don't have the right amount of income to deliver, you're standing on shaky ground. This unstated expectation may be one reason so many people hate and fear asking for money.

Effective performance management techniques, fortunately, have nothing to do with this "perform or else!" mentality. Their purpose is to examine quantifiable performance at every stage of the process, including stages that occur upstream, to find obstacles, bottlenecks, and wasted effort, and alleviate or remediate the process accordingly. Punishment is strictly off the table, out of the room, not eligible to even enter the building.

Once you are all comfortable with completing Scorecards, you are ready to start tracking the Donor Moves process. Assign low, achievable targets here, just as you did for Scorecard completion. Again, your first objective is to get your development people accustomed to figuring out how to persuade a donor prospect to progress from Donor Move X to Donor Move Y, on a regular basis. Start with a very simple target: "Your assignment for this week is to review all the open gift/grant opportunities you're currently working on, and identify the latest Donor Move achieved for each one."

Fulfilling this assignment means that your gift officers must evaluate all the open opportunities in their portfolios, and decide where to locate each one on the Donor Moves continuum. The outcomes may surprise you; they have often surprised me. If your gift officers have been focusing on what they did last, or what they think they ought to do next, they might not be clear about which Donor Move was last achieved by the prospect. Consider this a teachable moment. Get the rest of the team involved in the conversation, to make sure everybody "gets" the learning.

Once everyone has demonstrated the ability to identify the latest Donor Move achieved, it's time to assign some performance targets. These may be just as (seemingly) simple as the first assignments you set for Scorecard completion. Consider assigning each officer the challenge of achieving at least one move in the coming week. The move could be any one of the Donor Moves, achieved by any prospect that's currently active. The gift officer's job, then, is to persuade a prospect to achieve the next Donor Move in the sequence, be it moving from One to Two, Two to Three, Three to Four, or any later stage.

Misunderstanding Donor Moves

Donor Moves themselves represent another Zen-like "mountain." You have introduced the process, laid out the sequence, calculated conversion ratios, and talked at length about the way these milestones demonstrate the donor's giving process. So far, so good. But when it comes to the first review meeting, suddenly everybody gets it backwards. If, or when, they do, ignore your frustrations. You have identified another teachable moment.

Your shop may be one of those that already uses leading indicators to track pipeline progress. But if not, it's likely that the first time around, people may become confused. They may ignore the moves, define opportunity stages a different way, or do something else. It's common to see this exact misunderstanding among development teams new to the methodology, and I've grown to welcome it. Somehow people need to struggle with the concept, misunderstand it, or even get it backwards before they make the necessary breakthrough in understanding. When they do break through, their understanding and appreciation of the learning grows exponentially. Consider this misunderstanding an uncomfortable but necessary step in the evolution of the methodology.

Adding More Targets

If you, the leader, maintain the weekly review meeting schedule, you will begin to see more confidence and deeper understanding take hold. Add more complex or ambitious targets every week or two. Examples include:

- Raise the number of overall moves you want to team to complete. If last week it was "at least one," maybe this week it should be "at least two."
- Choose specific moves. Where the first assignment was "any move at all," the next could be "move at least one opportunity from Move Three to Move Four."
- Assign a target for identifying one prospect in your Move Zero database, and moving that prospect to Donor Move One.

If there are enough gifts at Move Four, the point where the prospect negotiates the details with you, it may be acceptable to assign a target for achieving Move Five, but if not, don't make it a major focus on the review. Stay focused on embracing the Donor Moves concept. Pay a lot of attention to the early-stage indicators, Moves One through Four. At this stage, calm and confident leadership and attention to recognizing leading indicators will produce better pipeline results.

READING THE STORY THE NUMBERS TELL YOU

Reading the "story the numbers tell you" is substantially different from management by anecdote. Meetings based on management by anecdote follow a familiar framework: "Okay, Mary, which gifts are you forecasting this week/month/quarter? Joe, it's your turn; which grants are you expecting to close? Sue, didn't you say you expected that check from the corporate partner? Oh, you mean they changed their minds?" Among other things, the parties to this sort of meeting tend to spend their time ignoring the reports of the folks on the hot seat because they're mentally trying to make their own performance sound better than the guy who reported last, or at least better than it really is. Or praying that the bell will ring before it's their turn. Unfortunately, little learning takes place in meetings of this type.

SMART Way performance review meetings are all about learning, thanks to the data you're gathering. Where in the past it may have been all about "what have you done for me lately," now it's all about "what can we learn to sustain or improve?" As the leader, continue to engage your team in interpreting the data. Some additional questions you'll find effective include:

- What do these data suggest about our effectiveness, efficiency, and productivity?
- Are we on track?
  - If so, what would we need to do to sustain that level of performance?
  - If not, what would we need to do to reach that level of performance?
- Could we raise the performance target, and if so, by how much?
- Would raising it be beneficial? Why?

Your leadership skills are essential in transforming the development shop from the tactical to the strategic. Without applying those skills, the whole initiative will evaporate and return to business as usual. It's the leader that makes or breaks the adoption process. Stick with it.

WHAT WE COVERED

- The components of Fundraising the SMART Way—the Prospect Scorecards, Donor Moves, and target setting—will not improve results without effective leadership.

- It takes careful leadership skills to drive adoption of the new approach. People will invariably return to their old, familiar habits without such leadership.

- Establish frequent meetings to review performance against the various SMART Way indicators. Hold these meetings weekly for a while; drop back to a less frequent schedule only when you are convinced the team has absorbed the concept, but never less than once a month.

- Start the process by setting Scorecard completion targets, then over time progress to setting targets for Donor Moves.

- Show your team how to "read the story the numbers tell you." As they become more skillful, their results will begin to improve.

WHAT YOU CAN DO

- Schedule weekly performance review meetings for the next 8 to 12 weeks. Let everyone know that attendance is mandatory, but if one or more of them can't make a particular meeting, they will catch up the next time. Hold the meeting anyway, as long as you've got at least one person to work with.

- Remember that crafting the SMART Way components is one thing, while using them is another. Use the inevitable misunderstandings and resistance as teachable moments.

- Gather all data before the meeting. Do not waste any meeting time on capturing data. If any participant has failed to record data, or has done so incorrectly, state that the review is based on the data captured, and encourage the participant to update before the next meeting.

- Assign modest targets at first. A good target to start with is "complete at least one Scorecard by the end of the week." After your team demonstrates proficiency in Scorecard completion, start to introduce Donor Moves targets: "Move at least one gift opportunity to the next Donor Move."

- You never know where the next insight is coming from. Make sure that all participants speak up during the meeting. If you ask a question and nobody volunteers an answer, call on someone at random.

- Be willing to modify any part of the model, from Scorecard statements to performance targets, but do so only if there is evidence to support such a change.

CHAPTER 8

The Breakthrough:
Continuous Improvement

Of all the myriad business processes that keep a nonprofit functioning, the fundraising process may be the most strategic, even if it's not the first thing your constituents think about when your charity's name is mentioned. Without steadily growing income, you can't fulfill your mission. Yet fundraising is the function least likely to be touched by the benevolent hand of continuous improvement. And that's a shame, as so many development executives have bemoaned after they were shown the door. Asking people to produce better results without giving them the tools to do so is either unfair, ill-informed, or both.

In my quest to apply performance management disciplines to the function of fundraising, I discovered, or maybe I should say rediscovered, the importance of continuous improvement. Without the disciplines of continuous improvement, the productivity and effectiveness of fundraising efforts might not change all that much. It's easy to slide back into management by anecdote and what-have-you-done-for-me-lately.

While the Scorecard, Donor Moves, and development drivers provide the metrics, and your reporting methods provide business intelligence or feedback, you still need ways to analyze and interpret results and decide what, if anything, needs to be changed. This is where the formal skills of continuous improvement come into play. I introduced some techniques in Chapter 7, such as the use of open-ended, nonjudgmental questions to read the story the numbers tell us, and the concept of the emotionally neutral zone. In this chapter, we will go into more detail about two of the most valuable methods of continuous improvement, root-cause analysis and the Plan-Do-Check-Act cycle.

You don't get continuous improvement simply by trying harder or attempting to "explain" your way out of unflattering data. You get it by using a strategic approach to meet or exceed constituent expectations. According to Robin Tyndhall, a contributor to eHow.com, a well-executed program of continuous improvement can ensure the success of any organization or organizational function with a focus on four premises:

- Success means meeting or exceeding the needs of external and internal customers.
- Most business problems are driven by process problems.
- Employees must be involved.
- Good data drive good decision making.

For us nonprofit people, "external customers" are our funders and advocates as well as the recipients of our programs and services, while "internal customers" are staff, board, and volunteers. I like Robin's description because it reminds us that performance is a group effort, and so is performance improvement. You never really know where the next great idea or innovation is going to come from, but the odds of finding it are much better if everybody's involved.

I also like this description because it emphasizes looking from the outside in, assessing performance by seeing how it has an impact on others, such as funders and clients. It can be difficult to break the habit of fundraising based on the tin-cup mentality, the old "give to us because we need it" approach, until you set up some metrics and reports describing what donors and clients actually do in response to those efforts.

THE PLAN-DO-CHECK-ACT CYCLE

To realize continuous improvement requires two techniques for analyzing recent performance: the Plan-Do-Check-Act cycle and root-cause analysis. In practice, you'll probably end up doing both of these simultaneously.

The Plan-Do-Check-Act (PDCA) cycle is the easiest to explain. First, make a "Plan" that describes what you have set out to accomplish. Next, go out and "Do" what the plan tells you to do, for a certain period of time. (A week is good, at first.) After that, "Check" the results obtained by comparing them to the original plan. Finally, take action to modify the plan or decide to take no action—the "Act" part—and then continue doing whatever the plan says.

Rinse and repeat.

Go through the whole cycle regularly. That's the point of process management: you do it, whatever the process may be, over and over again, reviewing your actual results, learning from those results, and adopting incremental changes or major innovations regularly, in response to the data you've collected, to get better results. Faithful use of PDCA leads directly to continuous improvement. It also engages everyone on the team in learning from past effort.

Root-cause analysis is a set of orderly, systematic methods for conducting PDCA. Both techniques will transform the way you currently manage fundraising performance, for the better.

ROOT-CAUSE ANALYSIS DONE RIGHT

The purpose of root-cause analysis is to discover the "root" of the problem, the earliest point in the process where a "defect" or loss of productivity first occurs, because it's easier and cheaper to solve the problem at that point. Out of a little, teeny pebble grows a snowball, eventually an avalanche, burying everybody in its wake. You want to find that pebble and snatch it off the trail, so the avalanche never happens.

To perform root-cause analysis effectively requires data captured at various points of the process. Since Fundraising the SMART Way^{TM} allows you to track a variety of results, it provides the diagnostic data that support root-cause analysis. The standard way to visualize the problem and its potential roots, or inputs, the so-called fishbone diagram shown in Exhibit 8.1, is helpful. It's called a fishbone because it looks like the skeleton of a fish.

Our fish has only three "ribs," or major input categories: Fundraising Skills and Behaviors, Operational Considerations, and External Market Conditions. Later on in this chapter, we'll add the "sub-ribs," describing the various nuances of each input category (Exhibits 8.2, 8.3, and 8.4). In the SMART Way model, we recommend examining these three input categories in the order shown next.

The first step in root-cause analysis is to define the problem you'd like to solve. The problem statement simply states the perceived problem. In this

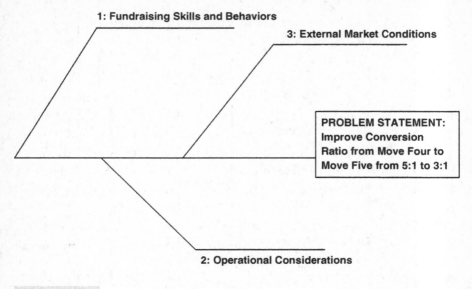

1: Fundraising Skills and Behaviors

3: External Market Conditions

PROBLEM STATEMENT:
Improve Conversion
Ratio from Move Four to
Move Five from 5:1 to 3:1

2: Operational Considerations

EXHIBIT 8.1   **SMART WAY FISHBONE DIAGRAM: INPUT CATEGORIES**

case, we've isolated the problem to read "Improve Conversion Ratio from Move Four to Move Five from 5:1 to 3:1." The problem statement merely describes the problem; it doesn't refer to the solution.

People tend to state the "problem" they're attempting to solve too broadly. For example, I wouldn't have been surprised to see a problem statement that says "raise more money." That statement covers so many possible inputs, it's nearly impossible to figure out what to do better. You're better off scrutinizing your actual data and pinpointing a specific problem. Data analysis helps you break the problem down into manageable parts. It's a whole lot easier to figure out how to improve a conversion ratio than it is to "raise more money."

The regular use of root-cause analysis does a great job of eliminating the blame game, an all too familiar organizational malady. When results are at undesirable levels, it's tempting to make it somebody's fault. I've seen this game played more times than I care to admit. It's always something like "*our* performance would be just dandy if *those guys over there* would do their jobs right!" The blame game is effective at evading accountability, and it hides problems, particularly those that can be solved, under the proverbial rug.

Like everything else in fundraising, it's too simple to say this or that result was undesirable because somebody else messed up. Fundraising is nobody's fault, while getting desirable results is everybody's job.

Another Leaky Bucket Insight

Leaky Bucket statement 9 asks how you manage things when fundraising results fall below desired levels. This statement got the highest proportion of "none of the above" answers, about 22 percent, suggesting that nearly a quarter of participants don't do much of anything to manage their undesirable results. That's a shame; poor or undesirable results provide excellent opportunities for learning and improvement.

The most popular options for this statement were "hold more special events," and "write more grant applications," both of which came in at 49 percent. As many fundraisers have learned to their regret, once you hold more than one or two signature events a year, you quickly reach the point of diminishing returns. Writing more grant applications may also chew up more time than the outcomes justify. But what is worst about these tactics is their failure to tell you anything at all about why the undesirable fundraising results appeared in the first place, or what you might consider changing to get better results. Both options—more events, more grant applications—are tactical. They are the Hail Mary passes of fundraising, stuff you "throw" at the problem that might make you feel busier but offer no guarantee of improved performance.

Once you get into the habit of root-cause analysis, you'll find yourself seeking out undesirable results, and more and more of them will appear. You no longer fear these undesirable results. Instead, you use them as a springboard for improving productivity.

The first step in root-cause analysis is identifying a result you don't like and want to change.

Input Categories and Subcategories

Fundraising results are affected by three categories of input, each containing three or four subcategories. Evaluate the impact of each category and subcategory in the same order whenever you find a result you want to change or replicate in future cycles. Always start with the first category and the first subcategory, go on to the next, and try not to skip any steps. This diligent approach will save you untold wasted hours and anxiety.

If you follow this approach, you're more likely to identify the true root cause. If you stop after the first input category, you might miss the actual root cause and put a lot of time and energy into a temporary fix.

Under ideal circumstances, such analysis is conducted in a group setting. Your regularly scheduled performance review meetings provide the perfect opportunity. With practice, you and your team will become proficient at it, able to identify and select the best result to analyze, do the analysis step by step, make a group decision about what changes to adopt, and appoint someone to be accountable for doing it, all in about an hour, from one to four times a month.

For the most part, you will use the methods of continuous improvement to keep fundraising performance consistent. But sometimes you'll encounter an unexpected result severe enough to be life threatening. Hey, these things happen. Look what happened to the economy on September 11, 2001. Literally overnight, it came to a screeching halt, followed by the housing bubble, and then was thrown back into chaos during the Great Recession of 2008. What are you supposed to do then?

The best answer is to use the same, deliberate, cool-headed methods that you would for ordinary, cycle-by-cycle continuous improvement. Methods of continuous improvement truly shine when there's a crisis. For those of you who saw the film *Apollo 13* (or actually remember the incident), what was so striking was the astonishing level of creativity and teamwork called forth when the lunar mission experienced an on-board explosion, depleting the oxygen supply and electrical power of the spacecraft. Engineers on the ground in Houston analyzed the problem, isolated causes, and selected improvements that kept the astronauts safe and alive for the rest of the mission. I certainly hope that losing part of your donor base won't put your actual life in jeopardy. But why shouldn't you be able to benefit from such orderly, systematic, thoughtful methods of problem definition and resolution?

The categories and subcategories of performance analysis include the following:

- Fundraising Skills and Behaviors
  - Scorecard Accuracy and Application
  - Questioning Skills

- Adherence to the Donor Moves Process
  - Level of Execution
- Operational Considerations
  - Technology Issues
  - Unclear Lines of Authority
  - Misaligned Goals
- External Market Conditions
  - Local-Market Changes
  - Regional/National-Market Changes
  - Global-Market Changes

Evaluate each category, and each subcategory, in the same order every time you encounter undesirable results. If you don't go through each category and subcategory, you may well overlook significant, often unexpected inputs producing substantial negative impact on results.

Category 1: Fundraising Skills and Behaviors

Always analyze this category first, because fundraising skills and behaviors are within the span of control of the development shop. Therefore, you and your colleagues can make certain improvements without the approval of other executives or departments. These are typically the easiest and least expensive fixes, but they are by no means comprehensive solutions.

The four subcategories of Fundraising Skills and Behaviors are:

- *Scorecard Accuracy and Application*—Having well-defined, accurate, objective criteria for evaluating donor potential, then investing more development effort in those with high potential, correspondingly less in those with low potential.
- *Questioning Skills*—Using carefully designed questions and the related skills of rapport building to engage high-potential donors, build relationships with them, and influence their gift-making decisions.
- *Adherence to the Donor Moves Process*—Keeping the focus on actions taken by donors that demonstrate the results of gift-officer activities.
- *Level of Execution*—Working hard enough, cultivating enough opportunities, conducting sufficient stewardship activities.

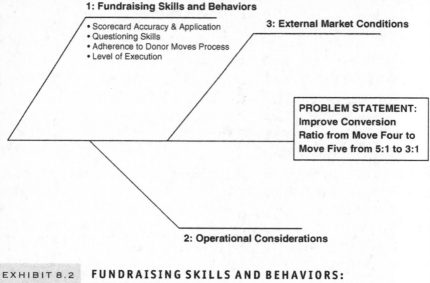

1: Fundraising Skills and Behaviors
- Scorecard Accuracy & Application
- Questioning Skills
- Adherence to Donor Moves Process
- Level of Execution

3: External Market Conditions

PROBLEM STATEMENT:
Improve Conversion
Ratio from Move Four to
Move Five from 5:1 to 3:1

2: Operational Considerations

EXHIBIT 8.2   **FUNDRAISING SKILLS AND BEHAVIORS: SUBCATEGORIES**

To solve the problem of improving the conversion ratio from Move Four to Move Five, we would discuss each of the subcategories, asking questions like these:

- *Scorecard accuracy and application.* Did we cut corners; is our Scorecard accurate enough; have we diligently asked the right questions and scored the prospects correctly? If the answer is no or maybe, then that's an issue that deserves further attention.

- *Questioning skills.* Are we using the right questions the right way at the right time, or do we need to revise them? Should we test some new or different questions and compare results to the original probing questions?

- *Adherence to Donor Moves process.* What tactics are we using to persuade prospects to move from Move Four to Move Five? What are the reasons prospects give us for failing to achieve Move Five? Are some opportunities at Move Four actually ready for the "closed-lost" pile?

- *Level of execution.* Are we working hard enough, scheduling enough meetings with retained donors or new prospects? Could we do more without losing quality? Are we losing time by deploying development resources to non-development activities?

People obtain the requisite skills through formal and informal education and field experience, of course, but the nuances of skills and behavior are deeply affected by the prevailing culture within your particular nonprofit. While it is desirable to recruit fundraising staff with great skills, training, and credentials, remember that every new agency, even every new campaign is just a little bit different from the ones you encountered in your last position. The fact that your favorite tactics worked for the Cancer Society is no guarantee they'll work for the ACLU.

Regrettably, those who lack fundraising experience, which typically includes the rest of the staff and board, may assume that good fundraising skills are all it takes. Not so. Keep in mind that the other two categories, Operational Considerations and External Market Conditions, may impact fundraising results just as much as the skills and behaviors of the development staff, and sometimes have an even more powerful deleterious effect.

Scorecard Accuracy and Application   Always look at this subcategory first, since it's all about your team's ability to select and work with prospects offering the best potential. There are two aspects to this subcategory: accuracy and application. Scorecards become more accurate, more correct, through use. Sometimes you'll discover that the original statement, importance weight, or prospect scale was off. Maybe you could assign some prospect scores on a binary basis, selecting a score of 5 if the quality or fact exists, or a 1 if it doesn't, but more familiarity will allow you to refine the list of possible scores. If you are still relatively new to the SMART Way process, be willing to upgrade your Scorecard a few times based on deeper knowledge.

In terms of application, you could have the most exacting Scorecards in the universe, but if your team's not using them, what difference will they make? You know your team is applying their Scorecards if you have the evidence to prove it. Gift officer files will be filled with completed Scorecards, and most active prospects will rank "A" or "B." If you're the team leader, it's up to you to help your gift officer determine if a "C" or "D" prospect really justifies the investment of more time.

Most of us find it a bit challenging to stop pursuing those C-list and D-list prospects. At the very least, you might think, "I've already invested all this time; I've got to make it work!" In such cases, the combination of excellent leadership and coaching from your supervisor, plus a correctly completed Scorecard, will help. It really doesn't matter if the prospect is warm, friendly, and hospitable or was referred to you by a senior executive or board member who hasn't really assessed the potential offered. If the prospect doesn't show evidence of high potential donor value, don't throw your valuable hours away.

Following is a summary of questions used to evaluate Scorecard accuracy and application:

- Have we scorecarded each prospect we added to the pipeline?
- Have we made any assumptions about scoring the prospect, or did we ask the right questions?
- Are we still calling on those C-ranked prospects, or have we concentrated on the A's?
- What could or should we do differently to adhere to the practice of Scorecard accuracy and application?
- Is Scorecard accuracy and application the root cause of undesirable results or merely a contributor?

Note: During root-cause analysis, it's always "we" collectively. It doesn't really matter if Jack was a bad boy or Jill was an overachiever.

Questioning Skills   Look at questioning skills second. What questions are you using to build your relationships and gain rapport with your prospects? The suggested probing questions, introduced in Chapter 4, help you open a dialog with donors and prospects. Experts at this skill set discover that they no longer need to pitch the merits of their organizations quite so heavily. Heavy-duty pitching tends to be "me focused," all about why the organization is so wonderful and how much it needs the money. But this is the time to find out if the prospect is good enough for you, not the other way around. You're trying to channel Cousin Judy, remember?

Conventional wisdom says listening is the most important skill, but I beg to differ. If you ask the right questions the right way, then you will be more likely to hear (i.e., listen to) the answers you need to decide if this prospect or donor justifies investing more time. This is the primary reason for adding specific questions to the Scorecard. The time and effort you put into crafting the questions repays itself handsomely. This way, you have a consistent set of questions; they are used by everyone doing cultivation work; and thus their answers can be judged and evaluated, creating a more reliable benchmark.

Following is a summary of questions used to evaluate questioning skills:

- Did we rely on the suggested probing questions? If not, why not?
- Did we discover insights that provoked revising the questions or adding to them?
- What did the use of the questions tell us?
- What could or should we do differently to adhere to the practice of questioning skills?
- Is questioning skill the root cause of undesirable results or merely a contributor?

Adherence to the Donor Moves Process   This third subcategory tends to create a lot of confusion, because fundraisers are much more accustomed to describing their own activities, not those of the donor. Two common errors crop up. Gift officers may fall back into tracking their own activities, regardless of the language used to describe the stage reached, or they may assume that prospects will repeat certain moves several times during the cultivation process. While it's true that prospects will tell you more and more about themselves over time, they will achieve Donor Move One only once. It's been achieved when you have enough information to complete a Prospect Scorecard. Similarly, they will achieve Donor Move Two only once, or at least once per gift opportunity, when they let you know they're satisfied with your agency's bona fides, even though they will without question want to know more and more about *you* over time.

But the most likely problem is a failure to record the achievement of each move for each opportunity. Entering the information into your donor-management application shouldn't be daunting; in most instances, you'll only need to look up the opportunity record and choose an entry from a pull-down menu. Sometimes you just get lazy and delay the update until "later" when you've got a batch of opportunities to update, or you're just too busy to interrupt what you're doing, so you wait until later. If you're anything like me, once you finally sit down to bring your records up to date, you might not remember which prospects did what when.

People will tell you their records are not up to date, right at the start of the review meeting. They might even try to update the records during the meeting, while people are viewing them. In my opinion, these are distractions. Nip that one in the bud. If you're leading the meeting—well, even if you're not—state that its purpose is to review the data gathered to date. Period. If the data are not up to date, conduct the review as if they were. Tell people that's the game plan: whatever data are in the reports are the latest, greatest, most faithful data and that's what you'll all work with. Then go ahead and hold the review meeting. In due time, team members will recognize that it's in their best interests to enter the information in a timely manner.

Following is a summary of questions used to evaluate adherence to the Donor Moves process:

- Did we move the targeted number of gift opportunities to the next Donor Move? Why or why not?

- Did we update data describing the prospect's achievements of moves? Why or why not?

- If we had better, more accurate, and/or more timely information about our pipeline, what would that tell us?

- What could or should we do differently to adhere to the Donor Moves process?

- Is there something in adhering to the Donor Moves process that is the root cause of undesirable results or is it merely a contributor?

Level of Execution   The term *level of execution* is a snazzier way of asking if you're working hard enough. Are you? Well, it depends. You might be very busy without producing desirable results. You might get great results without being overly busy. Level of execution helps you correlate outbound effort with the results produced. That's how you figure out if you're working "hard" enough. By contrast, being burned out and exhausted doesn't necessarily show if you're working at the correct level of execution.

The Donor Moves process helps you keep tabs on level of execution. In Chapter 6, you learned how to set targets for Donor Moves by calculating the total number of gifts it would take to reach your income targets, first assigning that number to Donor Move Five, the point at which the donor commits the gift, then working backwards, increasing the number of moves to be achieved at each earlier stage. Use a 1:1.5 conversion ratio until you establish a more accurate benchmark. Track actual moves against moves targets, and at the same time, track total size of pipeline compared to total size of actual income. Your pipeline always needs to be about three times larger than your actual income target. Over time, you might be able to shrink the conversion ratio down to two or two-and-a-half times, once you've established a baseline.

In due course, you should be able to say, "Gee, we are too far below our pipeline target and our target for actual income, to be able to meet our goals." Then use those magic, motivating words: *"What should we do differently now to give us better results next time?"* This approach improves teamwork, keeps people's heads in the emotionally neutral zone, and provides suggestions through active collaboration. Among other things, your team will stay motivated.

Following is a summary of questions used to evaluate level of execution:

- Did we track all major opportunities through the Donor Moves process?
- If we didn't track everything, what should we do to improve record keeping?
- If we did track everything, and our actual performance remains undesirable, at which point does our Donor Moves process encounter an obstacle or bottleneck?
- What could we do differently to move more prospects from Donor Move One to Donor Move Two, Two to Three, Three to Four, and so on?
- Did we set our targets or conversion ratios too high or low, and if so, how should we modify them?
- What could or should we do differently to adhere to tracking level of execution?
- Is level of execution the root cause of these specific undesirable results or merely a contributor?

Category 2: Operational Considerations

Lots of things can happen outside of the development shop but inside the four walls of your organization that can get in the way of productive fundraising. For the most part, the fundraising staff can't fix or improve these things without engaging the support, money, or authority of another department or executive. And you have to be diplomatic and discreet, or risk alienating your partners in the other departments or governing board. Development executives who manage this set of inputs successfully have learned how to make a

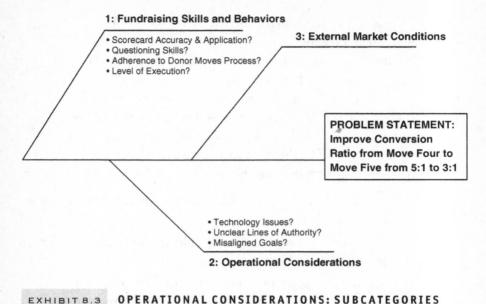

1: Fundraising Skills and Behaviors

- Scorecard Accuracy & Application?
- Questioning Skills?
- Adherence to Donor Moves Process?
- Level of Execution?

3: External Market Conditions

PROBLEM STATEMENT:
Improve Conversion
Ratio from Move Four to
Move Five from 5:1 to 3:1

- Technology Issues?
- Unclear Lines of Authority?
- Misaligned Goals?

2: Operational Considerations

EXHIBIT 8.3   **OPERATIONAL CONSIDERATIONS: SUBCATEGORIES**

business case for taking the undesirable results seriously and investing resources—people, time, money—to ameliorate them.

Back when I was in corporate sales, my fellow salespeople and I often grumbled about what we called "the sales prevention department." We meant the internal obstacle course we often had to run to avoid scuttling the sale or make it difficult to deliver the solution. Nothing is as frustrating as losing a sale because somebody or something *in your own company* stands in the way.

Many operational issues lie outside the control of the development shop. A fundraising prevention department may lurk somewhere in the hallways of your agency.

See Exhibit 8.3. Subcategories of Operational Considerations include:

- Technology
- Inadequate or Unclear Definition of Roles
- Misaligned Goals and/or Unclear Lines of Authority

Technology   The technology resources at your disposal are never neutral. They always contribute to or detract from the successful achievement of desired results. Technology is highly mutable; the pace of change keeps accelerating. It's easy to misuse it, run it incorrectly, or select it without considering the needs of the various departments or users, all of which makes your technology investment (and your information technology [IT] staff) a sitting duck for the blame game. Let's keep blame off the table and assess the usefulness of your technology to produce desired results instead.

If your organization has a donor management or constituent relationship management (CRM) platform, and your development staff fails to learn how to use it properly, it's hard to "blame" poor results on the technology itself. Before you get to that point, make sure that the in-house IT staff, the vendor, or a third-party consultant trains all users. Boom, you've already eliminated the notion that the problem lies in the application itself and put the focus back on operator error.

That's all well and good until you discover the training never took place, no provision was made for training new hires, or the IT department put your requests at the bottom of its priority list. To fix problems like these, you have to be able to build your own "case for IT support," so to speak, to convince senior management that supporting the fundraising team with the proper, appropriate technology tools will be good for the agency as a whole.

Consider if the "technology problem" is one of the following issues:

- There are no tools or modules in the available technology that support cultivation, opportunity management (pipeline tools), or marketing and outreach (ability to maintain your list of subscribers, segment the list, use it for e-mail marketing and the like).
- Tools and modules are available, but clumsy, inflexible, difficult to use, or no one ever successfully loaded the prospect/donor database into the tools, which may require special skills.
- The database has not been cleaned up or updated since who-knows-when.
- It's impossible to add additional data fields, such as those required by the SMART Way model, or to pull particular reports.
- Your version of the software application is out of date and the vendor won't support it anymore, but the budget's been cut and you can't upgrade.
- Your support requests never get a response from the IT department.

If any of these underlying causes turns out to be the root cause, make your case by demonstrating how much it's costing you to live with the problem, even if the cost is measured only in staff time. Here in the second decade of the twenty-first century, it should be possible to add a custom field, capture data from that field, design a special report, and have it produced on an automated schedule, without inordinate effort or expense.

Unclear Lines of Authority   Sometimes a board member thinks she has the right to tell you whom to cultivate and how to do it. Sometimes the CEO countermands the instructions you received from your boss, or a more senior gift officer tells you, the new grant writer, what to do. Such lack of clarity becomes wasteful and counterproductive quickly, so it should be avoided.

It may be that the lines of authority seem unclear because communications have broken down. Maybe the director of development forgot to tell you that board member Smith is in charge of a special project and needs your help. Stuff like that can be cleared up by a simple conversation. The real problem appears when it seems like no one is in charge. If that's the case, here's what you might see:

- It's hard for you to answer the question "to whom do you report?" because today you report to the CEO, tomorrow to the head of the board's Fund Development Committee, the day after to the chief financial officer.

- You have no performance targets or targets that are contradictory.

- Some of the functions that support fundraising, like marketing or stewardship, are set up in silos and report to different executives. Coordination and alignment are difficult or nonexistent.

- Fundraising goals and income targets are assigned in an arbitrary fashion, with no consideration for track record or resource capacity.

- There is no clear "chain of command," and as a result, you never know to whom to appeal when you need help.

Problems like these may be murky and difficult to pin down. These sorts of issues are frankly best dealt with ahead of time. If you're not sure who's in charge, pull that issue out into the open—diplomatically, of course. If you lack performance targets, consider drafting suggested targets and bringing them to the attention of the executive to whom you report.

Sometimes the board may decide to increase fundraising goals significantly, but won't let you (or the CEO) hire additional staff or invest in additional marketing. That's a setup for failure. Assume board and senior leaders have good intentions, but become deft at proving an unemotional business case justifying the additional resource capacity required to achieve the new targets.

Misaligned Goals   No part of the organization stands on its own. Programs can't exist without funding, funding can't exist without accounting, accounting can't exist without staffing, and so on; all functions need to operate in harmony. Organizational harmony requires proper alignment of goals and objectives. Without a purposeful effort, it's easy to create goals in a vacuum, in direct conflict with one another.

The classic example of misaligned goals is where the program staff has a goal of adding so many new clients next year, which will require certain additional expenditures, but the accounting department's goal is based on the amount of money it can cut from the budget. Somebody could end up in trouble; these goals may be incompatible.

Occasionally, you'll find misaligned goals within the fundraising department. If senior leadership wants you to concentrate only on donor retention and completely ignore donor acquisition, there's a fundamental misalignment. Donor acquisition, which is always required, costs more than donor retention, but without new donors, there's a limit to the extent of possible growth.

Consider the implications of misaligned goals in the following scenarios:

- The programs department will launch a series of new initiatives this year, but there are no plans to raise the money to pay for them.
- The finance department has launched an austerity campaign and has decided to eliminate reimbursement of travel expenses for members of the fundraising team.
- Someone on the board found out about a block grant to fund some programs that are not closely related to your organization's mission. Yet that board member has so much influence over the CEO, she has demanded that you apply for the funding, regardless of the cost of your staff's time and cost of lost opportunity.

The evidence of misaligned goals is often subtle. Furthermore, they are not within the span of your control, just like most other operational considerations. Make every attempt to describe the consequences of misaligned goals, using emotionally neutral language and describing the eventual cost to the organization of such misalignments.

Category 3: External Market Conditions

Nonprofit organizations need effective ways to sense what's happening in the external market, just as for-profit organizations do. Nonprofits need to have some way of knowing or anticipating changes in the broader economy, the ways that local, regional, or national governments underwrite social or educational services, the impact of emerging technology, and a raft of other issues. Unfortunately, there's a whole lot of evidence showing that they don't have good ways to do so. Here's just one example: In Florida, where I live, many social service agencies have received the bulk of their funding from a single government agency, or from a small group of such agencies, ever since these nonprofits were chartered. Over the past decade, however, those government agencies, and the current state legislature, have reduced their own budgets, severely restricting the amount of money available to their client social service organizations. Whether the legislature did this out of political expediency or as a result of lost tax income doesn't really matter.

What has been the response of the social service organizations? A few of them had enough wisdom to begin diversifying their fundraising sources, bringing in executives who could muster a base of new individual donors and corporate contributors to create sustainable income. Too many, however, took ineffectual approaches that failed to address the problem of replacing lost government funding. They engaged in some (or all) of the following:

- Sending busloads of stakeholders up to Tallahassee, the state capital, to protests the budget cuts, of course inviting the press to attend. For the most part, the budget cuts were not reversed.

- Conducting town hall meetings in their local communities to protest the budget cuts and inviting the press to attend. Again, the budget cuts were not reversed.

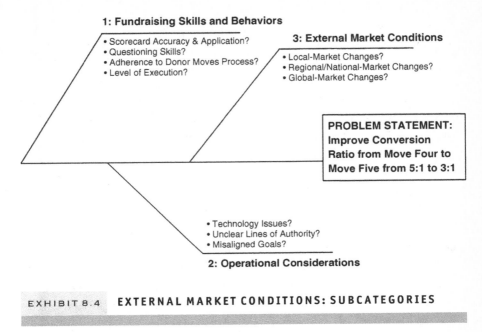

1: Fundraising Skills and Behaviors

- Scorecard Accuracy & Application?
- Questioning Skills?
- Adherence to Donor Moves Process?
- Level of Execution?

3: External Market Conditions

- Local-Market Changes?
- Regional/National-Market Changes?
- Global-Market Changes?

PROBLEM STATEMENT: Improve Conversion Ratio from Move Four to Move Five from 5:1 to 3:1

- Technology Issues?
- Unclear Lines of Authority?
- Misaligned Goals?

2: Operational Considerations

EXHIBIT 8.4   **EXTERNAL MARKET CONDITIONS: SUBCATEGORIES**

- Spending years discussing the pros and cons of adopting other means of raising money through philanthropy but failing to take decisive action.

- Hiring a "fundraising expert" because that person "knows everybody in town," then firing the expert after six months because "she didn't raise any money."

For-profit companies and many entrepreneurial start-ups do a better job of anticipating changes in local-, regional-, or global-market conditions. For these companies, failing to keep an ear to the ground would be unthinkable. Organizations that get really good at this are considered nimble, a compliment describing leadership's willingness to bob, weave, and flex in order to exploit an opening in the market, or to build a seawall preventing greater disaster. Nonprofit organizations would do well to emulate these techniques, especially now, as traditional funding models are morphing and as the stalwarts of philanthropy, those of the World War II generation, are dying off.

Local-Market Conditions   Pay attention to what's going on right within your local community. Be aware of who's been hired, fired, retired; changes such as these may present unanticipated opportunities or threats. Also stay aware of the way major nonprofits exercise their own fundraising. Do you know your competitors? Have you ever analyzed the value propositions they rely on to win over donors or grant makers? Find out if the larger local foundations are reducing their funding or emphasizing grants for capacity building over grants to underwrite programs.

Local-market conditions may have an impact on the availability of qualified new staff recruits. Maybe you'll want to emulate the way other local nonprofits use social media or conduct special events. At the very least, you'll want to try not to schedule your annual awards luncheon on the same day as the biggest nonprofit in the county holds theirs.

If your organization serves only the local community, local-market conditions are the most important for you to be aware of. Yes, you should be aware of market trends at the state, regional, national, or global level, but the local market will carry more weight.

Consider responding to local-market conditions by asking:

- What do we know about our local market in terms of [availability of desirable new hires, levels of foundation giving, needs for our services, etc.]? If we don't know much, what would be the best way for us to find out?
- If we discover some negative pressures in the local market (spell them out, of course), what should we do to respond, if anything? Why?
- To what extent do these local-market conditions affect our fund-raising results?

State-, Provincial-, or Regional-Market Conditions   On the whole, similar considerations apply. However, you need to know the extent to which a change in market conditions at the state or regional level will impact your organization. Many nonprofits based in South Florida, who serve only people in that area, receive state funding. I'm sure there are similar models in your state or country as well. It's in the nonprofit's interests to understand what's going on at the state level, and plan the way they'll respond ahead of time to avoid the last-minute panic.

If your organization serves a wider community in geographical terms, then it might well be that the larger marketplace—the state, the region, the province—will have an impact on your agency's survival, sustainability, or capacity.

Most nonprofits will be impacted at both the local and regional levels. Consider responding to state- or regional-market conditions by asking:

- What do we know or need to know about our regional market in terms of [availability of desirable new hires, levels of foundation giving, needs for our services, etc.]? If we don't know much, what would be the best way for us to find out?

- If we discovered some negative pressures in the regional market (spell them out, of course), what should we do to respond, if anything? Why?

- To what extent do these state-, provincial-, or regional-market conditions affect our fundraising results?

Now you get to ask another question: could conditions in the regional market cancel out local conditions or amplify their impact?

National-, International-, or Global-Market Conditions   Even if your nonprofit serves a tiny geography, it still might be affected by the global marketplace. Here's a positive example: the rapidly growing adoption of high-tech communications media has turned Planet Earth into a global village. You might just be able to adapt a technique perfected in rural India and make it useful to your organization in Wales (or vice versa).

From a more negative perspective, of course, we have all recently lived through—or are still living with—the global economic upheavals of the years since 2008. We're also starting to see the impact of changing climates, the appearance of "food deserts" even in developed countries, and looming challenges of finding drinkable water. These are scary times, and it's likely that no one will be unaffected.

So you've got to ask yourselves if your organization is at risk from these global forces. Certainly, if your nonprofit has a global reach, like the Red Cross/Red Crescent societies, those boards and staffs must evaluate and anticipate changes in global-market conditions, and provide support to the regional and local affiliates. Global conditions may impact almost any nonprofit, depending on the conditions. For example, the 2010 eruption of the Finnish volcano Eyjafjallajökull (say that three times fast) shut down air traffic for six full days followed by intermittent disruptions for another week or two. About 107,000 flights were canceled and billions of dollars, euros, pounds, and [insert favorite currency here] were lost. The ripple effect of this disruption certainly had an impact on any charities directly in its path, but it also had a more disbursed effect. Any nonprofit (or for-profit) executive who had to change travel plans, was unable to attend certain meetings, participate in conferences, or deliver conventional services knows that he or she lost money.

Most nonprofits will be impacted more at the local and regional levels, but some of them will also experience the impact of global conditions.

Consider responding to global-market conditions by asking:

- What do we know or need to know about the global market in terms of [competition for financial and natural resources, availability of educated personnel, potential political threats, etc.]? If we don't know much today, what would be the best way for us to find out?

- If we discovered some negative pressures in the global market (spell them out, of course), and we could see a reasonable chance that these pressures would affect us now or in the future, what should we do to respond, if anything? Why?

- To what extent do these global-market conditions affect our fund-raising results?

And now you get to ask the question you already asked about regional-market conditions: could conditions in the global market cancel out local- or regional-market conditions or make their impact even worse?

The Value of Resistance

Anticipate some resistance when you begin reviewing SMART Way data. Meeting attendees don't participate. They flog themselves by stating that they didn't do the work or didn't update the records. Somebody suddenly misunderstands the purpose or description of a piece of data and goes ballistic. Maybe a comment takes the meeting off course, down a rat hole, pulling the whole meeting out of shape and concentrating on he-said, she-said stuff. They'll call the Scorecard into question, say that the Donor Moves targets don't make sense, or simply have a meltdown because you're showing performance data.

Don't be surprised if you see such responses, especially during the first few weeks. Welcome these challenges to the status quo; they are evidence that the team is in the process of accepting the new changes. It means that somebody in the group, or maybe everybody, is struggling to understand the new techniques and fit them into their assumptions and preconceptions around doing the work of fundraising. Experts in team building will tell you that such a period of resistance, complaining, and general fussing is a necessary though uncomfortable stage in the evolution of the team. The Tuckman model of team development refers to this period as the "storm" stage, as in "form, storm, norm, perform."

As uncomfortable as it is to work through resistance, it's a necessary and even healthy aspect of team development. Great leadership and meeting management skills can guide the team safely through such storms, by refusing to become engaged in the bickering, drawing attention back to the data in question, or simply waiting out the tempest and then redirecting back to the meeting agenda.

Thanks for sharing. Next?

Reporting "Up"

Process management theory states that the people closest to the problem are the best people to solve the problem, and we built the SMART Way model to give those people a meaningful voice. Gift officers themselves are the ones who learn to apply the components and then interpret the data, seeking opportunities to improve their performance. But every development officer has to report to somebody higher up in the organizational hierarchy. Even if the only fundraiser is the executive director, he or she has to report to the board. In return, the boss (your immediate supervisor, the chief development officer, or the board) holds you accountable for results.

The conventional way we've done such reporting relies on our old pals management-by-anecdote and what-have-you-done-for-me-lately. Too bad these techniques (1) fail to provoke or deliver any learning or insights, (2) tend to come across as negative or punitive, and (3) bias the organization toward desperation measures like throwing more events.

The higher you go up the food chain, the more meaningful it becomes to show consolidated charts and graphs. Consolidate the data, not to hide or obscure anything but rather to accelerate learning and interpretation.

It's fascinating to see how much healthy dialogue can be provoked by a summary slide showing financial results in four bullet items, while all the energy tends to leave the room when the board reviews the twenty-six-page line-item budget. The gift officers do the work and keep the data up to date, while the supervisor, manager, or board of directors evaluate progress, make or confirm suggestions about improvement initiatives, and otherwise provide a safe, empowering environment for continuous improvement.

If your experience with reporting up has been negative or painful, it may be tough to overcome your anxiety about the level of transparency required to effect continuous improvement of fundraising results. But remember, management by anecdote tends to turn positive conversations into negative ones, while viewing consolidated tables, reports, charts, and graphs tends to turn negative conversations into positive ones. I know which route I prefer!

What We Covered

- The term *continuous improvement* refers to a succinct, defined set of techniques used to isolate undesirable results, identify areas justifying improvement initiatives, implementing certain initiatives, then reevaluating performance to see if the improvement produced more desirable results.

- Two major techniques used in continuous improvement are the Plan-Do-Check-Act (PDCA) cycle, and root-cause analysis.

- PDCA moves the group's attention away from outputs and activities and toward the regular, cyclical review of performance data, to keep development officers focused on the process as a whole, not just the tactics.

- Root-cause analysis adds to the group's ability to collaborate, where all participants seek out the point upstream at which the selected problem, defect, or mistake originated, where it is likely to be cheaper and easier to fix.

- Both techniques are effective at eliminating the blame game, and reducing the stress, anxiety, and "ask reluctance" so common to people doing fundraising work.

- Adopting the skills of continuous improvement reduces the temptation to jump into ill-considered and potentially costly tactics such as running too many events.

WHAT YOU CAN DO

- Set simple and achievable targets for your next review meeting.
- Guide the team through the last two steps of the PDCA cycle, Check and Act. You completed the Plan stage by assigning targets, and the Do stage by recording the data and producing reports. Now conduct the Check stage, with a group discussion about what did or didn't work.
- Proceed to the Act stage, after deciding what changes to the plan, if any, the group would like to make. Assign someone to be accountable for making the changes, but don't let them do the work during the review meeting. Delegate them to do it outside the meeting.
- Guide the team to use root-cause analysis. During the first meeting, you may simply want to introduce the model, drawing it up on a whiteboard or flip chart, then test for understanding by discussion.
- Choose a clear, simple problem. The clearer and simpler, the more effective your analysis will be.
- Consider each input category and subcategory in turn to identify the earliest point in the process where the "root" of the problem first emerged. Follow the guidelines included in this chapter.
- Come to group consensus to choose the cause and implement an improvement initiative suggested by the team, if any. If the initiative falls within the span of control of the development shop, take steps to pursue it without further ado.
- If the root cause lies in the areas of operational considerations or external market conditions, determine the most diplomatic, business-like way to describe the problem and its impact to the responsible executive. If you're uncomfortable doing so or if by doing so you cross internal boundaries and need to confront a more senior executive, by all means recruit the support of your supervisor, director, or senior leaders.

CHAPTER 9

Applying SMART Way Methods to Mass-Market Fundraising

Throughout this book, I have advocated for the adoption of scientific management disciplines more common to the for-profit world, to improve fundraising performance. My mission is to adapt some of the most beneficial and impactful tools developed in the for-profit sector, so that they can and will be used with similar enthusiasm to improve the capacity and mission achievement of the nonprofit industry. While it would be simplistic to say that nonprofits are completely unlike for-profits, and equally simplistic to say that they are entirely alike, there is no escaping the fact that the underlying disciplines of quality management, process management, and greatness, as described by Jim Collins in his monograph *Good to Great and the Social Sectors*[1], apply just as well to both sectors.

Regrettably, the data suggest that these disciplines have not yet become standard nonprofit operating procedure, to the detriment of the industry.

Mass-market fundraising employs all the techniques familiar to consumer marketing: advertising, e-mail marketing, search-engine optimization, lead tracking, lead nurturing, and related methods. The feedback derived from these techniques collates information about the words, phrases, campaigns, and techniques that worked well, which didn't, and which group of prospects was more likely to respond to this versus that. It touches the largest amount of prospects at the best cost/benefit ratio per touch. Mass-market fundraising

---

[1] Jim Collins, Good to Great and the Social Sector: A Monograph to Accompany Good to Great. © 2005. HarperCollins Publishers Inc., New York.

achieves favorable cost/benefit outcomes at least in part because it relies on automated techniques that far outpace the human capacity to remember the data, record it, and put together reports on it. Where you could get insights and feedback from maybe 5 or 10 people a week, your automated technology can handle feedback from tens of thousands of people a day, collate it in fractions of a second, and give it back to you in formats you can understand.

Because of the way mass-market fundraising works, it could be the bridge to the adoption of business disciplines that drive continuous improvement. Before we get into the details here, let me first draw a distinction between what I'm calling mass-market fundraising and the kind of fundraising required to acquire major donors and major gifts, by describing the difference between major-account sales and transactional or mass-market selling.

SELLING TO MAJOR ACCOUNTS VERSUS TRANSACTIONAL SELLING

You participate in transactional selling every time you go to the grocery store. Transactional purchases are the kind made daily by consumers. It doesn't matter much if you're buying toothpaste at the supermarket, ordering a book from Amazon, or picking up a carton of copy paper from Staples; in every case you make a transactional purchase. Your purchase doesn't cost the retailer much money. Of course, the retailer needs to make many such sales to make a profit, because retail profit margins tend to be razor thin.

There are at least two selling layers behind your point-of-sale purchase. Before you picked up your toothpaste, a wholesaler sold pallet-loads of that toothpaste to the supermarket's purchasing agent. The cost of selling that pallet-load will be higher, but so will the price and the profit margin. Behind *that* sale, the manufacturer made an even larger sale to the wholesaler.

As a transactional buyer, you just want a tube of toothpaste, preferably at a decent price. The supermarket chain doesn't send salespeople to your house to discuss your toothpaste preferences. They figure out your preferences ahead of time using sophisticated marketing techniques. These techniques provide psychological insights to develop the advertising that gets you into their stores. If it's a consumer product like toothpaste, the manufacturer probably shares some of the costs for conducting the analysis and doing the advertising.

Procter & Gamble won't know if you bought your tube of Crest at the Kroger down the street yesterday because you saw that ad on daytime TV the day before. But all that marketing and advertising, data from past purchasing patterns, and all sorts of other data on buying habits, produces a demonstrated impact on your decision to buy Crest rather than Colgate. Advertisers have been using statistical data and psychological research about decision making for decades, since long before the advent of electronic marketing. Electronic or interactive marketing has changed the playing field by making this information available to every business no matter how small, automatically, at very low costs. And guess what. All that science and discipline pays off handsomely in profits and satisfied customers.

Now let's talk about the major-account seller. The wholesale distributor *does,* in fact, send out that fleet of salespeople to call on the supermarket chain's purchasing agents. Well, to be correct, most of those salespeople work the phones; they don't drive around as much anymore. The wholesaler's salespeople sell in large quantities. They pay attention to the supermarket's purchasing power; the more the supermarket can purchase at any given time, the lower the price per unit. There are also lots of conditions to be met around delivery-time windows and other esoteric stuff that matter a lot to the supermarket because they affect net profit margin, all of which makes it easy for you to buy your favorite brand of toothpaste.

Behind the wholesaler's business, the manufacturer deploys even more sophisticated selling methods. Their salespeople actually *do* get out on the road, visiting with the wholesalers and in some cases directly with the larger chains. Those salespeople, who may be called major-account, national-account, or even global-account managers, act as consultants and advisers to their clients, seeking to understand and align with their needs and preferences, learning how they measure success, and creating close, reciprocal relationships to achieve long-term customer retention and high lifetime customer value. Their conversations with these major-account buyers have little to do with the technical nature of the product, and lots more to do with the impact the relationship will have on the buyer. (Major-gift officers: does this sound familiar?)

Sales professionals who specialize in this type of selling may make only a few sales in the course of a year, but each one is large, producing significant amounts of revenue. These salespeople earn lots of money from base salary and commissions, and they deserve it.[2] The work they do is mentally and physically strenuous, requiring lengthy preparation, professional development, skill, confidence, and the ability to tolerate rejection and uncertainty.

They also know that if transactional sales do not take place at the desired level and frequency, they will find it more difficult to justify the next major sale in the first place. After all, why would Kroger buy a million tubes of Crest if they're not convinced a million consumers will buy them? Directly or indirectly, successful major-account sales rely on the foundation of successful transactional sales.

THE MAJORS VERSUS THE MINORS

Fundraising 101: many small gifts where the cost of acquiring them is spread out over many people; a few large gifts where the cost of acquiring them is notable but the return on effort (ROE) is worth it. Major gift work brings in the big gifts; mass-market fundraising brings in all the people who want to "buy" your particular brand of "toothpaste."

The SMART Way™ model is a great fit for fundraising in the major category—major donors, major gifts, major grants, and super-sized corporate sponsorships. Just like major-account selling, the long-term value of these funding sources provides a justifiable return on the big investment required to identify those jumbo gifts that can take years to cultivate. It makes sense to fill out a Prospect Scorecard for such funders and track the potential gift through the Donor Moves process, a level of effort that's not justified for every single $5 gift.

Just as with major-account salespeople, development officers who specialize in major-level funding work extremely hard. It takes them a comparable amount of skill, training, experience, confidence, willingness to work without a net, ability to tolerate rejection, and so on. They deserve to be paid well for such lonely and difficult work. But, also, just like major-account salespeople, major-gift officers benefit directly and indirectly from the work done to acquire small to midsized gifts from small to midsized funders. You could say that successful major-gift programs rest on a foundation of small and midsized gifts.

---

[2] Wouldn't it be great if major-gift officers could earn similar incomes? See Dan Pallotta's remarkable book *Uncharitable* for more discussion on this theme.

Ever since GivingUSA began publishing its annual report on U.S. charitable giving in the early 1970s, individual giving has provided the largest proportion of all donations to all charities, ranging from about 81 percent in 1973 to about 71 percent in 2012, the last year for which figures are available. Note that the decline in the proportion of individual giving does not reflect an absolute decline in giving; other sources, such as foundations and corporate contributions, grew in proportion. The Giving USA 2013 Annual Report on Philanthropy shows that considerable amounts of giving came in the form of large gifts, ranging in size from the $1 million given by Lady Gaga to support Hurricane Sandy relief, to investor Warren Buffett's annual billion-dollar-plus gift to the Gates Foundation. These "mega-gifts" produce a significant proportion of overall charitable income, but they are few in number. The report actually lists each of these super-gigantic gifts in one of its tables.

These gifts and the donors who make them are obviously "major," and therefore justify the effort and expense of major-account marketing, cultivation, solicitation, and stewardship. The cost of this work is significant, so the gift officer needs to be reasonably certain that the gift, and subsequent gifts from the major donor, will be large enough to offer decent ROE.

Small and medium-sized gifts outnumber major gifts. Direct-appeal campaigns produce relatively modest size gifts from online donations, ticket sales for special events, and the annual appeal. They're transactional. Many such donations, especially the first gifts from a donor, are like "impulse buys"—you were inspired by the flyer or the text message and clicked the "yes" button to have $5 transferred from your account to the annual walk. The cost of the mass marketing—the postcard campaign, e-newsletter, and web site upgrades and maintenance—may carry what looks like a big price tag, but produces high ROE, by touching thousands of individuals and attracting many gifts at negligible costs per gift.

Growing Your Own Ideal Donors

The exchange of value between your nonprofit's value-added strengths, and your ideal (major) donor's value-sought is the source of the marketing language used to attract potential donors of all shapes and sizes. The value statements crafted into your Scorecard describe small donors as well as large. Therefore, all of your messaging is attractive to everyone who shares a passion for your mission, regardless of capacity for giving or willingness to give big today. Those who are attracted to your value exchange may start out by giving a few dollars to a text-messaging campaign, but they can grow up into major funders if you cultivate them properly.

A core tenet of the SMART Way philosophy is that *every* donor you cultivate has the potential to become an ideal donor because each one will share your values—a passion for your mission and an appreciation of your programs and services. Each one will be moved by the same messaging that moves your major funders; they just can't, or aren't ready, to give you the big bucks.

To Find Donors, Stop Looking

Inexperienced nonprofit executives, such as the founder–executive directors of grassroots organizations, often tell me that they don't know how to "find" donors. They get desperate and may make poor decisions, such as forgoing salary or health benefits, throwing themselves on the mercy of the "usual suspects," the biggest local philanthropists or corporations, without doing much research, or running special events without considering the hard and soft costs of such events.

> **IMPORTANT!**
>
> If you think you should "donate" your services as executive director because you can't raise enough money to pay yourself, please stop thinking that way. Remember, don't cut the budget; increase the income.

The SMART Way model and the use of effective inbound marketing techniques take the "finding donors" problem and turn it inside out. You don't find the donors anymore—they find you.

All the work you did in Part 1 helps the right donors find you before you even figure out the cost of postage for that direct-mail campaign you're planning. The technology you currently use to run your web site, social presence, and e-mail campaigns also gather so much insightful data automatically about your target audience that there's no meaningful excuse for *not* being able to "find" donor prospects.

The problem of finding donors is probably most prevalent and damaging in small start-ups and grassroots organizations. Your nonprofit might not have such problems, but I'd like to elaborate on the issue a bit because it's such a great example of the failure to embrace another set of business disciplines that could have a powerful, positive income on results, fund-raising and otherwise. These are the disciplines of inbound marketing.

Inbound Marketing

Inbound marketing refers to the broad scope of techniques and technology used to drive people to your nonprofit's electronic presence. They attract strangers to your site, social-media presence, and blog, who then convert themselves to visitors, leads, and customers. Strangers are first-time viewers; visitors are strangers who come back more than once; visitors become leads by taking some sort of action such as signing up for your blog; leads become customers, better known as donors, volunteers, candidates for board service or employment, and clients for your programs. All forms, links, or other ways to interact are instruments for "converting" visitors to higher levels of engagement.

Inbound marketing works two ways simultaneously. It attracts people to you while collecting data showing which words, phrases, and conversion forms were most productive, and which were least. Frequent review of Web analytics and other reports drives continuous improvement. Effective inbound marketing helps people to find you and converts them from cold to warm leads. They are "warm" because they have demonstrated their interest in your agency, cause, or programs by signing up. Virtually all of this work happens automatically. By the time you phone a person who reads your newsletters, "likes" your project on Facebook, attends the annual picnic, and gives small gifts online, he or she has built a relationship with you and your nonprofit. Those people don't say, "Go away, kid, you bother me" when you call. They're more likely to say, "I'm so glad you called!"

Now, before you can conduct inbound marketing, you have to know quite a few things about the audience you're attempting to attract. Who's most likely to want to be involved with your charity? What are they searching for when they do a Google search looking for a charity? What words, phrases, terms, and concepts capture their imaginations? What calls to action are most likely to get a response?

The rigorous analysis you completed in Chapters 1 through 4 has already told you the answers. Leverage this information throughout your inbound marketing. You already know:

- How to articulate your agency's value-added strengths, which describe what makes your nonprofit worth raising money for in the first place.
- How to describe your best funders' value-sought, the charitable motivations, philosophy, personal experiences, and so on, that motivate them to seek opportunities to give to charity.
- The exchange of value between your agency's value-added and your ideal donor's value-sought.
- Which value statements are most likely to motivate major funders to take action.
- Which probing questions are most likely to uncover the funder's charitable motivations, philosophy, and preferences.

Developing such insights is a discipline of greatness. It's not simply good for commercial business ventures or for the nonprofit sector as a whole. Any venture committed to providing betterment to its audience should know such information, whether you define betterment as a new car for your wife or the reduction of the homeless population in your community.

It's not within the scope of this book to teach you the techniques of inbound marketing; you can learn the how-to's from many sources, including your 22-year-old VISTA volunteer. Millennials speak inbound marketing fluently. And five minutes on Google will help you find dozens of experts offering help in branding, search-engine optimization, lead-nurturing campaigns, and the entire panoply of interactive marketing techniques that have proven so effective for the for-profit world in the past few years.

What is within the scope, however, is the exhortation to figure out what will persuade your target market to seek you out. And inbound marketing provides such plentiful, accurate, and testable ways to do so, you would make a big mistake if you failed to take advantage of it.

Reciprocal and Interdependent

To implement Fundraising the SMART Way, you conducted interviews to find the words, phrases, and other key concepts used by, and therefore attractive to, your best funding sources. You also devised a number of metrics and reporting methods that show you where you're getting desirable results and where you're getting undesirable ones. You pull reports and analyze them on a regular basis to identify opportunities for improvement.

Inbound marketing techniques are tightly aligned with the SMART Way philosophy. They ratchet up the amount of available data derived from your constituents to a granular level, detailing the effectiveness of words, phrases, conversion forms, marketing messages, campaign tactics and so on, at a level impossible to achieve the old-fashioned way of one phone call or personal visit at a time. Inbound marketing is a self-correcting mechanism:

- First, you interview a few current donors and other supporters to find out how they describe their interest in your nonprofit. This is "human" work; you've got to do it one live person at a time.
- Then you validate the keywords and terms they used, by evaluating the frequency of their use, then using keyword suggestion tools and other technologies. You're looking for the phrases used most commonly, either the same phrases used by your interviewees, or equivalent terms. This is also human work, but now you are "having a conversation" with automated technology.
- Next, integrate these terms into your electronic content, including web site copy, blog and social-media postings, e-newsletter articles and titles, YouTube videos, and the like. This part of it is where you combine science with art. More human work; somebody has to write up the content.
- Now engineer some calls to action in these outbound messages. A call to action invites the reader to do something that shows interest. It might be as simple as "subscribe to our newsletter" or as complex as "register here to participate in creating the community garden! A gift of $10 will purchase seeds for one crop for an entire season." A little more human work goes into preparing this stuff.
- Finally, pull reports from the analytical tools available on your site, blog, or e-newsletter. Every one of these media gathers such analytical data. Now, it's NHI—No Humans Involved.

If you don't have the initial data, you can't leverage the technology. If you can't leverage the technology, you won't be able to validate, refine, or update the data (messaging).

It's not an option to have one without the other.

Doing the Work

You have to work inbound marketing to reap its benefits. You simply have to put in the time to learn the skills and create the lead nurturing. It doesn't usually cost all that much to acquire the software applications, and many of them are free, but you have to use them diligently to get results. You won't have much of a following on Facebook, for example, if you don't update frequently. The subscription list for your blog will remain tiny if you don't send out blogs every week or so. The real cost of these tools is not the ticket price, it's the hours of effort required. If you don't know how to use them, or if updating them is a poor use of your time, for heaven's sake, hire somebody to do it for you. There are lots of people who can do the work for you, often at great (low) prices.

The more you work it, the larger your following, and the more insightful your reports become. All those people who follow you in the social stream, read your newsletters, and comment on your blog become your Move Zero database, the list of potential donors who have declared their interest.

Once you've got a following, you can sort them into smaller groups based on the calls to action to which they respond. If you have 1,000 subscribers, and 200 of them clicked on the link to view the pets currently up for adoption at your no-kill animal shelter, then those 200 ought to get invited to the dog-adoption fair you're holding next month. The ones who didn't sign up for the party will get additional direct appeals, but the ones who accepted, showed up, and then adopted a dog have now declared themselves qualified for a personal interaction of some kind.

This flow chart was originally designed to demonstrate the use of inbound marketing to cultivate customers. Simply change the word *customers* to *funders,* and it fits perfectly for the nonprofit sector. Apply a different set of inbound-marketing methods to attract strangers to your web site, while others are more effective at converting them to visitors, leads, funders, and sources of referral or "promoters." These concepts hold true, regardless of the web site platform you employ to maintain your site.

People continue to tell me they don't have the time to do social media (or e-mail marketing, lead nurturing, or search-engine optimization) or they "tried it once" and "it didn't work." If your nonprofit doesn't need any more money to serve clients, run programs, pay staff, and keep the lights on, then that strategy will work just fine. But if you have decided to

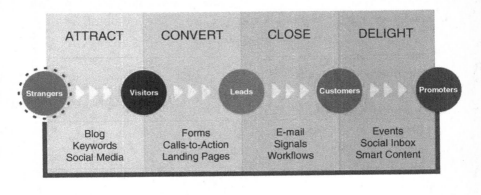

EXHIBIT 9.1   **THE INBOUND MARKETING EVOLUTION**
Source: © 2013 HubSpot, Inc.

revolutionize your fundraising performance, then you must master these skills and techniques, and give them time to work for you.

The "Go-to-Market" Strategy

Go-to-market strategies are another for-profit discipline that could have a powerful positive impact on the nonprofit sector, but they also seem to be underused or, worse, unknown.

The go-to-market strategy refers to the various channels a company will use to connect with its customers and the organizational processes it develops to guide prospect/customer interactions from initial contact through fulfillment. As the owner of a for-profit business, I spend a lot of time thinking about our go-to-market strategies, as does virtually every other for-profit executive in sales, marketing, and even product development. In big corporations, there are whole armies of people devoted to developing and refining these strategies.

Yet I have never heard a single nonprofit executive use the term or refer to the concept, including the marketing people who work for performing arts companies, where ticket sales play such an important role. If I'm wrong about this, please let me know by e-mail, Facebook, LinkedIn, or Twitter; you'll find all my contact information at the back of the book. I'd really love to be proven wrong on this one.

Instead, I see a great deal of pointless milling about, bumping into walls, tossing around tactics. Instead of saying, "What's the best way to gain mindshare or market awareness," they say, "Let's get referrals from our board members; they'll know the right people." But how many board members actually produce those referrals? "Not too many" is a more accurate answer than "Oh, all of them!" Let's not even bother to mention the well-intentioned special events, garage sales, auctions, and so on.

In the for-profit world, go-to-market strategies play a critical role in the successful sale of the company's products and services. They are used to announce a company's presence in the market, introduce a new product or upgraded version thereof, and other methods of bringing the company's products and services to the attention of the target audience. What's key to go-to-market strategies isn't just the tactical (do this, that, and the other), but the feedback from the target audience. Automated strategies have the capacity to gather statistically significant amounts of data that are later used to drive future sales.

Mass-market fundraising techniques can be used brilliantly to deliver similar levels of meaningful data to capture the attention of more and more individuals who share your nonprofit's values and want to support your mission and programs. The use of automated methods, such as those of inbound marketing, give you insights you can't get otherwise and since they're self-correcting, your results get better and better over time.

MASS-MARKET AND TARGET-MARKET FUNDRAISING

Mass-market fundraising tactics include the broadest, least selective techniques aimed at a larger target audience. If you decided to purchase or rent a list from a list broker to use for a direct-appeal campaign, your search criteria would most likely be limited to a relatively broad set of criteria such as the classic demographics of age, gender, level of income, and zip code. You would probably also want to include more specific criteria such as level of annual charitable giving. The messaging you'll use must appeal to the broadest base of constituents possible. Typical mass-market campaign tactics include:

- The annual appeal campaign, where you ask everybody on the list to give at a modest level.

- The "special" appeal campaign, where you ask everybody on the list to support a particular program or serve a particular group of individuals.
- Online donations pages.
- Text messaging campaigns, where you ask as many people as possible to donate money (often tiny amounts like $5) using their mobile phones.
- Special events, especially those that do not require formal attire. These would include town hall meetings, picnics, fairs, athletic events such as the "Corporate Run," and the like, where you ask as many people as possible to show up, join the race, and so on in exchange for a donation or pledge.

Target-market fundraising may use those very same campaign tactics, but now the messaging must be more specific and the anticipated returns (donations) will be larger. If you have a special campaign to recruit sponsors and exhibitors to participate in your annual walk-a-thon, you'll use target-market techniques. These techniques pitch the same campaign, but the messaging is considerably more targeted ("If you'll sponsor our Annual Pillow Fight, you'll get your name out in front of 4,000 new people in just one day!") Where the attendee might shell out $10 to attend the pillow fight, the presenting sponsor might give you $5,000, and exhibitors would probably pay $500 or more just for the privilege of advertising their wares.

Target marketing is also achieved by the technique of lead nurturing, another automated technology. Lead-nurturing campaigns start out by drawing the prospect in through keywords and other messages, then converting those same prospects to more specific campaigns. For example, let's say you publish your e-newsletter this week, and it includes references to two events you're planning, the Doggy Adoption Day you're holding next month at the county park, and the mobile pet neutering program that is slated to start this coming January. Your newsletter contains a link to register for the adoption day, and another link to get more information on supporting the neutering program.

I read your shelter's newsletter, and since I've decided to get myself a dog, I register for the adoption day. My next-door neighbor likes cats, not dogs, and she's passionate about getting feral cats neutered, so she signs up to get more information about that program. As soon as I raised my hand about the Doggy Adoption Day, the magic automated inbound marketing elves prepared a series of messages drawing me closer to the agency, before and after the event. Meanwhile, my neighbor receives a series of messages about her interests. Over time, these messages convince me to make an annual gift to the shelter, and convince my neighbor to become a volunteer team captain in the project to find and neuter feral cats throughout her community. Eventually, she's invited to serve on their governing board. She ends up leaving a portion of her estate to the shelter.

Mass-market and target-market fundraising are mission-critical fundraising techniques; they bring in billions of dollars a year for U.S. charities. But they have additional benefits that might not be so obvious. They'll help validate your Scorecards and improve their accuracy through the use of Web analytics and other data-gathering techniques. They'll make it easy for you to nurture those who have declared their interest in your nonprofit, but who are not yet ready, willing, or able to participate at a higher level. They give you data useful for continuous improvement.

Best of all, they bring you the "embryonic" donors, volunteers, and others whom you want to bring along through babyhood (initial gifts) through adolescence (regular gifts growing in size over time) all the way to grown-ups (major donors and givers of estates and bequests).

SMART Way Management Controls

The management controls fundamental to the SMART Way approach have a beneficial impact on mass-market fundraising. To begin with, the Scorecard defines donor criteria using objective criteria and standards. These standards allow you to control or raise the accuracy of your messaging so it attracts the right donors. It's also easy to establish measurable performance indicators for mass- and target-marketing campaigns, knowing that the establishment and careful tracking of such indicators drives continuous improvement. Here are a few examples of indicators that could be used to track the performance of any small-gift appeal, campaign, or event, such as:

- Total number of new names added to the invitation/subscription list.
- Number of new-name attendees.
- Number of returning attendees.
- Number of new corporate sponsors or exhibitors.
- Number of returning corporate sponsors or exhibitors.

And let's not forget some other, more specialized metrics. If you want to convert some of your minor donors to giving at a higher level, a good performance indicator might be "number of times a board member or senior executive engages a new event attendee in conversation," or "number of follow-up calls or visits made by peer solicitors."

And, of course, your technology has been doing a great job all along, keeping track of every time a smaller donor clicked on a link, made another gift, raised their level of giving, or stopped giving for more than so many years. If a for-profit company can send you a "we miss you" message after six months, give you an update about new products and services, and maybe even an incentive to buy again, why can't your charity do something similar?

Embracing the Next Generation(s)

A final comment about age diversity is in order before we end this chapter. For many years, most major donors have been members of the so-called *traditional generation,* a term referring to people born before or around the end of World War II. The youngest of these people are now entering their seventies. Although they have been the major target for major-gift work, they're no longer a "sustainable" market; they're dying off, and the Baby Boomers, born after the end of WWII, are approaching retirement age. Now let's factor in the huge cultural chasms that exist between Traditionals and Baby Boomers, Boomers and Generation X, and Generation X and Millennials. The cultural icons, messages, types of special events, and forms of charitable giving that work for Traditionals are so different from those that appeal, say, to Millennials, that they might as well be from different planets. Traditionals hand-write their messages; Millennials consider e-mail an extinct form of communication, preferring the text message and the tweet.

Woe unto your development efforts if you fail to take these diverse cultural attitudes and communications preferences into account. What works for one group could, and probably will, backfire for another. The donating community is going to change more frequently, and in more dramatic ways, at an accelerating pace over the next couple of decades. If you want your nonprofit to survive, be prepared to absorb that change.

Your mass-market fundraising strategies make up the "platform" for understanding such differences, deriving accurate perspectives on communications preferences and methods of engaging cultural differences. Use it often, but use it wisely and well.

WHAT WE COVERED

- Mass-market fundraising, and its first cousin target-market fundraising, provide two benefits simultaneously. They allow you to reach the most potential supporters at the least cost per touch, and they automatically collect data and provide analytical feedback reports that help you refine and improve the accuracy of your messaging and funder-selection strategies.

- Mass-market fundraising is the incubator for major-gift work. The value statements built into your Scorecards will work for all donors regardless of giving capacity or willingness to give. Once you gain the attention and engagement of an individual who shares a passion for your mission, use low-cost, automated techniques over time to "evolve" that small, entry-level donor into a major giver, peer solicitor, or even a board member.

- The proper, effective use of automated inbound marketing techniques means that potential donors find you. You don't have to look for them. Or at least you don't have to spend as much time and money looking for them.

- Mass-market fundraising must be tailored to the cultural norms and communications preferences for each major age cohort. What moves Traditionals to take charitable action might not work for Millennials and vice versa.

WHAT YOU CAN DO

- Review the interviews you conducted with donors and board members, looking for commonly used words, phrases, and concepts. Conduct keyword research to determine which of these words or phrases is most likely to be persuasive, and consider the use of more powerful alternatives if the original content doesn't make the grade.

- Work with your IT department or an outside marketing expert to craft web site, e-newsletter, and blog content rich in the use of these keywords and phrases. Lock them into your web site. Send out newsletters, blogs, and other messages using the keywords.

- Scrutinize Web analytics reports and other feedback from your marketing technology; use it to suggest ways to improve content, calls to action, inbound links, and so on. If you don't know how to do this, get outside help—now.

- Develop lead-nurturing strategies. Use them.

- Review mass-market performance as often as you review major-gift performance. Add ways to track the evolution of donors from small to mid-level to major.

CHAPTER 10

Radical Thinking about the Fundraising Revolution

For too long, the fundraising discipline has been more art than science. Art is great in its place, especially when we define it the classical way, as a trade or craft utilizing a system of principles and methods, like "the art of winemaking."[1] Here's the problem of relying on art: it can take decades of practice and experience, preferably under the mentorship of others who have already accrued similar experience, to be any good at it. That's probably the best way to become a great bassoonist, ceramic artist, or ballet dancer, but it doesn't work very well in business.

Business, be it for-profit or not-for-profit, is no longer willing to support such long apprenticeships. The profit margins simply aren't there. And in a nonprofit world where the infamous overhead ratio continues to hold sway, few organizations are willing to tolerate the cost of paying unseasoned development officers (higher overhead costs, right?) if they can't raise three times their salary—by next Thursday, please.

Since there are only so many fundraisers left with 40 years of "art" under their belts, and since most of them will probably hang up their cleats in the next few years, now what do we do?

Now we add some science to the mix. It's management science, fortunately, not astrophysics or string theory, which is good; for the most part, management science is easy to understand and adopt. Everything we've discussed in this book has been based on methods of management science that

---

[1] www.thefreedictionary.com/art

have been field-tested for over 50 years. Simple things like adding documented qualifying criteria, leading as well as trailing indicators, performance targets, and success measures can have a powerful positive impact. Advocates of such management control can attest that the use of these scientific mechanisms doesn't simply save time or money. It also brings about innovations and breakthroughs that might never have come to light otherwise.

A few examples of the scarcity of management disciplines in fundraising may suffice. See if these comments sound familiar:

- "People just aren't interested in our cause."
- "Our organization has been operating for 20 years, but we never know if we're going to make budget or not."
- "We need more money, but our board just won't help us raise it."
- "Why should we use e-mail or social media for marketing? Our donors don't like technology."

These are just a few of the thousand-and-one self-defeating comments I hear from nonprofit executives, over and over. I've heard them regularly over my 20 years serving nonprofit organizations, and would really like *not* to hear them for the next 20, but unless the nonprofit industry decides to reexamine and reinvent the way it funds itself, I fear that I might.

By contrast, let's pretend for a moment that you are the chief sales officer of a well-managed for-profit company, and you hear sales versions of the preceding comments. How would you respond? I can tell you, you wouldn't respond by throwing up your hands and saying, "That's just the way it is," or even "try harder." You'd be more likely to respond like this:

- *"People just aren't interested in our products."* "Well, let's create interest! Let's create a market! Who on our marketing team is the best at creating interest?"
- *"We've been operating for 20 years, but we never know if we're going to make budget or not."* "Hmm, let's improve our strategic and sales-planning processes. Let's also find out if our accounting software meets our needs. Maybe we need to recruit a better chief financial officer, too."
- *"We need more money, but our board just wants us to cut costs."* "Wait a minute. We've already got a decent sales staff, support team, and sales-force automation; how can we work with them differently to get better results at the same or lower costs?"

- *"We don't use e-mail marketing or social media. Why should we? Our customers don't like technology."* "Let's try it anyway. There are data out there proving those technologies help, even with customers like ours. Let's find some good, forward-thinking marketing professionals and get their advice."

Do all businesses use such enlightened methods? No, of course they don't. But they don't simply surrender to poor sales performance either. They make efforts to change. They invest money. They market and advertise. They recruit better salespeople, train them, coach them, and equip them with good technology and effective methodology. The best businesses invest heavily to improve the way their organizations operate, and then strive to adopt the habits of greatness.[2] Effective for-profit companies operate with the mind-set of growth and potential, where poor or undesirable performance triggers purposeful efforts to improve, not simply self-flagellation.

Speaking very broadly, nonprofit organizations are more likely to apply continuous improvement techniques to their programming, and only their programming, long before they'll apply it to the ways they manage the fundraising function. Somehow, fundraising has to do better all by itself, without the benefit of tools, metrics, or even much attention from management, unless you count negative attention ("what-have-you-done-for-me-lately"). Thus, fundraising operates, and will continue to operate, with a mind-set of constraint or limitation, status quo, and cost avoidance. Ironically, this mind-set has produced fundraising practices where poor productivity is *built in.* In other words, we're managing the development function to make sure it will lose money.

IMPORTANT!

Running your fundraising shop with a mindset of constraint, limitation, status quo, and cost avoidance builds poor productivity into the effort.

While senior management and the governing board certainly would like to raise more money, they burden their fundraising staffs with practices that are wasteful, even counterproductive. The lack of metrics, guidelines,

---

[2] Jim Collins, *Good to Great: Why Some Companies Make the Leap . . . and Others Don't* (New York: HarperCollins, 2001).

benchmarks, and reporting methods pushes the development team to rely on tactics, swapping out one tactic for another out of desperation or relying on the accidental talents of the 40-year veteran fundraiser you've managed to keep on the payroll. That's pretty much like putting a nerdy 12-year-old in the boxing ring with Evander Holyfield and then punishing the poor kid when he loses the round.

In the discipline of fundraising, we must change the mind-set of limitations and cost avoidance to the mind-set of potential. If we nonprofit people fail to challenge the prevailing mind-set, we're in trouble—trouble that will grow worse, not better.

Time for Radical Thinking

There's certainly evidence that our industry is becoming more professional, although there is a long way to go. On the bright side, we've seen a significant increase in graduate schools offering degrees in nonprofit management. As recently as July 2012, Seton Hall University identified 331 different graduate schools doing so. There has also been a corresponding proliferation of software applications, training programs, books about nonprofit issues, consulting practices, expert services, and so on. Those increases are useful signals that the market for the discipline in question is growing. These advances are good leading indicators suggesting, one hopes, that down the road practitioners will be better equipped.

My concern is that, in spite of such proliferation, development shops still aren't getting better or different results.

Available research continues to demonstrate a significant gap between the real and the ideal, which is where we opened this book. AFP's Fundraising Effectiveness Project, Giving USA's Annual Report on Charitable Giving, and our own Leaky Bucket study show troubling evidence: flat or declining levels of income and size of donor base, failure to define or use metrics, and other methods for managing development performance; all of which paint a picture of an industry in trouble.

Now if the industry in question were the makers of typewriters or vinyl LPs or whalebone corsets, we might simply say "the market has disappeared" and move on.

But the "market" for human services, education, behavioral health, medical research, habitat conservation, sea-level rise, the disappearance of Arctic ice and the preservation of musical instruments of the Renaissance isn't going away anytime soon. Market demand for these "products" of the nonprofit industry is growing, not shrinking. A growing market with a declining funding stream? That's not only a troubling picture; it violates basic rules of the market-driven economy, which is all about demand and supply. In the market economy, when demand is up, suppliers thrive. By the way, that's the same economy in which nonprofits operate. If demand for our programs and services is up, yet we can't fund the "supply" side, what are we doing? Cui bono?

It's time for us to answer the question that Lenin so famously posed back in 1902, the one that led to the Russian Revolution: "What is to be done?"

FUNDRAISING AND THE RUSSIAN REVOLUTION

Lenin wanted to depose the czarist regime and provide better economic conditions for the Russian people, mostly serfs living in grinding poverty, without any rights to property or even, in some cases, to their own lives. Talk about the need for human services! Too bad the Russian Revolution was such a bloody mess. There are varying opinions as to whether it succeeded in its aims of redistributing wealth and providing equality of opportunity.

The Fundraising Revolution I envision is a bloodless one, with more benevolent, lasting outcomes. It will facilitate ways for the nonprofit sector to build more sustainable organizations, organizations that enjoy more predictable, consistent financial support.

The tools of this revolution have been accepted and leveraged effectively for decades in the for-profit sector. They have improved working conditions for millions of workers. They have also produced phenomenal benefits for us consumers as well. Without the disciplines of continuous improvement, you and I would not own smartphones or tablets. It took decades of continuous improvement in information technology to create these tiny, relatively inexpensive devices, which have more computing power than the mainframes of the 1980s and 1990s, and far less likelihood of component failure.

It might seem as if smartphones just somehow sprang into being overnight, but in reality their origins go back at least 60 years, to the time of the first computers around the end of World War II. Those puppies were enormous, hugely expensive, difficult to operate without all kinds of specialized training, and prone to component failure. In fact, one of the places we first saw the emergence of Six Sigma was in the manufacturing of computer chips. Six Sigma is the level of quality management that reduces failure rates to about 3.4 in 1 million opportunities. That means if you make a million computer chips, you'll only have three or four that don't work and have to be thrown away. Imagine the amount of time, money, and lost-opportunity cost saved by such rigorous management. These advances in quality management drove the cost of computer power down, down, down to the point where we have miniature gadgets almost anyone can afford that do more than the old mainframe could do.

So why not use these same techniques to improve fundraising results? Why not develop quality management techniques that improve the fund-raiser's success rate from 1 donor out of 10 prospects to 1 out of 1.5? Why not reduce the costs of engaging those donors from the hundred-plus dollars you'd probably spend to get them to attend your luncheon, down to the pennies it costs to get that donor to "like" you on Facebook?

Think about it. Imagine how great it would be if you could raise much more money, with much less effort. That's the revolution I'm talking about, a revolution in the way we manage and control fundraising efforts that just might produce revolutions in the ways we serve the greater good.

Overthrowing the Status Quo

Revolution, however, implies some serious overthrowing somewhere in the mix. In political revolutions, it's usually the current government that's being overthrown, often with a lot of bloodshed. In the fundraising revolution, we don't need to overthrow the government, fortunately, although we might just need to tackle some notions held by the governing board. And let's trust that the bloodshed will be limited to the occasional paper cut.

In our case, the "overthrowing" part has more to do with overthrowing traditional cultural constraints. Cultural constraints are more or less invisible to the user. Anthropology teaches us that what is natural, comfortable, correct, or civilized to us will often seem incorrect, wrong, unnatural, uneducated, barbaric, or worse to those from other cultures. And vice versa. Did you know that in some parts of highland New Guinea, it's considered impolite to wipe your nose when it's running?

The "art" of fundraising needs to be rethought and rebuilt on a basis of effective management science. Long-standing traditions and cultural constraints have produced a discipline with big ambitions and enormous responsibilities, operating on an unstable foundation, which:

- Throws tactics—events, grant applications, on-line auctions, you name it—at the problem, without considering the true costs of those tactics.
- Fails to use undesirable results as a way to trigger deeper learning and continuous improvements.
- Assumes that staying abreast of rapid changes in communications technology is of low priority.
- Concentrates on a population of donors—the so-called "traditionals" aged 65 and older—that's literally dying off, but fails to reconfigure its methods to attract younger populations.
- Doesn't entirely understand the value of establishing, documenting, and tracking performance against effective metrics and therefore either ignores metrics altogether, or uses metrics that are obscure or nondiagnostic.
- Violently eschews the notion of performance incentives such as commissions to reward and motivate its best producers.

Each of these examples represents a "leak" of fundraising productivity. You can plug these leaks by simply reversing the conventional wisdom:

- Welcome the evidence of undesirable fundraising results, since these demonstrate the need for improvement initiatives.
- Stay abreast of evolving communication technologies; master and leverage them to drive further improvements.
- Embrace the communications preferences of a broad range of cohorts, whether they differ due to age, gender, levels of education, or ethnicity. The marketing and advertising industries already have the data, so we don't have to do the original research on what makes people tick.
- Adopt performance metrics. Use them.

And as far as commissions are concerned, even people who are deeply mission driven are, at least to some extent, "coin operated." Commissions and other financial incentives tend to be motivating to high-performing salespeople. However, the Ethical Guidelines of the Association of Fundraising Professionals declare that financial incentives are inappropriate for development people. Although I have always complied with these guidelines and will continue to do so, I am starting to wonder if it's entirely appropriate *not* to give financial rewards to our best performers. Just like those major-account sales professionals, fundraising work is extremely difficult and ego demanding. How come development officers get the short end of the stick?

For my part, I'd prefer to see practitioners of the fundraising discipline expand their thinking about how and why they could improve results through the adoption and adaptation of the fundamental business practices provided by Fundraising the SMART Way™ or like models. Let's figure out how to bring in more money, from very well qualified and engaged donors, and make it a habit to analyze and interpret performance data for continuous improvement. It seems to me that embracing such habits would give us the data, the evidence to make a solid business case for changing the rules.

ADOPTING THE MIND-SET OF POTENTIAL

Brothers Chip and Dan Heath wrote a book called *Switch: How to Change Things When Change Is Hard,*[3] about converting from the so-called "fixed" mind-set to the "growth" mind-set. They say that the fixed mind-set is one of limitation, constraint, and loss of opportunity, while the growth mind-set is one of potential. I found one theme particularly impactful. The authors tell us that those with a growth mind-set are likely to welcome poor results, failing grades, and other disappointing evidence with delight because it inspires them to do better, take chances, experiment, and learn how to improve. Growth mind-set people interpret such evidence as a benefit, not as punishment.

In fundraising, we have perfected the fixed mind-set. If the only response to undesirable results is "throw another event," it's safe to assume that our development officers will (1) throw another event, even if they think it's a bad idea and (2) feel defeated because they're not really sure what they might have done better, or at least differently, that would have produced better results in the first place. The failure to provide effective management controls leaves performance *un*-managed.

Where the setting of quantifiable performance targets has never taken place, people simply do not know whether they're performing up to

---

[3] New York: Random House, 2010.

standards or not. The lack of documented performance expectations is a great example of the fixed mind-set.

Where the only performance indicator is cash in the door, our people never really know where they wasted time or effort. This is yet another instance of the fixed mind-set: you'll know you've done well just because you raised the money, but if you haven't raised the money, all you know is that you're a loser for failing to raise more dough. You won't be able to see where you might have gone astray earlier in the cycle.

Where there are no generally accepted criteria for prospect selection, our people may chase unqualified or under-qualified prospects, creating an increasingly unsatisfactory cost-benefit ratio. Yet another fixed mind-set: any old prospect will do as long as you stalk them long enough and win their donations by force; surely if you just bought one more lunch or made one more phone call or leveraged one more mutual friend, you could have brought in that gift.

Where prospects are acquired through personal obligation or because of the leader's charisma, our people may unknowingly contribute to low rates of donor retention. It's not uncommon to find donors who give because they "love the CEO" or because they have some obligation to the development officer or peer solicitor. Guess who follows the solicitor when he or she resigns from the board, retires, or quits.

REVOLUTIONIZING THE WAY WE MANAGE PERFORMANCE

Individuals with a mind-set of potential will often find ways to improve their own performance. But to impact the performance of an entire organization requires changes in the way that organization is led and managed. The fundraising revolution will not be complete, or even take place, unless we also revolutionize the way leaders lead the organization and managers manage it. To revolutionize the way we lead and manage fundraising performance, then, we need our leaders and managers to change the way they think about their organizations, obtain actual data on performance, interpret them, and engage their people in ways to bring about the improvements desired.

It's just not good enough for senior leadership or the governing board to tolerate the lack of transparency and accountability that currently plague the fund development discipline. It's not good enough to evaluate fundraising performance based solely on the trailing indicator of dollars in the door. It's certainly not good enough to ask your development staff to raise more money if they aren't sure why your organization deserves to be funded at all, much less at a higher level. Nor is it good enough to expect the development team to work as hard as they do, without the support, guidance, and feedback that comes from the use of thoughtful metrics and guidelines.

The first, most profound change must come from the very top of the organization and be expressed in its mission and core values. If the organization is worth raising funds for, then there are three pertinent questions for organizational leaders to ask:

- What have we designed our organization to accomplish?
- Are we accomplishing it, and how do we know?
- How much money *should* it cost us to accomplish it? In other words, are we spending enough?

These questions don't appear to be asked often enough. When it's time for the board to discuss money or approve next year's budget, the conversation tends to focus on bookkeeping minutiae and cost avoidance. Certainly, that's been the case in my personal experience, but there's also data to support my impression. After all, the Leaky Bucket study shows a minority of nonprofits tracking their overall income or income by funding category. If the organization's leadership doesn't even track income, how can they know if they're spending enough money, much less too much?

Leading the Revolution

I would like to issue a challenge to those who serve nonprofit organizations in a leadership capacity, asking them to rethink what leadership means. This may seem like a lofty goal for a mere methodology for sustainable fundraising, but it's not. If leaders' charge is to set direction and inspire others to follow, then the first task is to determine how the organization will go about changing the world, or at least their corner of it. To do so requires a willingness to do two things: challenge the vision of what the organization can accomplish; and seek evidence showing how far the organization may be, at any point in time, from fulfilling that vision.

The Leadership Techniques   Therefore, the first thing I challenge non-profit leaders to do is to *set aside enough time to consider the mission and vision of the organization regularly.* Effective leaders must review and reconsider this most strategic of issues, at length and without interruptions. Reviewing your purpose for 90 minutes at the annual board retreat is simply not enough time. In fact, one of the reasons governing boards exist at all is to provide regular opportunities to discuss high-level strategic issues such as the organization's ability to achieve its mission, or reasons to modify the mission based on new evidence. Unfortunately, few governing boards appear to honor and concentrate on such critical decisions, but that is the subject of an entirely different book.

Challenging the vision is not easy. Day-to-day working pressures can obscure it, and the endless stream of apparently urgent demands leaves little time to consider the deeper strategic issues, especially the ones your organization was originally founded to address. But if the leader is not devoting time to these big-picture issues, attention to detail can actually pull your organization off course, and quickly, too. Busy-ness is not only distracting; it's the enemy of strategic thinking.

The only way to devote sufficient time to such big, high-level, strategic issues is to devote the time. Period. Put the time on the calendar and make it sacrosanct. Unless you're actually giving birth or having a heart transplant, you simply have to hold those meetings and devote the right amount of time, making sure it's devoted to one thing and one thing only—how close are we to achieving our mission? If you don't devote at least an hour a month to this task, you're cheating yourself, but even worse, you're cheating the recipients of your organization's mission.

If you're really, really super-busy, then an hour a month isn't enough; raise it to an hour a week. If you think that's impossible because you're too busy, you're probably doing too much of the "doing" work, you're not delegating enough, or you need to hire more staff.

Now that you've set aside the time you need, what do you do with it? You assemble your key advisers, including other members of the senior leadership team. If you have a board that's willing and able, you bring them into the conversation, which means that you ought to devote the majority of all board-meeting time to strategic thinking, and relegate all mundane and trivial stuff to the consent agenda. You share evidence—reports on current data—showing the organization's current performance according to a few vital indicators of performance, the ones that are most diagnostic of your organization's ability to achieve mission and vision. You compare the current status to the desired status. And as a group, you consider the big questions:

- Are we meeting our interim goals and targets, and if not, what should we do about this?
- Will our current trajectory allow us to reach our target in the time allotted?
- What else could we do for our clients that would bring about such desired changes in the world sooner, or more effectively?
- Are we satisfied with our progress or not?
- In what way is the need for our services growing, declining, or remaining the same?
- *Are we spending enough money to achieve our aims?*

Once the meeting is completed (and it's always completed on time because you've learned how to manage such meetings effectively), publish your decisions internally, providing them to your staff lieutenants as guidelines and instructions for the next review cycle.

Then you get to do it again next month.

CASE STUDY   **THE CONSENT AGENDA**

Most governing boards use the Consent Agenda format, where all standard committee reports and other mundane items are collated together, and the group votes on their acceptance en bloc. Typically, the Consent Agenda is introduced at the start of the board meeting, thus opening the door for lengthy discussions about Consent Agenda items, and reducing the time available for strategic discussions.

Your governing board will spend more time on strategic discussions if you move the Consent Agenda to the last 10 or 15 minutes of the meeting. This simple change will reduce the amount of time board members can quibble over Consent Agenda details.

Great leadership skills may be exercised at any level of the organizational hierarchy, and they should be. You can use similar skills and techniques, even if the only performance you're evaluating is your own. In that case, think strategically about your personal capacity for achieving or contributing to the achievement of the mission. If you manage a group of other contributors, consider the group's collective ability to contribute to the achievement of the mission. Fundraising the SMART Way is optimized to support leadership techniques and encourage insights into the health of the fundraising process, including the accuracy of the organization's funder-selection strategies.

In all cases, use the techniques of continuous improvement, reviewed in Chapter 8, to get the most benefit out of these regular reviews of performance against plan.

The Information   Leaders make decisions based on the information they review. Come to think of it, the business world often describes leaders as "decision makers," and those with career ambitions often say, "I want to become a decision maker!" Decision makers who lack accurate, up-to-date information run the risk of making bad decisions. Therefore, getting the right information is the other critical element required to lead the fundraising revolution at your organization. Access to such information is a prerequisite for the exercise of effective leadership. Without it, "leadership" may be relegated to micro-management, pep-rally motivation, or off-with-their-heads-style punishment. The big question here is this: what is the right information?

Fundraising the SMART Way produces the kinds of mission-critical insights and observations that have been largely lacking up to now, through analytics I like to think of as "navigational aids." If you were sailing a boat out on the open ocean, you would seek key information to aid your navigation, primarily from your compass, GPS, and sailing charts. Before starting your journey, you lay out the course you plan to follow, which is analogous to the strategic fund-development plan. You then peek at the compass, review your charts, consult your GPS, and listen to the Coast Guard's weather channel to discover the unexpected, and make tactical or strategic decisions about getting from here to there under these specific conditions. If you're on course, dandy; if you're off course, get back on. The threat of bad weather or pirates might make it more difficult to regain your desired progress, but at least your navigational aids give you ideas about how to cope.

The performance reports of Fundraising the SMART Way are the navigational aids of the fundraising process. They work pretty much like compass, sailing chart, and GPS, laying out the strategy and reporting on progress toward the "destination" using tables, charts, and graphs. As we have seen, however, fundraising professionals are more likely to lack such navigational aids than they are to have them. Without appropriate feedback from the process, it's nearly impossible to resist the temptation to "try harder," work longer hours, disregard qualifying criteria, engage in a tactical frenzy, or panic.

What information do you need to see, and how should you see it?

The first thing that comes to mind, of course, is actual income raised, preferably income recognized by the accounting system. (You can't spend "income pledged" or "income promised"; you can spend it only after the check clears.) As we have seen in the Leaky Bucket study, the most frequently reported fundraising information is income, either total income, income by funding category, or both. If you only measure or report on income, you're not seeing the whole picture of productivity.

Fundraising the SMART Way captures critical data from two sources that can be cross-referenced to give deep insights into health of the development process. These are the funder's rank and score as calculated by the Scorecard, and data about the pipeline, demonstrated by progression through the series of Donor Moves. These data place the income-received indicator into a meaningful context diagnostic of development productivity.

Data about rank, score, and Donor Move provide at least the following six insights:

1. A way to view the pipeline in table form, collating all information about pending gifts or grants, providing the forecast and specific insights about cycle times.

2. Distribution of prospects and current funders by rank, which shows the team's ability to identify and invest appropriate time in A- and B-ranked donors, while reducing time spent on the C's and D's.

3. Distribution of forecasted income by rank, showing effectiveness of concentrating on high-potential funders.

4. Distribution of opportunities by rank, Donor Move, and level of income, which maintains predictability and consistency.

5. Level of attainment of income per funding stream, as compared to the target for each stream.

6. Dynamic progress of each major opportunity through the pipeline, making it visible, and establishing accurate baseline information about cycle times from move to move.

Reports such as these have not been widely used in the fundraising discipline, but they should be. They are effective at assessing the current level of productivity and identifying root causes, managing the deployment of resources, and getting feedback from the process indicating needs for and opportunities to embark on improvement initiatives. In the field of process management, we refer to such data as "the voice of the process." Fundraising the SMART Way gives a voice to the fund development process, a voice that has largely been silent up until now.

IMPLICATIONS FOR INFORMATION TECHNOLOGY

The fundraising revolution will be forged by the exercise of great leadership, and enabled, by and large, by technology harnessed properly. Even if your shop and/or donor base may be small, you must utilize information technology to capture critical data, collate and report on them, and use them to conduct preliminary analysis. The right technology, deployed the right way, allows the benefits of Fundraising the SMART Way to become manifest.

Unfortunately, most platforms for constituent relationship management lack certain data fields key to the SMART Way model, especially the funder's Scorecard rank. Fortunately, those same technology platforms offer enough flexibility so your information technology (IT) department or outside support team can add them. If your organization has a functioning CRM platform, you are ahead of the game, especially if it already contains the entire database of current and prospective funding sources and those all-important Move Zero names. A centralized database of contacts gives you a great place to start. It's advisable to collate all contact information in one central database, and flag contacts in a variety of ways so you know who gets this newsletter, who gets that one, who gets invited to the gala, and who's related to whom.[4]

---

[4] If you have not invested in such a platform, you need to think about it; the field now offers some highly sophisticated, flexible, and affordable options. Just make sure you can modify the installation to capture, collate, and report on performance data.

First, let's address the need to add Scorecard information into this database. Your CRM platform, assuming you already have one, holds all the contact information for each entry in the database. A SMART Way Scorecard is typically a macro-enabled spreadsheet that automatically calculates the prospect's rank and actual score. It can be created as a simple Excel spreadsheet, and then linked to the contact record, or it could be custom-created within the native capabilities and language of your CRM software, which will probably be an expensive undertaking.

Once you've completed the Scorecard, you may transfer prospect rank and actual score to the CRM platform's contact record, either by entering them manually in custom fields, or by setting up an import/export function. Then store a copy of the completed Scorecard as an attachment to the contact record or in some other file folder on the agency's system. The funder's Scorecard rank is critical when you collect analytics on the fundraising process. If you make it a standard part of the contact record, you'll be able to pull reports including such information, for example, to obtain a list of all current A-ranked donors.

It should be possible to engineer the Scorecard template into your CRM platform using its native programming language, but unless your shop is quite large, and you have very competent programmers, it might not be worth the effort. We are finding that it's simpler to build Scorecard templates as a spreadsheet, then update the contact record either manually or through an import/export routine. In the long run, it's just as effective and a whole lot less costly.

If your CRM platform includes an opportunity management module, most likely that module will contain predefined opportunity stages. Typically, opportunity stages describe actions or behaviors taken by members of the fundraising staff, such as initial meeting, discovery call, facility tour, gift proposal. SMART Way Donor Moves replace conventional opportunity stages with a relatively short list of actions describing the donor's behavior, and thus tracking the donor's giving process (as opposed to your "getting" process). Most opportunity management modules will allow you to relabel the opportunity stages, meaning that you can simply have the IT department change the stage descriptions to Donor Moves, as defined in Chapter 5.

The third component is a way to record performance targets, including the following:

- Targets for total income, preferably for the year and for each month or accounting period. Setting forth such targets and interim targets facilitates the tracking of progress against plan.

- Targets for income by category, where applicable, following the same rules as above.

- Targets for each Donor Move or opportunity stage, stating the ideal or targeted number of occurrences per move, per month, and per year.

- A pipeline multiplier target, usually either 2×, 2.5×, or 3× the size of the target for actual income.

Targets can be represented in your reports. If your report is a bar graph showing distribution of forecasted revenue by donor rank, you can add a target line running across the bar graph showing the desired level of revenue per donor rank.

While most CRM systems provide both standard and custom reports, it may make more sense to export SMART Way data to a low-cost reporting tool such as Excel, SQL, or Crystal Reports, rather than attempting to craft the reports from within the platform's native capabilities.[5]

IMPLICATIONS FOR THE GOVERNING BOARD

Since the governing board represents the highest level of leadership in nonprofit organizations, the business analytics we've been discussing will enhance their ability to lead the organization and advise its senior executive. Whether your organization's governing board participates in fundraising or not, the members of the board still need to have the same kind of information—strategic, accurate, timely, and diagnostic—your executives do. I believe they'll welcome it, too, after seeing how much confusion and anxiety resides in nonprofit boards when it comes to raising money.

---

[5] Interested readers may obtain a copy of our reporting templates at www.wiley.com/go/smartfundraising. You can use the template as an add-on to your CRM platform, or as a specification for the IT department to follow.

I'm all too familiar with the tensions that tend to persist between board and staff when it comes to fundraising. It's a hot potato; you throw fundraising to the board (I can't raise money unless you do it for me!) and they throw it right back to you (Aagghh!!! We hate to ask for money, etc. etc.), creating conflict where none should exist, and actually making it more difficult to conduct the board's most important role, namely, that of setting direction and holding the CEO accountable for achieving desired results.

Once the board is equipped with appropriate information, there's a shift. The board can now assess the situation with accurate and timely reports and make informed decisions and recommendations. The right information gives the governing board what it needs to act on behalf of those they represent, offer support to the CEO, and maintain accountability for results.

Imagine this scenario. It's time to give the board a report on fundraising, something you have always hated to do because no matter what you say, the conversation always seems to go haywire. Up to now, you've always reported fundraising progress one anecdote at a time—and watched the discussion spiral downward and out of control. Now, however, you can show progress in context, simply by sharing a few graphs:

- How actual pipeline activity compares to established goals and targets.
- How effective the development team has been at identifying and pursuing more qualified prospects rather than wasting time on the usual suspects.
- Where bottlenecks have occurred in the process, and what you and your team have done, or plan to do, to relieve them.
- Where operational considerations and external market conditions have imposed obstacles or restrictions requiring a response, and how you will solicit support from other departments or service providers to resolve or work around the challenges.

These insights into fundraising performance convert the fundraising conversation from frustrating to positive. Even if progress is slow, there's always evidence of *some* progress, providing a richer conversation and avoiding the blame game.

Those of you who are blessed with sophisticated boards, who understand and provide good governance, will see ways in which this new approach will benefit board, staff, agency and clients, as a whole.

Those of you who don't feel quite so blessed may have some reservations. If you feel that your board is apathetic, hostile, or doubtful about your ability to achieve desired results, you might not think that spreadsheets and graphs can make any difference at all. I'm happy to say that they do and will. Your reservations, while valid, are likely to dissolve, or at least diminish. Both parties, board and staff, must, however, agree to change their ideas about what happens in board meetings.

Steven Bowman has said, "The role of the board is not to meet and receive reports about how busy the senior executives are . . . [T]he role of the board is to make the choices that create the future for the communities they serve. Creating the future is all about being aware of what is happening in the strategic environment; focusing on the things that are likely to have an effect on your organization; choosing what needs to be modified, created, or stopped; and repeating this process continuously."[6]

The level to which the organization is funded, the degree to which income is predictable and consistent, the extent to which funding diversification has been managed—all of these elements make up the "strategic environment" Bowman describes. When the fundraising report is delivered as a series of anecdotes, the board cannot see the strategic environment; they only see a bunch of disconnected stories about donor prospects. And since they're only human, they are more likely to remember the bad news (and give you a hard time because of it) than they are the good. They are actually *unable* to translate these one-at-a-time stories into a coherent whole. When people are asked to make decisions based on faulty, incomplete, or inaccurate information, they make bad ones.

In my opinion, since so few boards have access to the orderly, diagnostic, and dispassionate reports produced by the continuous improvement model, too many of them opt to continue the tactical frenzy: throw more events, complete more grant applications, go hat in hand and beg for more bucks from the usual suspects. They just don't have the tools to suggest anything better.

Earlier in this chapter, I said that we're setting up our development shops to *build in* a lack of productivity, which means setting them up to

---

[6] Steven Bowman, "Choice, Future, and Communities: The True Role of the Board and Governance." In *YOU and Your Nonprofit Board*, Terrie Temkin, PhD, ed. (Rancho Santa Margarita, CA: CharityChannel Press, 2013), 8.

fail. We place obstacles in the paths of development officers who are already working at a heroic level of effort, simply by our failure to provide them with appropriate metrics, guidelines, and reporting methods. If I've persuaded you to think radically about the fundraising revolution, then you'll start wondering how to identify these obstacles to performance and replace them with strategic tools and methods designed to produce success.

In the same vein, I call upon the members of governing boards to rethink their responsibilities in regard to funding. Notice I said "funding," not fund-*raising*. Currently, I would argue that we have set up our boards to fail as well as our development shops, at least in terms of the fiduciary responsibility of boards to represent the interests of the owners, a population that's not always easy to define, but most likely means the community in general, and those within that community who need the help and support your programs were designed to provide.

In too many nonprofits, board members are shortchanged by a combination of "sins of omission" such as the failure to provide metrics, by purposeful practices that tie board members' hands, and by plain old ignorance about how a random group can become a high-performing team and collaborate to make good decisions. These boards are uninvolved, or try to micro-manage staff, or believe their roles include stuffing the envelopes and serving the chicken salad. Such boards have never sought, nor taken advantage of, the enormous body of knowledge currently available about governance, so they end up making it all up on the fly. They may not even know such a body of knowledge exists.

These are the boards most likely to suggest counterproductive fundraising tactics that cost a lot but don't deliver much benefit. Unfortunately, if the board tells you to throw another event, their "suggestion" takes on the force of law. Pity the poor CEO or development director who refuses to follow the "suggestion."

Just like executive leaders, boards also need access to information about funding so they can make informed decisions. If you'd like your board to stop suggesting yet another golf tournament, gala event, or evening at the home of the local celebrity, try giving them copies of the same tables, charts, and graphs you're now relying on. Give them the analytics and business intelligence allowing them to visualize the fundraising process as a whole.

PARTING REMARKS

Fundraising is everybody's job, but it's nobody's fault. Great fundraising professionals may have the biggest Rolodexes in the world, and hold degrees and credentials galore, but they simply do not work in a vacuum. It's possible for the greatest fundraising Superman ever to flop upon moving to another agency.

Success in funding your organization to sustain current operations and build capacity for the future requires the coordinated efforts of the entire agency, from the board chair to the office temp who's sitting at the receptionist's desk today. Poor fundraising results are not the fault of the development officer, the director, the CEO, the board; they are organizational results and thus require organizational remedies. I'm not saying that every staff member (including the office temp) has to pitch every poor soul who walks in the door. What I am saying is that leadership needs to adopt the techniques of performance excellence throughout the entire organization, and constantly seek better, more cost-effective and more innovative ways to achieve the mission and fulfill the vision. And that includes moving fundraising onto the same disciplined platform.

Some of the most effective, exciting and innovative techniques have become standard operating procedure in the commercial world. I see no reason why the social sector should not adopt such practices, and every reason why it should. We can engage the tools of capitalism in benevolent ways. We can use them, just as for-profit businesses do, to bring awareness to our causes, engage broader followings, give the human impulse toward charity more room and space.

When we do, the business function of raising money through philanthropic means will become more consistent and even more user friendly. Even more important, it will enable you to change the world.

About the Author

Ellen Bristol (Pembroke Pines, FL) came into the nonprofit sector after more than 20 years of experience in the corporate world, where she specialized in major-account sales of information technology equipment. Since 1995, the year she launched Bristol Strategy Group, she has developed a solid track record as consultant and author in the fund development arena.

She is the developer of the methodologies Fundraising the SMART Way™ and its for-profit version Selling the SMART Way®, as well as the designer of the accompanying software application, The SMART Way Scorecard, available in both nonprofit and for-profit versions. She is the author of the e-book *De-Mystifying Fundraising: Seven Steps to Fundraising Success*, co-author of *The Leaky Bucket: What's Wrong with Your Fundraising and How You Can Fix It*, and a contributing author to *The Nonprofit Consulting Playbook* and *YOU and Your Nonprofit Board*.

In addition to her writing, Ellen has also developed the SMART Fundraising Game, a game to show board directors and non-fundraising staff what fundraising is really about. She is a board member of the Association of Fundraising Professionals (AFP International), Broward (Florida) Chapter, and the Professional Advancement Division of AFP, where she sits on the Research Council.

About the Companion Website

This book includes a companion website containing a variety of resources to make it easy for you to adopt the principles of Fundraising the SMART Way™, including:

- The Best Practices Library, containing a series of white papers illustrating elements of the SMART Way methodology.

- The Opportunity Risk Calculator for Nonprofits, a live spreadsheet to calculate the estimated opportunity risk associated with your development time.

- The Fund Diversification Calculator, a live spreadsheet to calculate the relative proportions of income you currently enjoy, plus a second sheet for forecasting desired changes in diversification.

- Templates for conducting the SWOT Analysis, Value-Added Analysis, Donor Value-Sought Analysis, and Exchange of Value Analysis.

- Templates for developing your own SMART Way Prospect Scorecard profiles and Donor Moves pipeline.

- The complete template for SMART Way Prospect Scorecard 2.0, containing Scorecard profiles for all three major funding categories. This workbook also produces reports and graphs of strategic importance to development officers, development directors, CEOs, and the governing board.

To access the site, go to www.wiley.com/go/smartfundraising (password: results123).

Index

NOTE: Page references in italics refer to exhibits.